Selling Is a Team Sport

**Turn Your Whole Organization
into a Living, Breathing,
Selling Machine**

Eric Baron

PRIMA PUBLISHING
3000 Lava Ridge Court • Roseville, California 95661
(800) 632-8676 • www.primalifestyles.com

To My Girls,
Lois, Andrea, and Deborah

PRIMA PUBLISHING and colophon are trademarks of Prima Communications Inc., registered with the United States Patent and Trademark Office.

All products mentioned in this book are trademarks of their respective companies.

Library of Congress Cataloging-in-Publication Data

Baron, Eric.
    Selling is a team sport : turn your whole organization into a living, breathing, selling machine / Eric Baron.
        p. cm.
    Includes index.
    ISBN 0-7615-2530-0
    1. Selling. 2. Sales management. 3. Teams in the workplace. I. Title.
    HF5438 .B266 2000
    658.8'1--dc21   00-036325

00 01 02 03 HH 10 9 8 7 6 5 4 3 2 1
Printed in the United States of America

HOW TO ORDER

Single copies may be ordered from Prima Publishing, 3000 Lava Ridge Court, Roseville, CA 95661; telephone (800) 632-8676 ext. 4444. Quantity discounts are also available. On your letterhead, include information concerning the intended use of the books and the number of books you wish to purchase.

Visit us online at www.primalifestyles.com

Contents

Acknowledgments   v

Introduction   ix

Section I   Selling as Problem Solving

Chapter 1:   "Whatchagot?" or Why You
              Need Organization-Wide Selling   3

Chapter 2:   Problem Solving 101: Maximizing
              the Chances of Success   27

Chapter 3:   Problem Solving 102: Actually Doing It!   51

Section II   Putting It Across to the Customer

Chapter 4:   Needs-Driven Selling   75

Chapter 5:   Merging Needs-Driven Selling
              and Problem Solving   87

Chapter 6:   "A Table by the Window, Please,"
              or the Importance of Positioning   113

Chapter 7:   "Elementary, My Dear Watson,"
              or Analyzing the Situation   135

Chapter 8:   "May I Recommend . . . ?"   167

Chapter 9:   Resolving the Issues (Hallelujah!)   187
Chapter 10:   Last Call! We're Closing!   211

Section III   Unleashing the Power of Sales Teams
Chapter 11:   So What Are These Things
              We Call Sales Teams?   225
Chapter 12:   What, Another Meeting? Count Me In!   241
Chapter 13:   The Team Hits the Field:
              Making Joint Sales Calls   253

Section IV: Making Organization-Wide Selling a Reality
Chapter 14:   It's All About Culture   271
Chapter 15:   Putting It in Perspective   287

Index   293
About the Author   301
About The Baron Group   303

Acknowledgments

The creation of *Selling Is a Team Sport* has taught me many lessons. The big lesson learned has been the enormous amount of teamwork required in producing a book for publication.

I owe a debt of gratitude to Lois de la Haba, of the Lois de la Haba Literary Agency, who is my agent and my friend. She believed, from the start, that what I have to say is relevant. Her boundless energy, enthusiasm, and professionalism resulted in selling this book to Prima Publishing.

Hank Saroyan took my "text book" and transformed it into a light and readable story. Working with Hank has been one of the many unexpected rewards associated with this project.

Kristen Wainwright of the Boston Literary Group pointed me in the right direction at the right time. Her support and encouragement helped me move forward when I needed guidance.

The people at Prima have demonstrated an approach to teamwork consistent with what the book proposes. I am grateful for the guiding light of Ben Domintz, founder, CEO, and chairman of Prima. With Ben at the helm, we were able to turn the manuscript into a book that relayed the message of organization-wide selling.

David Richardson, associate acquisitions editor, envisioned what the book could be and became the driving force behind it. He has been a constant source of guidance and support. Tara Mead, project editor, has provided valuable editorial assistance in many ways, especially by always thinking in terms of the reader.

As developmental editor, John Bergez also played a critical editorial role. His immediate grasp of the material and his ability to crystallize and simplify the key points energized the project and greatly improved the manuscript.

These acknowledgements would not be complete without expressing my gratitude to George Prince, founder of Synectics® Inc., who had a major impact on my life. George has always given people the permission to be themselves. As my mentor he opened avenues of learning I never imagined. Many of his revolutionary ideas appear throughout the book.

Rick Harriman, managing director of Synectics, has had a profound affect on my career for more than twenty-five years. His friendship, support, and continued encouragement will always be remembered and appreciated.

My partner and friend, David Hauer, consistently adds perspective and humor to my life. This project has affected the daily workings of The Baron Group, demanding of him great tolerance and flexibility. He has certainly met the challenge, and I am grateful for his support.

David Richter, my lifelong friend, is someone who has always believed in me and in what I could do. The number of times he gave me a friendly kick in the butt to keep me focused would be hard to recount. I will always be grateful for his friendship, support, and unique business insights.

I could not have accomplished this task without the support of Doris Anderson and Francine Mendence, of The Baron Group. They put in countless hours, often long after the office closed, to ensure that I met my deadlines. Thanks also to Lisa Balsam-Solinga, who carefully documented references and attended to other aspects involved in making the manuscript accurate.

And, of course, I want to thank the most important people in my life, my immediate family. My wife Lois has walked in step with me throughout this journey and has been absolutely unwavering in her support. She has often been my guide, sometimes my crutch, and always my inspiration. My daughters, Andrea and Deborah, who as young adults have become my best friends, always manage to remind me of what is really important. And finally my parents, Sydney and Sylvia Baron. My late father taught me the value of hard work and personal sacrifice. My loving mother has always been supportive of my efforts and has done so much to instill confidence in my ability to meet difficult challenges.

I am eternally grateful to all of you for your role in making this happen. The book is called *Selling Is a Team Sport*. One of the things I learned in this process is that writing can be a team sport as well.

Introduction

This book introduces the why's and how's of what I call *organization-wide selling*—a way of doing business in which everyone in the organization participates at some level in the sales process. It shows, in detail, the skills involved in making your entire company a living, breathing, customer-driven, selling machine.

Why "organization-wide" selling? Because, like it or not, the reality is that almost everybody is selling commodities today. Regardless of what type of business you're in, whether you provide sophisticated services or everyday household products, there are tons of competitors offering similar products and services with comparable quality at about the same price. And they are backed by organizations that are as impressive as yours with people representing them who look just as good as you do.

To make things even scarier, the competition comes from all over the world, sometimes from places you probably couldn't locate on a map. And if that isn't bad enough, if you have the advantage now, you can be sure that one or more of the companies that pose little threat today will catch up and surpass you tomorrow.

I'm sure this isn't a revelation to you. You know you're working in an extraordinarily competitive, rapidly globalizing environment. Whether you are a sales professional who confronts these issues in the front lines every day, a CEO developing strategies to deal with the challenge, or a middle manager trying to implement the game plan, you've probably given the subject a lot of thought.

One of the conclusions you've undoubtedly reached is that you have to figure out ways to differentiate yourself from your competitors. This book is based on the simple idea that the single best differentiator you can leverage is the people who make up your organization—provided you know how to deploy them effectively as value-adding resources that can knock the socks off your customers.

The reality is that companies that don't leverage all of their resources will find themselves at a significant disadvantage compared with companies that do. For your company to position itself strongly in today's environment, it must instill in the minds of each and every employee that he or she is an integral part of the sales process. Everyone—and I mean everyone—must keep the customer in mind at all times. Customer satisfaction must drive every decision. Providing outstanding customer service must become the norm. Working together as teams toward that common goal is no longer the fantasy of those cerebral thinkers in Organization Development. It is the way to survive and thrive in the bare-knuckled world where you compete.

I don't blame you if you're skeptical. For decades, people have talked about the power of cross-functional teams, making matrix organizations work, instilling creativity throughout the organization, applying team selling principles, and effectively using resources from throughout the company. Although some companies have made these concepts work, most haven't. That is why I wrote this book.

I started my career with Union Carbide in the late 1960s. As a chemical engineer, I entered the sales profession as a technical representative in Carbide's Chemical and Plastics Division. I spent eight years there and held positions in sales, sales management, marketing, and, by accident, sales training. While in this final position, I met the people at Synectics® Inc. Synectics has been teaching, researching, and applying concepts associated with creative problem solving, innovation, and teamwork, among others things, for more than forty years.

I joined Synectics in 1976 and spent five years with that wonderful organization. It was during that time that I became intrigued with the similarities between problem solving and selling. Because I wanted to explore this in more detail, I left Synectics in 1981 to cofound Consultative Resources Corporation (CRC) with Kate Reilly and Jonathan Whitcup. At CRC, we explored these concepts and developed programs to teach them. In 1992 I ventured out and founded The Baron Group to devote more time to researching and teaching the subjects covered in this book.

Selling Is a Team Sport evolved from that final venture. At first the focus was to introduce the problem solving approach to selling. But as time passed, I realized that I couldn't give the subject the depth it needed without investigating team selling. I then realized that to make any of this happen, organization-wide selling must be the fundamental principle to be introduced to the marketplace.

What I've come to believe can be put into five words: Selling is a team sport. The day of the rugged individualist is over. As one successful salesperson in a focus group boasted recently, "I love to go head to head with those 'lone rangers' out there. They're easy to handle. As long as they go at it alone and I'm backed up by a whole bunch of powerful, viable resources, I see no way that I can lose. It's not even a fair fight."

So how does organization-wide selling happen? It starts with sales professionals who think of themselves as problem solvers, who routinely bring a problem-solving mentality and sophisticated problem-solving approach to every interaction, both internally and externally. From there it moves to the creation of multifunctional sales teams that exist for one reason only—to provide outstanding customer satisfaction. From sales teams, the approach spreads throughout the entire organization until everybody is constantly thinking about the customer, from the kid in the mail room to the machinery operator in the plant to the senior vice president of sales and marketing (or, for that matter, of finance).

Creating this kind of organization doesn't happen overnight. At ground level, the sales professionals who manage the relationships with customers and prospects need to learn state-of-the-art skills in what I call problem-solving selling. This approach involves such concepts as consultative selling and needs-driven selling. However, problem-solving selling goes beyond these familiar ideas and raises the sales interaction to a higher level.

Beyond the sales professional, cross-functional sales teams need to know how to work together, how to apply proven problem-solving principles, how to tap into their collective expertise, and how to leverage resources from throughout the organization. And everyone in the company needs at least a basic understanding of the sales process and what the organization is trying to achieve in its relationships with customers.

At the highest levels of management, executives need to communicate the message and support it with incentive and recognition programs. Mission and vision statements have to be updated, training has to be implemented and sustained, support systems need to be reworked, and experimentation needs to be encouraged.

Yes, there's a lot to do. But it can be done. I know, because I've seen it happen.

So who should read this book? The short answer (and one I'm sure my publisher likes) is, everybody in the company. More modestly, I've thought of myself as writing primarily to executives, sales managers, and sales representatives, but also to the managers in other functional areas who need to understand the concepts so they can participate in the process. At times, particularly in teaching the nitty-gritty skills of problem-solving selling, I address myself directly to the sales professional. But when I do, I'm imagining that the CEO and the senior management team are listening in, as are representatives from all other company functions. My hope is that all employees are paying serious attention, because the goal is for everyone to feel a sense of ownership when it comes to the customer. That is what organization-wide selling is all about.

The book consists of four sections. Section I, "Selling as Problem Solving," introduces the fundamental concepts of organization-wide and problem-solving selling. It demonstrates how the highest level of selling occurs when sales calls are transformed into problem-solving opportunities, and why this transformation calls for utilizing resources from throughout the company.

Section II, "Putting It Across to the Customer," takes a fresh look at the sales process by exploring the specific skills involved in what I call problem-solving selling. The chapters in this section introduce a specific selling sequence and the skills required to make it work. Depending on your background, some of the information will be quite new, while some may be a review of lessons you've learned in the past. This section provides a framework for people to use in any selling situation, whether alone or as part of a sales team.

Section III, "Unleashing the Power of Sales Teams," explains what sales teams are, what their reason is for being, how they are formed, and how they can work together successfully. These chapters investigate the roles and responsibilities of team members as well as such management topics as team building, strategizing, performance assessment, motivation, and compensation issues.

At the end of each chapter in sections I through III, you'll find a section called "Memo to Management." Even though I'm writing this book for managers as well as the people in the sales organization, these sections are an opportunity to speak directly to the issue of what management can do to implement the specific ideas discussed in each chapter. If at times you find these sections a bit irreverent, I hope you'll understand that this is just my way of getting across how vital it is for managers to stretch if organization-wide selling is to be more than just a new flavor of the month.

Section IV, "Making Organization-Wide Selling a Reality," is where managers and executives take center stage. It is addressed primarily to the leaders who bear the responsibility of providing the energy, enthusiasm, and passion to get the message out and to implement the program. I hope the sales pros and everyone else listen in, because a key part of the message is that organizational change must start at the top but build from the bottom. In short, it involves everyone. I investigate the issues involved in cultural change and what everyone has to do to make the dream a reality.

That's the program, in a nutshell. It all comes down to one central idea: In an age of commodities, the way to differentiate your organization is to use all your resources to demonstrate to the customer that you do bring something unique to the table—you and your people. That is what no other organization has to offer. This book tells you how to leverage that uniqueness.

The organizations that will thrive a decade from now are those that have mastered selling as a team sport. It's time to learn how to play the game. You have nothing to lose but some bad habits and scores of missed opportunities. And what you can gain will boggle your mind. Not only will you ensure the loyalty of your customers, but you'll also find yourself and the people you work with deriving much greater satisfaction from your work. Besides, you do want to win, and my book will show how to do that more often than you ever imagined.

Selling as Problem Solving

CHAPTER 1

"Whatchagot?" or Why You Need Organization-Wide Selling

Sal Murphy arrived early, took a seat in the lobby, straightened his tie, and thought about his approach to these kinds of cold calls. When summoned, he entered the small but impressive executive office. Inside, the prospective client, Betty Cornstarch, Director of Purchasing, was cordial, though a bit aloof. After a word or two of chitchat, Sal cleared his throat and began briefly to explain how his firm could be of value to her business.

Betty sat in her chair, hands clasped behind her head, Lee Iaccoca-style. In the midst of Sal's pitch, she sat forward and said, "Look, Sid, or whatever your name is, I know you guys are good and come highly recommended. I was impressed with what I read about your stuff, but what could you possibly offer us that we're not getting from the two firms who have been keeping us happy and out of trouble for the last seven years? My boss dislikes change and he's known these guys since he got here. I just thought you should know that before you go on."

Internally, Sal shuddered, wondering how long a drive it was to his next appointment, and how hot the interior of his car would be by the time he got back to it. Externally, he loosened his tie and set his jaw for a tough and probably frustrating waste of time.

Stripped of power and immediately on the defensive, Sal thought, "So this is that hot lead with tons of potential that we spent all the time preparing for, and here I am out of the game before kickoff. All that prep time with the team for this?"

After a sentence or two under this pressure, Sal began to sweat. Then, completely discarding his planned approach, he cut straight to the sales pitch—hawking specific goods and services at a healthy clip, stopping briefly along the way to see if the buyer's demeanor had changed. It hadn't.

Sal continued, delivering what by most standards would have been a decent initial presentation. He knew his products and services cold. He talked about his company's unique approach to managing relationships. He boasted about the outstanding sales team that he managed, how they met regularly to develop solutions for their customers, and how pleased so many of those customers were with his company's performance. He proudly enlightened Betty about how teamwork was a valued cultural norm within his organization, both internally and externally. He went so far as to explain how the company's mission statement made specific reference to the fact that everyone in the organization played a unique role in providing outstanding customer service and guaranteeing unparalleled customer satisfaction. He uttered the magic word "partner" three times. He talked until the words, running by on cue cards in his head, ran out. Unfortunately, most of them landed on the floor.

When Sal finished, Betty thanked him, stood up, extended her hand, and showed Sal the door. No deal was broached, no sale was achieved, no next steps were nailed, and, although the meeting ended neutrally, Sal knew it probably didn't make sense to waste any more time pursuing this company. It was not the call he had anticipated. It was not the call he had carefully planned. It was not the call that his sales team members who had worked with him in the preparation phase expected. And it was not the kind of call that the leaders of the company envisioned when they put together their new mission statement. It was, quite frankly, your basic sales-call disaster.

Sound familiar? Any of us who have spent time in sales have been there. Probably more times than we care to remember.

Exchanges like this one happen every day in the marketplace. That awful, defeating question or statement from prospective customer to salesperson, couched in a thousand different forms, is hurled across desks, phone lines, and conference rooms like blinding serves in a table tennis tournament. The resulting standoff is one of the greatest difficulties that a sales professional can run into on a cold call, a lukewarm call, or for that matter, any call. The customer has challenged the salesperson's right to exist, forcing him or her to get to the sales pitch right away, far too early in the process. The customer made it very clear, right from the beginning, that Sal would quickly have to explain to her what was different about his company and why she should spend any time with him at all. After all, things were proceeding quite well without Sal or his company, and she didn't see any reason whatsoever even to consider making any changes.

That's not a problem just for Sal. It's a problem for the entire organization he represents.

Differentiating Your Organization in Today's Environment

What happened to Sal is that he had stepped squarely on what I call the "Whatchagot?" land mine. Many salespeople have watched meetings with prospective customers blow up in their faces after stepping on one of these. Quite often, buyers deliberately utilize this tactic to derail and abbreviate the sales process. It forces the salesperson to enumerate prematurely the company's goods and services in a lifeless, non-engaging, and often inhospitable forum, whereby they can be summarily rejected—thus ending the meeting and saving time.

The problem isn't just that Sal let himself be forced into presenting prematurely. Managing the sales call is vital, and we'll spend a lot of time on that topic in this book. But sales technique alone won't cut it. Unearthing the "Whatchagot?" land mine brings to light two huge issues in the sales world of today—the "point of difference" issue and the "status quo" issue.

The first issue has to do with what makes your organization different from its competitors. The second concerns buyers' desire to find out quickly what they can get that their company isn't already getting, or why they should consider making a change and disrupting the status quo.

Perhaps the greatest challenge facing sales professionals and their organizations in today's business world is the need to differentiate themselves from the crowd. That's not a new problem, but differentiation is more essential for success than ever before. In today's cluttered, high-tech marketplace, all companies and sales forces are relegated to selling commodities to an inundated buyer group. Whether your company sells weed trimmers, baseball gloves, computer gear, financial services, Sheetrock, or steel-belted radials, scores of companies are offering similar products with similar specs, with similar resources behind them, and at similar prices. Nothing really stands out from anything else on its own merit, and if it does, it won't for long.

So what's the only thing that can differentiate one truckload of goods unloaded at the loading dock from another? Quality and service! Who reflects quality and service to a buyer? The sales organization. And who makes up the sales organization? You! That doesn't just mean you as a sales professional, manager, or trainer. It means you, Mr. and Ms. Executive. It means you, Mr. and Ms. Division Manager, and you, Mr. or Ms. Chief Engineer. It means, in fact, your entire organization.

Newsflash	*To differentiate itself in today's marketplace, an organization needs to demonstrate how the people who make up the company are different. And that doesn't mean just the sales force. It means everybody in the organization.*

Organization-Wide Selling

Most people within every organization touch the customer. Some do so directly; most do so indirectly. But virtually everyone touches the customer in some way.

Unfortunately, most of your people don't think in terms of the customer on a day-to-day basis. You know that. You experience it as a customer all the time yourself, whether you are calling about a credit card problem or an airline flight or the defective replacement part for your air conditioner. You know how it feels when the people with whom you interact really don't seem to care a heck of a lot about you or your problems. Conversely, you know how good it feels when they do show interest in you. And if you've ever had a company anticipate your needs, suggest creative solutions you hadn't thought of, or simply serve as a resource for solving your problems, then you know that that feels best of all. And you're almost certainly loyal to the company whose people treated you that way.

That kind of approach represents organization-wide selling, which we can define as everybody in the organization taking responsibility for the customer in everything they do. Everyone—from the vice president of sales to the plant manager, from the person running the contracts department to the shop workers on the plant floor—must consistently think about what they can do to provide outstanding customer satisfaction.

The reality is that if your company doesn't grasp that organization-wide selling is mandatory today, you will find yourself at a disadvantage compared to your competition. But most of your organization's people aren't salespeople, you say? They are if they have anything to do with solving customers' problems. And who in your organization isn't somehow involved in doing just that?

Selling Means Problem Solving

Let's return to Sal for a moment. One of the things that derailed his conversation with Betty is that Sal never had the chance—or I should say, never created the chance—to find out what Betty's needs really were. He was thrown by the "Whatchagot?" challenge into trying to talk about how his company was different from the rest, how it was customer-centered, and the like. The problem is, no matter how charming and convincing Sal's presentation was, his behavior belied his message. In talking about himself and his company, he wasn't listening to the customer.

Sure, Betty didn't give him much of a chance. Clearly, however, customers bring up the "Whatchagot?" challenge precisely because they want to know what your company can do for them that other companies can't. Bookstores are loaded with volumes about how organizations can address this issue. Yet the most exciting and vibrant way to prove a company has more to offer than its competitors is seldom discussed at all—and that is by demonstrating the inherent ability of salespeople, sales teams, and people throughout the organization to help their customers and prospects solve their business problems.

Inherent ability? You bet. As human beings, salespeople, even Sal, tend to be natural-born problem solvers. When they are in their offices planning their sales calls, plotting their territory, segmenting their markets, classifying their customers, and anticipating objections, they can be extremely creative. When they are participating in internal meetings or dealing with their own day-to-day problems, they often develop many innovative solutions. At off-sites, company retreats, or in training programs, salespeople come up with new ideas and approaches capable of resolving virtually any issue. The same can be said for people throughout the organization, who solve dozens of problems before lunch every day.

Yet, as shown by Sal and thousands of others on a daily basis, a salesperson can transform from that dynamic, problem-solving superhero into a predictable sales guy at the first hint of dissatisfaction, disinterest, or abject resistance. For some reason, she can't bring herself to use her problem-solving talents when facing a customer, no matter what the customer's disposition. As one of my clients complained after making a joint call with one of his people,

"I just can't believe it when in the customer's office, right before my eyes, this bright, articulate, creative salesperson transforms into a paperweight!"

Perhaps salespeople act this way because they feel creative problem solving is somehow inappropriate, or off target. Perhaps they feel it is too impromptu and they should stick with material they know well. Perhaps it is that they just don't know how to do it comfortably. Whatever the reasons, the opportunity to problem-solve in a sales call seems to lead salespeople by the thousands like lemmings over the cliff. To my way of thinking, that qualifies as thousands of missed opportunities every day.

Well, it's time for salespeople, managers, executives, and the entire supporting cast to drag themselves onto the shore, shake off the seawater, grab a branch, and climb back up that cliff into the fray. Salespeople need to think of themselves from this day forward primarily as problem-solving resources for their clients. If they do, they will immediately find themselves able to capitalize on what would otherwise have been missed opportunities.

How do organizations accomplish this change in approach? First, salespeople must learn how to turn the sales call, when appropriate, into a problem-solving session. That isn't easy, but, like riding a bike, once you get the hang of it, you'll never forget. Salespeople who master the appropriate skills will be able to help customers solve business problems and capitalize on opportunities they encounter because they'll be in the customer's trusted information loop. They'll realize that they can help customers develop their own ideas by using process skills to encourage them.

We'll talk a lot more about selling as problem solving in the rest of section I of the book. How to implement the approach in contacts with customers is the subject of section II.

> **Newsflash**   *Transforming sales calls into problem-solving opportunities is the highest level of selling. When salespeople and their sales teams learn how to do this, the results can be extraordinary.*

Salespeople who master the skills of selling as problem solving will be able to utilize the human capital at their disposal more effectively, whether it is the members of their sales team or other people within the organization. They'll be able to maximize the use of the company's products and services to accomplish these goals. This approach will enable them and their customers to create and develop ideas together. This creating-together habit will grow and continue, so that the people who make sales calls will be able to solve not just the problems at hand, but also unforeseen problems that crop up in the future.

Using this approach to selling, salespeople—and the organization they represent—will soon become a valued intellectual resource that buyers call upon when they have a problem to solve. As one corporate executive said in a focus group we observed not too long ago, "I want my salesperson to bring me solutions to problems I don't even know I have."

Think about that quote for a minute. Think about what that potential customer is asking your organization to do: provide "solutions to problems I don't even know I have." Not only is that a big statement, it's also an extraordinary compliment. And that's what salespeople need to learn how to do.

> **Newsflash**   *The most successful sales professionals are the ones whose customers eagerly anticipate their meetings because they know they will do some problem solving together.*

There's no better way to stand out from the crowd than to cultivate a problem-solving mentality throughout the organization. It takes the whole organization to accomplish this goal, because salespeople can't anticipate and solve customers' problems on their own. They're going to need cooperation from all departments to package creative solutions to customers' problems. They need to call on the technical expertise of people in the organization who don't normally think of themselves as salespeople. They need the synergies that result when a dedicated team focuses on anticipating and solving customers' problems. And the relationship that starts with the sales call needs to be maintained throughout the customer's dealings with the company.

Becoming a problem-solving resource is a proven way to differentiate your company that will work right away *and* last through the next umpteen waves of technical advances piling up on each other like rush hour traffic on the Hollywood Freeway. It helps now and it staves off obsolescence. Why? Because to be a problem-solving resource for your customers, you need to develop good relationships with them. And good relationships will always be in vogue; they don't become obsolete.

That's why professions that once frowned on formalized selling processes, such as law, public accounting, dentistry, managed health care, advertising, and even medicine, now pride themselves on the quality of their sales and marketing programs. Selling and marketing are simply the first step in building relationships. Down and out, desperate and disreputable stereotypical images of salespeople such as Willy Loman, the Flim-Flam Man, the Snake Oil Salesman, and WKRP's Herb, the sales guy, are less and less evident today. Honor, dignity, and recognition have taken their place, and this trend goes all the way to the top. Today the most senior levels of management boast about their contact with customers. John Alvord, when he was president of Connecticut National Bank, referred to himself as the "Number One Salesperson in the Company." The CEOs of Dell Computer and Home Depot referred to themselves as "Salesmen in Chief" when they were building their companies into super-organizations.

Salespeople today have the opportunity to do what many have wanted to do for decades—get involved in problem solving rather than simply hawk products and services. The time is ripe for *truly consultative* relationships with customers. Provided, of course, that the entire organization is geared to achieving this goal.

A New Look at Consultative Selling

The term "consultative selling" has been used for almost thirty years. Yet few buyers think that the salespeople who regard themselves as such are truly consultative. Many salespeople today are sensitized to using a "needs-oriented" or "needs-based" approach to selling—which suggests that the salesperson attempts to learn a customer's needs before presenting whatever it is he or she is selling. That's great in theory, but all too often it devolves to half a dozen cursory questions followed by the usual canned pitch. It doesn't *feel* consultative, as there is little engagement with the information brought to light by the questions and answers. And how could there be such engagement, if the salesperson isn't empowered to harness organizational resources in a creative way to meet the customer's needs?

Historically, *consultative selling* is supposed to be an approach to creating long-term, mutually beneficial sales relationships with major customers by helping them improve their profit margins through the use of the company's products and services. Mack Hanan first coined the term in 1970 in his landmark book, *Consultative Selling* (Amacon 1995). In this ideal scenario, the role of salesperson changes from *product supplier* to *problem solver* and *profit improver*. Initial writing in this area suggested that truly consultative relationships are *partnerships in growth*—an important element of which is the confidence the buyer has in the salesperson. Therefore, salespeople were asked to build a "climate of confidence" in order to function in a consultative manner.

From the time "consultative selling" was introduced those many years ago, salespeople, sales managers, and sales trainers have used the term in a variety of ways. Yet surprisingly few have represented it correctly. Most think that a "needs-oriented" approach to selling is, in and of itself, consultative selling. It is not. Determining a customer's needs before presenting anything is a great approach, but consultative selling goes far beyond that.

> **Newsflash** *Salespeople and organizations who are truly consultative most often leave their purely needs-oriented counterparts in the dust. So can you.*

Webster's Deluxe Unabridged Dictionary defines *consultative* as "having the *privilege* or *right* of conference." Webster is the only authority I've found to include the word *privilege* in defining this term. Everyone in the organization should take note of that word and remember it. *Privilege* implies that you must *earn the right* to suggest to another person a way to do something more effectively. It hints that to *assume* your opinions will be readily accepted is foolhardy and dangerous. Before you can consult, you have to pay some dues.

> **Newsflash** *People react negatively when faced with unsolicited ideas or feedback from persons not in their trusted loop.*

The notion that the opportunity to consult is a privilege would probably intrigue anyone who has ever worked with a consultant. Too often, even professional consultants offer their ideas and make recommendations without taking into account that the person on the receiving end may not want to hear what the consultant has to say. The result is that the consultant comes across as insensitive, arrogant, or just plain rude. Insensitivity and arrogance are behaviors that turn people off so effectively that they can't hear what's being said no matter what its value. It is one of the prices we pay for not being sensitive to *process*—a concept we'll discuss much more fully in subsequent chapters.

Newsflash   *Just because someone tells you they are hungry, it doesn't mean they want you to make them lunch.*

Later chapters will also develop in detail the skills involved in creating and maintaining a consultative relationship. For now, the important thing to realize is that salespeople who are backed by an organization-wide selling approach will have many ideas to bring to their customers all the time.

An example of how far-reaching a genuinely consultative approach can be comes from the early 1970s. In the chemical business at that time, everything "petroleum-related" was being rationed as a result of the Middle East oil embargo (just like gasoline to the public). Because of shortages of raw materials, in any given month manufacturers were allowed only a percentage of what they had purchased in that same period the previous year. As a result, many companies found themselves unable to produce enough product month-to-month to cover their fixed costs. Many were on the verge of bankruptcy.

Carl, a salesperson in this field who had many such customers, was able to prevent one of his customers, Company A, from going "belly up" by introducing them to another customer, Company B. The second company could provide the first with the rationed raw materials they needed, in exchange for access to some of *their* manufacturing equipment. This required some significant retooling on the part of Company A, but it was worth it to get the raw material needed for their biggest paying account.

Company B had an excess supply of the raw materials Company A needed, and Company A had some equipment that was 90 percent ready to do a job Company B had no equipment to handle. Through Carl's proactive and innovative efforts, these two companies were able to form a strategic alliance, benefiting both. Both companies came out ahead, and Carl suddenly had two devoted, long-term customers.

This case illustrates how—*with the customer's permission*—a creative salesperson can bring big problem-solving ideas to selling situations in such a way that all parties benefit.

All too often, in their zeal or insecurity, sales professionals fail even to notice the opening for this kind of creative partnership with customers. By using their inherent problem-solving abilities, by working effectively with their sales teams, and by listening to the ideas that their resources throughout the organization offer, salespeople can become genuinely consultative, and clearly differentiate themselves and their organization from the competition.

The Sales Team

So far we've focused mainly on how the individual salesperson needs to represent the kind of consultative, problem-solving approach that will distinguish the organization from its competitors. That's because it's the salesperson whom the customer first encounters. But—as may already be obvious—salespeople can't carry the freight entirely on their own. A truly consultative approach to selling requires *sales teams* that bring together different kinds of expertise and organizational resources.

The concept of teams within organizations has had a lot of airplay in recent years, but corporations have understood the need and value of teams at least since Henry Ford's original assembly plant. Sales teams, in particular, have been used in many organizations for many years. But today, the sales team has become a much more formalized structure. The world we live in demands the use of sales teams. It is primarily a resource issue: Every organization must compete with limited resources, and those resources must be leveraged. There is too much information out there for individuals to manage and use themselves. Hence the team concept becomes imperative. And the sales team becomes a necessity.

Of course, the notion of salespeople using the resources available to them is as old as sales organizations themselves. Most successful salespeople will tell you that they could never have accomplished what they have without the help of lots of people. When I started my sales career with Union Carbide many years ago, I had numerous resources available to me. I was the sales rep in the field, working out of my home in Evansville, Indiana. I had a customer service representative in the Cincinnati office. I had three technical service people in Bound Brook, New Jersey, available when we ran into quality problems. There was a credit guy in New York who kept an eye on my customers' ability to pay. There were distribution people in South Charleston, West Virginia, ready to expedite shipments in emergencies. We had marketing people in New York City helping promote what we sold and market research people in Tarrytown, New York, available to determine what new products and services to develop. Legal was there to review contracts and settle disputes. R&D was always looking to improve our product line. I had a district sales manager in St. Louis, who reported to a regional sales manager in Cleveland, who reported to a national sales manager in New York, and so on and on.

Now I probably boasted to my customers about the outstanding resources a company like Carbide had to provide the kind of quality service the customers required. I doubt I used the term "sales team" because I don't think it was used back then, but I'm sure I referred to our resources or subject matter experts or functional leaders or technical experts or whatever the appropriate label was at the time. But in no way, shape, or manner was this anything that resembled what we think about today when we think of a sales team.

What has changed significantly is the conscious attempt by organizations to leverage the resources needed to address the needs of the customer base. The sales team concept is the result of an evolutionary process in numerous sales organizations. In the early days of corporations, most salespeople worked alone. The salesperson was the front person who developed business with the company's customer base. As business became more complex, it became necessary for the salesperson to work collectively with other individuals to get things done. Over time, more emphasis was put into the development of groups.

There was a time twenty to thirty years ago when many companies were doing very interesting experiments to learn how to get the most out of the groups within their organizations. Salespeople found themselves in group situations more and more. Some enjoyed it, while others found it inhibiting. And as time went on, the concept of the group evolved to the concept of team. (Later on we'll look at the differences between groups and teams.)

Who is on the sales team, and how does it function? We'll discuss those questions in detail in section III. For now, suffice it to say that a sales team is made up of whatever functions touch the customer, either directly or indirectly. That means not only obvious candidates like customer service, marketing, product management, R&D, and fulfillment. It means production and manufacturing, quality control, engineering, and even finance. We'll see later on that this doesn't mean that all these groups and others are represented in every meeting of the sales team. But it does mean that all are involved appropriately in working *together* to anticipate and solve customers' problems.

An effective, motivated, energetic, and productive sales team can become a terrific problem-solving force within an organization. Teams can create their own identities. They can set new standards for innovation and partnership. Often they become quite visible and carry with them a sense of pride and even prestige. The end result can be a sales organization that has been transformed into a *living, breathing, problem-solving machine.*

Let me be very clear here. There are two specific and distinct reasons to have sales teams. The first, which I've already alluded to, is obvious: We need to provide our customers with the best possible solutions to their business problems, and if we tap into our collective expertise, we can maximize our ability to do that. Using teams to develop strategies internally, and bringing those people to meet with customers when needed, will result in our doing better work with our customers and prospects. It's that simple.

The second reason is not so obvious. As an organization tries to leverage those resources, it needs to provide its people with more of a *sense of ownership* when it comes to the customer. The people involved must feel that ownership whenever they do anything that has an impact on the customer. Although it is extremely important, this ownership variable too often is taken for granted or not given much consideration. That's a principal reason why organization-wide selling is such a powerful concept. If everybody feels a sense of ownership when it comes to the customer, they will be more committed to doing whatever they can to help the customer.

A quick digression: When I worked at Synectics®, Inc., I learned a wonderful expression that I use all the time: "Involvement is the prerequisite to commitment." If people feel more involved in the process, they will feel more committed to the results. Whether their recommendations are accepted or not, if they have the opportunity to express their point of view, and feel that what they suggested was heard and given fair consideration, they are much more likely to buy into the end result.

Newsflash *If you truly involve your team members and other resources available to you in the customer management process, they will do things for the customer that will knock your socks off.*

In today's marketplace, sales teams have become a necessity, not a luxury. It will be hard to compete without them. If you are going head to head with a viable competitor, and they are using the resources available to them and you aren't, you will find yourself at risk and working at a serious disadvantage.

The challenge for the company, of course, is how to transform its sales organization, which probably consists of many talented individuals, into one that is driven by well-organized, efficiently run teams. Many people need to be involved in this process, and if support doesn't begin at the CEO level and cascade down throughout the organization, it simply won't happen. Obviously, the sales organization must play the lead role, and the sales professional is a key player. But the evolution to having effective sales teams deliver outstanding customer satisfaction goes far beyond simply finding ways for salespeople to better leverage their resources.

It Starts at the Top

As he walked slowly through the parking lot to his car, Sal couldn't help but think about the impressive speech the CEO of his company had made at the national sales meeting just a few months earlier. His company was going to be one that was passionate about providing their customers with outstanding customer service. Customer satisfaction would be the number one priority. Everyone in the company, and he meant everyone, was going to think of themselves as sales professionals. And the CEO had given himself a new title—Chief Executive Salesperson.

Sal remembered how the troops had initially received the message with skepticism. It appeared to be just one more attempt to get them excited about their jobs—"the new flavor of the month," one of them had whispered during the speech. But as the company newsletter and promotional literature and daily e-mails reinforced this new approach, management was able to demonstrate that this wasn't just a lot of hype, and more and more people started to embrace the concept. As sales teams were formed and met regularly to work on customer-related issues, everybody saw the potential associated with the concept. When the new mission statement and company values were released and directly addressed these points, it became even clearer. When the new compensation program included measures for team orientation and customer dedication, everyone realized that this was not a temporary measure. And as traditional non-sales types started to come up with ways to help customers, they started to become true believers.

Sal shuddered at how with all that support behind him, he failed to make progress with this high-potential prospect who had been identified as a key target. He knew that he was the person who represented everyone in the organization when he made that first visit to the prospect. It was he who would have to explain how everybody in the company was thinking differently as they experienced what was actually a cultural change. As he reflected on the call, he realized that he let them all down. The customer never realized all that they could do for her.

At Christmas, Sal sent Betty a cute company greeting card, realizing as he sealed the envelope that she probably wouldn't even remember who he was.

Well, at least Sal's company had the right idea. Sales organizations today will find it absolutely necessary to do what the CEO in Sal's company did. If everybody in the organization is thinking about the customer, and thinking of themselves as salespeople, they will in fact prove they are different. It has to start at the top—at the very highest levels of the organization. If the message doesn't come from the executive offices and cascade down, it isn't going to happen.

Of course, words have to be backed up with deeds. Many CEOs and executive vice presidents and other senior managers talk about how customer oriented they are, but there is much research that reveals how little the customer is discussed at that level. The written word is important, but actions are more important. If a "customer-oriented" CEO, or any senior manager, does not spend time talking to salespeople and their managers, meeting with sales teams, or visiting customers, their actions strongly contradict their words. As a result, they won't be taken seriously by the people within the organization. And what they ask their people to do will probably be ignored.

But no matter how well the organization embraces the message, no matter how effective the sales teams may be, no matter what the company does to reinforce what they want people to do, it still becomes the role of the sales professional to communicate this effectively to the customer. If the salesperson's behavior does not reflect these changes, the customer has no reason to accept any of the promises he or she brings to the table.

Think back to Sal's encounter with Betty. In this scenario, Sal was suckered into responding in a perfectly predictable way, by attempting to meet the buyer's challenge head on—instantly proving beyond any doubt that good old Sal wasn't much different from any other uninventive, desperate, and predictable salesperson. He had failed in his effort to differentiate himself. He did not represent his sales team and the other resources within the organization the way he (or they) would have liked. And as the front person for his company, he did nothing to demonstrate just how different they really were.

Newsflash	*If you want to position your company as different from the pack, then you'd better not behave like the rest of the pack.*

Sal could have stood out as significantly different, if he had responded to the challenge in a more confident, relaxed, and unique way. Any effective response to the "Whatchagot?" land mine can be a remarkable way to differentiate oneself (and one's company) as worth the time to get to know, simply by avoiding the premature recitation of a prepared sales pitch. And at that moment, Sal was the company. If he could not differentiate himself, there was no way he could demonstrate the uniqueness of his organization.

Part of Sal's problem was that the organization had preached teamwork, problem solving, consultative selling—the whole ball of wax. It had issued a new mission statement. "Customer centered" was all but implanted on people's brains. What the organization had overlooked was that consultative selling isn't just a philosophy or a frame of mind. It's a set of behaviors, backed up by appropriate organizational structures and practices.

It's easy to talk the talk. But to walk the walk requires knowing how. To be able to introduce a problem-solving mindset to their sales calls, sales professionals must develop strong interactive skills, learn to work the subtle human dynamics of the sales process itself, and demonstrate total sensitivity to the customer's view of his situation. That's why so much of this book is devoted to the specific skills salespeople need to acquire to make organization-wide selling a reality.

Newsflash	*The entire company may think of themselves as salespeople, but it is the sales professional who has to demonstrate this first.*

As should be obvious by now, though, successful selling today isn't just about skills training and better marketing. As important as they are, Sal's skills wouldn't forge a lasting relationship with Betty's company unless the company culture fully supported what he was trying to do. The approach starts with the sales professional, then moves to the sales team, and eventually manifests itself throughout the organization (see figure 1.1).

The problem-solving mindset must saturate the entire organization. It's so easy to simply avoid working on a problem or taking advantage of an opportunity. It is easier to put a problem off than to roll up your sleeves and attack it. When organizations become more oriented toward problem solving, they can do great things.

Figure 1.1   Organization-Wide Selling

Newsflash   *A problem-solving mindset is something that everybody in the company must demonstrate if organization-wide selling is to become a reality.*

What all this implies is a cultural change. To change cultures, you need to change attitudes. You also have to change beliefs and behaviors. That's not easy to do. But it is doable, and section IV will detail what is involved in making it happen.

Getting from Here to There

We've so far discussed a number of ideas, but I hope I've made it clear that they're intimately related. Selling may begin with the sales call, but the key to successful selling isn't just being highly skilled at this special kind of human encounter. Selling isn't any longer only a matter of technique. What works today is developing genuine partnerships with customers, giving them the best possible reason to work with you and your company. In one sentence: Selling means problem solving.

At one level, this approach does involve technique—and a more than superficial understanding of what problem solving is and how it works. Salespeople need to become master problem solvers, and that can mean taking a very different approach from traditional sales calls. For that, training and study are required.

But techniques won't solve customers' problems. They'll just create the opening to do so by getting salespeople past the "Whatchagot?" land mine (and all the others customers put in their paths).

Genuinely solving customers' problems involves the synergies that come from creating effective sales teams. It involves the dedication of the whole organization: a mindset, a culture, and the structures and processes that back them up.

> **Newsflash**   *The "rugged individualist," a hero in sales days gone by, is about as relevant today as the three-martini lunch.*

The rest of this book details how to get from here to there. We'll look at what makes problem solving work, how to put the approach across to customers, how to forge dynamic sales teams, and how to implement a customer-oriented, sales-oriented consciousness throughout the organization.

I wrote the first draft of this book with salespeople in mind. I've been through those wars, and I'm excited about what I have to offer the people in the trenches. But whether you're a sales professional, a sales manager or trainer, an executive, a CEO, or just someone who realizes that everybody in the organization is a salesperson, I think you'll find something important and valuable in this book. The fact is, selling isn't just about the sales professional. Selling is a team sport.

MEMO TO MANAGEMENT

Nobody likes to hear it, but for the most part, we are all selling commodities these days. Wherever you look, someone is offering something that looks every bit as good as what you have to sell, promising the same excellent service, and ensuring the same backup from the people within the organization.

You and your people need to differentiate yourselves from the competition. Your salespeople can't do that effectively if they don't (or can't) use the resources available to them. The day of the rugged individualist is over. Teamwork and collaboration are critical components of successful selling.

Organization-wide selling is the key, but don't forget that from the customer's perspective, the organization is the sales professional. You have lots of Sals working for you. They are hardworking, conscientious, committed, loyal, and dedicated. They want to be successful, and they want the company to be successful. They certainly have the ability to reach their potential. Unfortunately, many of them don't. As a result, you don't.

If your entire organization is to become completely sales-oriented, the process starts at the top, but it manifests itself in the field. Sales professionals must learn that early in any relationship, particularly on the first call, presenting their products and services does not accomplish much. The role of the sales professional on that first meeting or even the first few meetings is to assess the customer's situation. If they do that well, when the timing is appropriate, they can make powerful recommendations that are developed by customer-focused groups within the organization.

Implementing this problem-solving, consultative approach to selling isn't easy. The trap that Sal fell in is common. Your support is critical. Without your constant reinforcement and positive role modeling, the points made in this book, no matter how valid, will fall on deaf ears. No organization ever becomes sales-oriented through and through without the active support and leadership of management. So it's worth your while to understand the approach to selling detailed in this book. You have nothing to lose but some of the frustrations and disappointments that result from the missed opportunities you experience every day.

When your sales representatives have the skills and resources behind them to transform every sales call into a problem-solving opportunity, they will elevate the sales process. They will clearly differentiate themselves. And you, and your whole organization, will reap the benefits.

CHAPTER 2

Problem Solving 101
MAXIMIZING THE CHANCES OF SUCCESS

In chapter 1, I stressed how important it is for people throughout an organization to bring a problem-solving attitude to all interactions that involve customers—both sales calls and internal meetings in which customers are discussed. The development of this mindset is a key element in adopting an organization-wide selling approach. Putting that mind frame into action, however, requires specific problem-solving skills. In this chapter and in chapter 3, we'll focus on these skills. While these skills are relevant to everyone in the organization, they are especially valuable to sales professionals.

Are We Selling, Problem Solving, or Both?

People have been talking about the link between selling and problem solving for a long time. Motivational speeches to salespeople often refer to helping customers solve their business problems. Commercials portray an organization's sales force as people with solutions to problems. Interviewers and recruiters often look for problem-solving traits when they recruit salespeople. Yet salespeople too often don't apply problem-solving skills when interacting with customers and prospects. In my view, they have the ability to do so, but they simply don't know how to make it happen comfortably.

Problem solving is also the link between selling and consulting. Helping customers solve their business problems is just what consultants are supposed to do. It works the other way, too: the most successful consultants are the ones who know how to *sell*—not just their services, but their ideas and recommendations. They may not think of what they do as selling, but that's exactly what it is.

Given the acknowledged similarities between selling, problem solving, and consulting, why don't salespeople attempt to be consultative, as Mack Hanan first suggested almost thirty years ago? To be sure, some of the most successful salespeople do take a consultative approach. Most, however, can't, because they don't have an awareness of the *process skills* involved in transforming sales calls into problem-solving opportunities.

> **Newsflash**   *Process sensitivity and skills are the keys to truly consultative selling.*

Salespeople as Natural Problem Solvers

Fortunately, the "selling as problem solving" approach is a congenial one for salespeople to learn. That's because salespeople tend to be natural problem solvers.

Here's why I'm absolutely sure about this. During the eight years I spent with Union Carbide in the late 1960s and mid-1970s, I was introduced to Synectics®, Inc., a forty-year-old international consulting firm with offices in the United States, Europe, and Asia. Many consider Synectics to be the most successful consultancy involved in teaching creative problem solving, innovation, teamwork, and their application to the business environment. Studying the Synectics approach to problem solving confirmed my belief that good problem solving and good selling involve many of the same traits and skills.

In its early years Synectics spent most of its time researching, teaching, and applying creative problem-solving concepts and techniques. Along the way, the researchers at Synectics began to notice that most of the things that went well in problem-solving sessions were quite *unintentional.* People in successful meetings had no idea *why* the meetings went well. Similarly, most good problem solvers were unaware of why they were successful at their crafts. Synectics was the first firm to attempt to quantify the problem-solving process, and quantify it they did!

When I joined Synectics, I quickly realized that successful salespeople, like good problem solvers, don't know exactly why they are successful. Most good salespeople find their success difficult, if not impossible, to explain succinctly. Yet one of the reasons I believe so strongly in the organization-wide approach to selling is that it relates very well to the natural strengths of the salesperson.

Why are salespeople natural problem solvers? Consider some of the traits that effective sales professionals have in common with champion problem solvers.

Successful salespeople are "people-oriented." Sales is a "people" business. Sales professionals are always using people skills at their customer locations, whether it's with the receptionist in the lobby, the factory worker who is using their product, the purchasing agent they call on, or the CEO they see every so often. They do the same thing when they work internally with people from the plant, the credit department, legal, marketing, or the members of their sales team.

Problem solving, too, is a people-oriented activity. Many individuals with good ideas aren't listened to simply because they lack good people skills. As Emerson said, "What you *are* speaks so loud, I cannot hear what you *say.*" Those who work effectively with people are more successful in problem-solving situations.

Salespeople are risk takers. The best anecdotes about salespeople usually involve moments of high risk. The biggest breakthroughs in sales often seem to occur when the participants are most anxious, uncomfortable, and unsure. Similarly, in problem-solving sessions, getting people to take intellectual risks almost always results in new and creative ideas. George Prince, the ingenious founder of Synectics, Inc., and my mentor, talked often about how the most creative ideas appeared when people were least comfortable.

Successful salespeople are curious and inquisitive. Neil Rackham, the highly respected author of *Spin Selling* (McGraw Hill 1988), has done some excellent research correlating the relationship between the number of questions asked and the number of successful sales attained by a salesperson. "There is a clear statistical association between the use of questions and the success of the interview. The more you ask questions, the more successful the interaction is likely to be" (14–15).

Salespeople who use questioning well are successful because they are better able than their competitors to unearth information and thereby determine more of their customers' needs. The result is that they are able to offer more "benefit statements"—statements that point out the value of products and services to a prospective buyer. As we'll see later, the ability to offer benefit statements that are *on target* is the result of effective *questioning,* not effective *presenting.*

Like good salespeople, effective problem solvers also rely on curiosity, learning as much as possible about the problem they are attacking. Surprisingly, however, knowing *too much* about a problem can work against generating creative ideas. With more and more detail, the tendency to "shut down" and "censor" ideas increases. Although salespeople should learn as much as they can about a customer, they'll never know as much as the customer does—and that naiveté can be very useful.

Successful salespeople are good listeners. The most successful salespeople listen effectively to their customers and respond accordingly. A salesperson who listens effectively will uncover more of the customer's needs, just as a problem solver who listens more effectively has a better understanding of the problem. In both cases, the result is more and better ideas for solutions.

Successful salespeople are results-oriented. That's what keeps them pushing forward toward the ultimate goal, the sale. Similarly, effective problem solvers always seem to be seeking that next bit of information or hidden clue about the issue at hand that might help unearth a workable solution.

Salespeople learn to handle rejection. When I teach sales seminars, I often ask the group to identify the things they like and do not like about selling. Invariably, the top of the "Do not like" list is "being rejected." Nobody likes the feeling of being told, "No, you weren't the one selected." This, it turns out, is one of the main reasons salespeople are reluctant at the end of a nicely flowing meeting to ask for the business. They know from past experience that they are courting rejection.

Of course, the reality is that in the sales profession we're bound to lose more deals than we close. Successful sales professionals come to realize that when customers say, "No," they're not rejecting the salesperson, but rather the idea at hand. That's important, because human beings have a natural tendency to reject new and different ideas. We all do this a lot, often with perfectly good intentions. Yet, when we find our own ideas rejected, too often we react by getting defensive, aggressive, or even passive. None of these responses is particularly effective or helpful, but they're part of the price we pay for being human.

Successful people in any field where rejection is one of the occupational hazards have found ways to get around the uncomfortable feelings that are aroused when rejection is encountered. They are able to creatively turn the rejection into an opportunity for problem solving.

Similarly, successful problem solvers know how to deal with disappointing reactions to their ideas. They might not like what they hear, but that doesn't stop them from continuing to try to solve the problem at hand. For example, one healthy reaction to rejection is to use criticism as the basis for improving an idea. If an idea is rejected because it is too expensive, a proactive response is, "Well, then let's figure out a way to get the cost down, OK?"

Salespeople and problem solvers who meet with recurring success tend to be good at this craft. Using criticism to advance the process of problem solving instead of shutting it down is a skill that can be learned and applied to any conflict situation.

Effective salespeople are tenacious. Most people realize that "stick-to-it-iveness" is a necessary part of good sales technique. We've all heard horror stories about the people who gave in too early versus those who hung in and eventually were successful. Research backs up that anecdotal evidence. Years ago, Xerox Corporation released some research findings showing how the average salesperson gave up on an account two calls below the number typically required to close a deal. That doesn't mean that if everyone made two more sales calls they would get the order every time. But it does demonstrate the importance of hanging in there longer than one thinks is necessary.

Whenever I speak to new salespeople, I say that I hope each of them experiences a customer for whom they have to wait several years before finally getting an order. The rookies' reaction typically is a sarcastic, "Thanks a lot!" Eventually, though, they learn that while some customers may take a long time to convince, nurturing that relationship can turn it into a long and meaningful one. There is no more satisfying feeling derived from selling, I believe, than finally doing business with an account that took a long time to deliver.

Similarly, problem solvers often devote considerable time to an idea that intrigues them, in spite of many flaws that are apparent when the idea is initially presented. Einstein was an aficionado of this school, saying, "If at first glance an idea doesn't have at least some element of absurdity, I have no hope for it at all."

As a matter of fact, the most exciting ideas to watch emerging from problem-solving sessions are the ones that at first seemed a far cry from being even *close* to a solution. The reason that such ideas can and do develop into viable solutions is that the problem owners are willing to invest the required time to develop the concept, work through the issues, and grapple with the concerns necessary to transform idea to concept and finally to solution. Ideas that seem least likely to work, yet still intrigue the group, often have a life of their own, exciting the thinkers and propelling them forward through the process toward solution.

Thomas Edison, when asked how he had been able to labor so relentlessly trying to find the right combination of metals for the first light bulb filament, replied, "I ached to give it all up, but something kept me going . . . the kind of thing you do when you're young and don't know any better."

Successful salespeople have the ability to use the resources available to them. The same is true of good problem solvers. One of the things I enjoy most is watching a group of people in pursuit of an answer build upon one another's ideas. The ability to hear someone say something and use that something to trigger a *new* idea is a skill that can be developed and honed. Groups can be taught how to use one another's ideas to trigger their own extensions of these ideas. Groups will invariably perform better than individuals in this respect because of this "pinball" factor—ideas bouncing from brain to brain, picking up momentum along the way. Sales teams can learn to do this, and the results can be mind-boggling.

The ability to use resources effectively is a key attribute that salespeople must develop to implement the organization-wide sales approach. This elevator goes to an even higher floor if she's willing to let the other guy have the credit. Over the years I have learned to revere an old adage given to me by my father: "There is no limit to what a man [*sic*] can do or where he can go, if he doesn't mind who gets the credit."

A Proven Problem-Solving Approach

The fact that good salespeople and good problem solvers share many traits gives us a running start on adopting a problem-solving approach to selling. Just as important is the fact that genuinely consultative selling is similar in structure and format to creative problem solving. The key is to learn to look at sales calls as problem-solving opportunities, and then use the appropriate skills to leverage these opportunities.

There are several approaches to creative problem solving. My favorite is the Synectics method, and not simply because I spent five years of my career working for that fine organization. Properly applied, it yields dazzling results time and time again.

The problem-solving methodology we'll focus on was designed primarily for group interactions, as opposed to people working alone. As such, it's directly relevant to the concept of organization-wide selling and to the use of sales teams. As we'll see, however, much can be learned from this methodology that will be of value to any problem-solving situation, including the solo salesperson's forays in the field. As I will emphasize repeatedly, that's because *a sales call is a meeting*—a unique kind of meeting, perhaps, but a meeting nonetheless. Consequently, understanding meeting dynamics can be a tremendous asset to sales professionals.

Newsflash   *The sales call is a meeting. All the dynamics of any meeting occur during sales calls.*

Content Versus Process in Problem-Solving Meetings

Meetings in general are difficult to manage well, and problem-solving meetings are perhaps the most challenging of all. Despite the countless books, articles, and papers that have been written about how to conduct meetings, not to mention the thousands of people who earn their livelihood as meeting planners and facilitators, the sad fact is that meetings rarely accomplish their full list of objectives. Many meetings achieve less than half of their intended agendas, and others are overall disasters. Surveys indicate that up to 70 percent of an executive's time is spent in meetings and that most executives feel that 70 percent of that time is not productive.

So what makes for successful meetings? Whenever I begin a training program, whether in consultative selling skills, innovative team selling, meeting management, problem solving, or sales management, I begin with the concept of increasing the Probability of Success (POS) of any interaction by understanding the following equation:

$$\textbf{POS} = f\textbf{(Quality of Thinking)} \times \textbf{(Climate)}$$

This formula, originally developed by Synectics, expresses the idea that the probability of success in any interaction is a function of two variables: the *quality of thinking* of the participants and the *climate* in which that thinking takes place. Whether the meeting involves six people or sixty, whether it's a sales call or a debriefing, a focus group, a coaching session, or a job interview, the same formula applies.

Quality of thinking refers to the *content* component of any meeting. "Content" is anything on the table that answers the question "What?":

- What is the task?
- What is the problem?
- What is the objective?
- What are the ideas?
- What are the issues?
- What are the results?

The other variable, *climate,* is where most of us crash and burn. "Climate" refers to the *process* component of the meeting. Process addresses anything that answers the question "How?"

- How was the available time used?
- How were ideas treated?
- How did it feel to be in the room?
- How was the time distributed among participants?
- How much fun was it?
- How much good listening took place?
- How relaxed or tense were the participants?
- How effectively did we work together?
- How speculative did we get?
- How safe was it to take a risk?

In briefest terms, climate refers to *how it feels* to be in the group and how the group behaves. Not only is climate one of the two key variables that determine the probability of success, but many people familiar with meeting dynamics know that climate also affects the other variable, quality of thinking, magnifying its effects on the potential for success.

Climate issues make up the *process* component of a meeting. When meetings don't succeed, it is most often because of a failure in process. Think of the last meeting you attended. If it was disappointing, I'll bet that it wasn't because of a shortage of ideas or because the people involved didn't have enough brainpower to address the task at hand. The ability to control the *process* of a meeting is the ability to make it succeed.

The same thing applies to sales interactions. Salespeople who understand process will be far more successful than those who don't. Look once again at Sal's doomed sales call. It was Sal's response to the "Whatchagot?" land mine—not the land mine itself—that caused the interaction to blow up in his face. If Sal had been more attuned to process, he might have responded to Betty's "Whatchagot?" challenge in a different way:

> Look, I'll be pleased to answer your perfectly understandable question, Betty, but I know I could better explain how we can be of value if you would first allow me to ask a few questions and learn a bit more about your situation. Would that be OK?

Using this response, Sal would have both defused the land mine and set the stage to learn something about Betty's situation. The moment Betty agreed, Sal would have regained control of the call while appearing to comply with her stated request, no matter how aggressively she worded it.

Sal's inability to manage process was costly in the short and in the long run—in the short run, because there was no meaningful next step, and in the long run, because there was little chance that he would even get another meaningful appointment. By the same token, when problem-solving meetings within the organization fail, customers—and the company—are the losers.

Newsflash	*Salespeople, sales teams, and sales organizations who use process as a conscious tool are at a distinct advantage compared to those who don't.*

Problem-Solving Roles and Responsibilities

One of the keys to managing the climate of a problem-solving session is to be clear about the roles and responsibilities of the participants. Let me briefly develop this idea as it applies to meetings. Later we'll apply it to one-on-one encounters with customers.

In any problem-solving meeting two roles typically emerge—the problem owner and the participants invited to help the problem owner. The issue is that nobody pays much attention to process. (See figure 2.1.)

The problem owner finds him- or herself managing both the content and process of the meeting. Typically, in this situation process tends to be ignored. That is why the role of the facilitator has become more prevalent during the past fifteen years.

Today, whenever possible, three distinct roles are found in problem-solving meetings: the *problem owner,* the *participants,* and the *facilitator.* (See figure 2.2.)

It's important to remember that the *problem owner* is *the person who called the meeting.* In pure meeting management terms, you

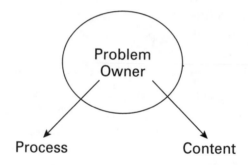

Figure 2.1 Typical Responsibilities of the Problem Owner

Figure 2.2 Alternative Distribution of Roles and Responsibilities in Problem-Solving Meetings

cannot "call" someone else's meeting. If you do, you will probably pay a price for it at some later point.

An example is the sales manager who walks into the product manager's office uninvited and tells her what she needs to do to improve the quality of the product. Or the advertising account executive who walks into a creative director's office and offers ideas about a campaign that he isn't involved in. In cases like this, you can anticipate a negative reaction because unsolicited ideas and feedback are being offered to solve the other person's "problem." That's what I mean by calling someone else's meeting.

Newsflash   *When you call someone else's meeting, you are setting yourself up for trouble.*

Now, calling someone else's meeting is something that sales professionals must do every day. Every time we make an appointment or drop by to see a customer to tell them how *our* company can improve things for *their* company, we are calling the customer's meeting. Normally, that's something to avoid, but in the sales world, calling customers' meetings is expected. The nature of our job as salespeople requires that we take the initiative. Nevertheless, it behooves us to be sensitive to the inevitable effects of calling someone else's meeting. It's easier for customers to accept our products and services if they are presented as solutions to needs the customers agree they have. So we have to be careful about *how* we go about making presentations or offering unexpected ideas. We'll take a hard look at this point later.

Outside of sales calls, though, a meeting belongs to the problem owner, who therefore serves as chairperson. When meetings deal with multiple issues, different people can become the problem owner at different times. If the group is working on a distribution issue, it would be silly for anyone except the distribution manager to assume that role.

Now here's where the content versus process issue comes in. Managing both the content and the process of a meeting is too much for one person to do effectively. The way to deal with this is to delegate some of the chairperson's responsibilities. The chairperson (the problem owner) takes responsibility for the *content* and *all content-related decisions* in the meeting: the wording of the task, which ideas to develop, whether to continue in a certain direction, when to abandon a particular concept, and to whom to assign the follow-up steps. In short, the problem owner is responsible for the "quality of thinking" half of the probability of success equation.

If the problem owner assumes all responsibility for *content*, then the *process* responsibilities *in toto* must be delegated. These duties are handled by the *facilitator*. The pure facilitator takes charge of all process responsibilities, ranging from menial tasks like arranging logistics, watching the clock, and taking notes to more sophisticated tasks like protecting ideas, serving as an idea catalyst, and managing conflict. The facilitator assumes the role of "traffic cop," directing verbal and idea traffic in the meeting to ensure it flows smoothly. In short, the facilitator manages the "climate" half of the equation.

There are, of course, exceptions to this clear-cut division of labor. One of the facilitator's responsibilities is to make decisions about applying methodologies if the group runs out of mental steam, is unwilling to speculate, or refuses to take the risks that could result in new and different ideas. In such cases, facilitators can't completely divorce themselves from the content of the meeting. But the primary role of the facilitator is to focus on process.

The facilitator must be aware of what is going on in the group as a whole and at the same time be sensitive to how the problem owner is reacting to ideas flowing from the group. It can't be stated too strongly, however, that the role of the pure facilitator is to manage the *process* only, and that it is usually inappropriate for that person to offer ideas or make suggestions.

When sales teams meet, as is the case with any group, they will do better if they have a facilitator. Usually different team members take turns assuming this role so that their sales-related input is not lost for the entire meeting.

As an aside, I should mention that an alternative to having a single facilitator handle all the process tasks is to assign facilitation responsibilities to various members of the group. The most common task that is handed off is that of the *scribe*. The role of a scribe is to capture in writing—whether on a flip chart, a white board, a steno pad, or a laptop—every idea, suggestion, recommendation, perspective, and thought that group members offer during the course of the meeting.

In their well-conceived book, *How to Make Meetings Work* (Jove 1976), Doyle and Strauss make a strong case for having one person act strictly as the scribe. The rationale is that recording the key points in a meeting is too difficult an assignment for one person to do in conjunction with all the other possible process responsibilities.

Other roles that can be handed off at the discretion of the facilitator include those of the timekeeper, who makes sure discussions are held within the predetermined time limits; the "gate-keeper," who ensures that conflicts are quickly resolved; the "modeler," who consistently models the kinds of behavior that aid the creative process; and even the "paper hangers," who make sure that ideas are captured on newsprint and taped to the walls so everyone can see what has been done. Sometimes keeping people involved in the process is important, even though their task may seem trivial. Having different team members involved in managing process can result in better meetings.

Problem-Solving Roles in Selling Situations

Now let's look at how these basic ideas about problem-solving meetings apply to sales calls.

As I said earlier, the same dynamics that affect problem-solving meetings are at work in sales calls. Consider what happens in a sales call: Information is shared. Ideas are offered. Decisions are made. Hidden agendas come into play. Emotions can be aroused. Action steps are assigned. Politics often play a role.

Sounds like a meeting, doesn't it?

Once salespeople learn to look at sales calls as meetings, they can begin to approach content and process issues in new ways related to the probability of success formula. The question for salespeople is, How do we resolve the issues that ruin meetings when we're in a selling situation? Or, to put it more positively, How do we manage the climate of the sales call so as to optimize the chances for success?

The process starts long before the "meeting" itself, and it continues long after. Salespeople should use a problem-solving approach when they plan their sales calls, when they conduct these calls, and when they do the necessary follow-up work after the sale.

To begin with, the most successful sales professionals are the ones who spend considerable time planning their calls and using the resources available to them. In anticipation of a sales call, they team—do a great deal of strategizing about both the content and the process of the meeting, preferably with help from some of the members of the sales team. They plan an agenda and define the outcome they want to achieve (which may or may not be a sale—it might be, for instance, getting acquainted with the customer and beginning the process of establishing a relationship). They consider how best to utilize the scheduled time and how to take advantage of their resources. In terms of content, they figure out what needs to be put on the table. They anticipate objections and think hard about how to address them.

The sales call presents a number of opportunities for problem solving besides the central task of helping the customer solve his or her problems. Put the customer at ease (problem solved). Confirm the agenda for the meeting (problem solved). Demonstrate understanding of the customer's situation (problem solved). Convince the customer you care about his or her problems (huge problem solved).

Notice that *these* problems are process issues. They have to do with the climate of this special kind of meeting. As we'll discuss in a moment, that means that effective salespeople need to master the skills of good facilitators.

The "follow-up" part of a sales call requires problem-solving skills. Serious salespeople know that what they do after the call, particularly after a successful cold call, presents a wonderful opportunity to differentiate themselves and increase the buyer's confidence that they have made a right choice. As the saying goes, "The real selling begins *after* you get the order."

Providing additional perspectives on what was discussed, offering an idea that occurred after the meeting, or simply putting some initial thoughts in writing can make an excellent early impression. Sending relevant information based on the meeting can go a long way. Offering recommendations that involve other people can also be a way to use creative thinking to demonstrate value after the call is done.

The opportunity to be creative before, during, and after the call is another reason salespeople tend to be good problem solvers. The sales job is one that requires a *consistent* problem-solving frame of mind.

Newsflash   *Successful salespeople use their problem-solving ability to differentiate themselves before, during, and after the sales call.*

Process Sensitivity as a Valuable Sales Tool

We've already seen that the *process* component of a meeting is the key variable in determining the probability of success. For this reason, salespeople who are sensitive to process and understand how to make it work for them are going to be way ahead of the game. When they meet with their sales teams, they will develop better strategies and make the people on the team feel more committed to the end result. Just as important, they will be more successful in their interactions with customers as well. They'll easily differentiate themselves from aggressive or laid-back competitors who don't know how to leverage process to add value to every customer interaction.

Salespeople dread losing control of a sales call, the way Sal did in his interaction with Betty. But "control" doesn't mean doing all the talking and forcing the customer onto *your* agenda. It means doing what a good facilitator does in a problem-solving meeting: being attentive to the climate of the session and using process skills to keep the flow going.

> **Newsflash**   *Salespeople who think of themselves as facilitators and manage the process of their sales calls will more comfortably control those sales calls.*

In short, salespeople need to moderate their sales calls the same way professional facilitators manage problem-solving meetings. How so? Well, a good salesperson must know how to draw out the prospective customers and clients who are reluctant to speak and slow down the ones who talk too much, without offending either. They must control the tempo and process of the sales call and make sure that the meeting stays on track. They must make certain that time constraints are respected, and take notes to remember what transpired. They need to know when to speculate and when to be rigid. At the same time, they are responsible for certain content outcomes, such as developing action plans and determining who has responsibility for implementing the next steps.

What this means is that the salesperson assumes the roles of both facilitator and participant when interacting with a customer. (See figure 2.3.) At the same time, the salesperson must treat the customer as the problem owner (even though the customer may not *know* that he or she has a problem) while encouraging the customer to act as a *participant*. Anyone else who attends the meeting (the resources) also plays the role of participant.

A mistake many salespeople make is to ignore facilitation and focus single-mindedly on the content they have to present. But salespeople cannot effectively describe the uniqueness of their company's approach if they don't understand the specific business challenges the customer is experiencing. That means learning as much about the customer's situation as possible.

Think about how Sal failed to use process as a tool to turn things around in his conversation with Betty. He responded to Betty's "Whatchagot?" challenge with a canned pitch about his products and services. It was well presented, but accomplished little. In today's marketplace, even a distinct advantage in goods and services will be quickly gobbled up, emulated or stolen by

Figure 2.3   Applying Meeting Roles to Selling Situations

competitors, leaving you in the same crashed car in the same gully at some later date. It's better to use process skills to turn the car around now, avoid the chasm, and build a meaningful, solid relationship with your customer. Then you can talk goods and services as a function of that relationship at a later, more relaxed time.

In Sal's case, eliciting information about Betty's situation would have enabled him to offer thoughtful answers that would justify at least considering "changing horses in midstream," and would identify exactly what Sal's company could offer that those other companies couldn't: real partnership. Because he didn't ask these questions, he didn't have the relevant information to accomplish his objective.

When salespeople understand meeting dynamics and consciously use problem-solving tools, encountering a "Whatchagot?" attitude won't stop them in their tracks. Why not? Because the *process-sensitive* sales professional can turn the situation around by simply getting the buyer to verbally review his or her situation. That isn't asking so much, is it? We're asking people who may have big egos to *talk about themselves* for a few minutes—in most cases, an irresistible offer!

Sure, sometimes it isn't that simple. But as with problem-solving meetings, facilitation in sales calls can involve managing conflict or counterproductive behavior. For example, in the face of one of those less-than-friendly "Whatchagot?" land mines, an upbeat response might be:

> Wait a second, Betty. The last thing I ever want you to feel is that you're wasting your time. Let me spend a few minutes learning about your situation. Then I can better tell you, based on what I learn, why it may be in your interest to hear what else we have to offer. OK?

Of course, there's a lot more to managing sales calls effectively than what we've discussed so far. That's what section II of this book is about. For now, the point is to think in terms of managing interactions with customers as problem-solving opportunities. Process sensitivity is an essential part of doing that.

Process Sensitivity Throughout the Organization

If creating an organization-wide selling approach starts with instilling a problem-solving mindset throughout the company, then process sensitivity needs to permeate any organization that wants to be perceived as customer-driven and sales-oriented. Attention to process will help the people within an organization work together more effectively to anticipate and solve customer-related problems. And it will help the salespeople and their sales teams perform better when interacting with customers.

Newsflash   *The more sales professionals, sales teams, and sales organizations understand about the dynamics of process, the more successful they will be in everything they do.*

Think about it. If all the members of an organization were better listeners, responded to new ideas more openly, conducted more effective meetings, used questions more appropriately, and in general were more sensitive to the human dynamics associated with interactions, they would be bound to produce more and better solutions. When people start to focus on *how* they interact and not just on *what* they have to say, they not only perform more effectively, but also derive more satisfaction from their jobs. And they *can* learn how to do it. It's simply a matter of being introduced to the necessary skills and having the support required to reinforce what they learn.

In this chapter, we began introducing these skills by looking at meeting roles and responsibilities and how they play out not only in meetings, but also in one-on-one sales calls. Chapter 3 completes this introduction to problem-solving methodology. So get ready for the advanced course, in which you'll learn a proven sequence of steps for creative problem solving.

MEMO TO MANAGEMENT

If you want your organization to adopt a problem-solving mentality to selling, it is incumbent upon you to foster an environment in which problem solving and creativity can flourish.

Partly that means making sure the skills taught in this book become part of everyone's repertoire. But it also means bringing your own process sensitivity to bear on the climate within your organization.

How? Encourage your people to bring new and different ideas and approaches to the sales process. Encourage risk taking. Accept failure, when it occurs, as a growth opportunity as opposed to an excuse to blame or punish people.

Challenge your people to think beyond the normal constraints. After a joint sales call with one of your people, suggest ideas that could have been offered to the customer. Include in your performance appraisals opinions about your salespeople's use of teamwork, creativity, and speculative thinking in working with customers. When people within the organization do great things on the customer's behalf, make sure they get loads of recognition.

As always, you have to walk the walk. When you invite salespeople and others within the organization to continually develop new ideas, many of these ideas will not be acceptable at first glance. That's a natural and necessary aspect of creative problem solving. If you shoot down or reject ideas immediately, it won't take long before ideas stop coming your way.

That doesn't mean you should pretend that you like an idea when you don't. But it does mean that you demonstrate your understanding of the idea, see the value in it, and, if necessary, use its shortcomings to spur even better thinking.

The concept of process sensitivity and how organizations need to focus on process may sound a bit esoteric or "touchy-feely." Nothing could be further from the truth. If your company is like most, it wastes tons of money every year because of process-related issues. Good ideas are lost or never surface in the first place. Important messages are never heard. Misunderstandings and misconceptions result in missed opportunities. The lack of effective teamwork leads to lost productivity—and lost sales.

There's no need to deny it. It happens all the time.

Changing this state of affairs requires more than your active support. Unless you demonstrate your own sensitivity to process, it will be hard for your people to take the message seriously. All it takes is one bad actor in any meeting to destroy the potential of the group. If management falls into that unfortunate role, the effect is multiplied.

Cultivating a healthy climate in the organization isn't just a humane value. It's not a matter of being "nice." It's a question of reaping the rich dividends that come from turning your company into a problem-solving, selling machine.

CHAPTER 3

Problem Solving 102
Actually Doing It!

Chapter 2 emphasized the importance of *process* and process sensitivity in problem solving. I'll have a lot more to say about the specifics of managing process in both one-on-one and group interactions as we go through this book. Now, though, it's time to put some flesh on the idea of problem solving itself.

This chapter is devoted to a structured process for group problem solving. Why is that topic important now? For three reasons.

First, if you're going to implement sales teams (or improve the ones you have), it's vital to train them in group problem-solving skills. After all, the whole point of having a sales team is to come up with better solutions to customers' problems. That's what is going to differentiate your organization—not the pizzazz that a sales team brings to presentations, but its effectiveness in solving real business problems. So sales teams need to know how to work as a group to solve problems effectively and creatively.

Second, sales teams and other groups in your organization conduct meetings all the time. Obviously, not every meeting is a problem-solving meeting. But if a team or work group can learn to problem-solve effectively together, the rest is pretty easy.

Third, if salespeople and their colleagues can learn to use these problem-solving concepts with customers, they can do extraordinary things. Although we'll be focused primarily on a group process in this chapter, later on you'll see in detail how these concepts can be ported to interactions with customers. But first your people have to learn and practice them, and what better way to do that than by solving some real company problems?

The approach to creative problem solving described in this chapter is based upon forty years of research by Synectics®, Inc. It has been proven to work in thousands of organizations around the world. It can work in yours.

A Proven Problem-Solving Sequence

Applying a point-specific sequence to a subject as intangible as problem solving may seem like a contradiction. After all, the very activity of problem solving suggests an abundance of freedom to accomplish what is needed without being hemmed in by any arbitrary structure. Yet, a well-developed sequence of activities can be helpful in a variety of interactive situations because, like a road map, it helps you pinpoint where you are on the journey to resolution and plot a course to where you want to be.

As shown in figure 3.1, the problem-solving sequence we'll study has five phases. The first three phases can be easily compared with what is usually called a brainstorming session. But there's more to problem solving than brainstorming. Phases 4 and 5 take the process even higher, moving a meeting beyond a forum for the generation of ideas to one for the development of workable solutions.

Each of these phases has one or more steps and requires specific skills in order to be effective. Every problem-solving meeting won't require the use of each and every phase, but in most, each phase will be used at least some of the time. With that in mind, let's delve into what happens during each phase.

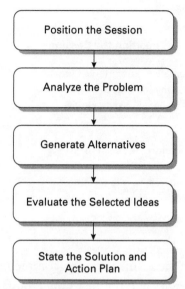

Figure 3.1   Problem-Solving Sequence

Phase 1: Position the Session

The purposes of this phase are to create the climate for the session, clarify the task (or the objectives), and review the ground rules for the meeting. (See figure 3.2.) Here is where you put the attendees at ease and lay the groundwork for the success of the session.

Create a Comfortable Climate   Salespeople know that warm-ups like friendly introductions help get a sales call off to a good start. Yet the same people who know that often fail to do the same thing when they kick off a meeting. It's always worth the time investment to set the climate. Regardless of how well the attendees know one another, or how often they have been in these kinds of meetings, ask each of them to say something before getting down to business. This gives each participant the opportunity to hear the sound of his or her own voice and feel involved in the process even before the real work begins.

```
Phase 1
Position the Session

1. Create a Comfortable Climate
2. Clarify the Objectives
3. Review the Ground Rules
```

Figure 3.2   Phase 1: Position the Session

Newsflash *In problem-solving meetings, people need to hear the sound of their own voices as early as possible.*

In calling for these introductory comments, you can tailor their nature to energize and pre-focus the group's pattern of thinking on the upcoming task. For example, if the session is focusing on changes within an organization, you might ask each person to talk about some meaningful change they made in their lives recently. Prior to a "new product" session, attendees could be asked to talk about some new product or activity they have tried in the past six months. In a sales team meeting called to discuss a specific account, each team member might be asked to say something they have learned about that account during the last month or so.

In general, anywhere from fifteen minutes to half an hour should be plenty of time for introductions in a problem-solving session. If the people do not know each other, you can allow a little more time for these introductory statements, but it is always best to avoid prolonged oratory by anybody.

As tempting as it might be to skip this step, don't overlook it. It's important to establish a healthy climate at the beginning of every meeting. Groups that don't have a comfortable environment don't derive as much enjoyment from their work as they might, and unhappy camps are filled with unhappy campers. Unhappy campers build campfires that go out.

Clarify the Objectives   Clarifying the meeting objectives at the outset is vital. In problem-solving meetings, the description of the objective is typically referred to as the *task statement*.

There are four ground rules for stating the task:

1.   Stated tasks should be specific.

2.   Each task statement must stand on its own.

3.   The task must be achievable in the allotted time.

4.   The task should not be stated as a question.

To illustrate, for a two-hour meeting, a task statement like "How can we increase sales?" is too broad; it requires too much background explanation to be worked on effectively in the given time frame. Also, presenting the task as a question may suggest that there is only one right answer, and create a mindset that hampers the free-form speculation needed for creative problem solving. One hopes that there are many potential solutions to the problem at hand.

In contrast, task statements such as "Determine ways to increase sales by 15 percent in the third quarter" or "Investigate ways to improve sales in the OEM market by year's end" provide a tight focus for the group about a very specific arena, making for a productive use of the group's time.

Review the Ground Rules   The last step in phase 1 is to review the ground rules for the meeting. This step includes explaining the roles and responsibilities of the participants, such as designating the problem owner, facilitator, and scribe; clearly explaining the process to be followed; and making sure everyone understands the logistics.

If participants understand the whys, wherefores, and benefits of the ground rules, they will usually comply with the facilitator's requests. That, in itself, will increase the chances of a more fruitful gathering. Sales teams will often establish their own ground rules that apply to all of their meetings. Sometimes they even post signs in conference rooms that highlight these ground rules. You have seen how sometimes they can have fun with these: "Leave the ego at the door," or "Hierarchy carries no weight here," or "If you're having a bad day, don't let it ruin our day."

A good job done in phase 1 will ensure that the meeting begins with the group feeling comfortable, understanding what is expected of them, and free of the confusion that usually besets meetings that simply start with no set-up. Again, it's worth the time.

> **Newsflash**   *Your sales team will work more effectively if they have specific guidelines and ground rules to follow whenever they get together.*

Phase 2: Analyze the Problem

In this second phase, the problem owner explains the events that led to calling the meeting and provides the information required to begin developing ideas.

If there is a controversial part of the problem-solving sequence I'm recommending, this is it. Participants in problem-solving meetings tend to want to know as much about the problem as they can find out. Their logical assumption is "The more information, the better." But this is *not* the case. On the basis of forty years of research, Synectics concluded that beyond basic facts, the more time spent defining and focusing on a problem, the *less creative* the session and corresponding solutions will be.

Why? Because as people learn more and more about the problem, they begin to edit and censor ideas in their heads. Ideas that seem worth offering when participants are operating with a surface understanding of the problem lose luster when the members learn that even vaguely similar-sounding approaches have already failed for some reason. The last thing you want people to do is hold back in a problem-solving session. Sometimes providing too much information gives them permission to withhold their ideas.

> **Newsflash**   *When you are in a creative problem-solving mode, "Less is more" when it comes to defining the problem.*

To get around this, Synectics recommends seeking just four specific bits of information about the problem during this analysis phase (see figure 3.3).

If participants can't contribute effectively without additional information, then get a few more facts. Generally, however, these four areas will provide more than enough information to get the group started. Remember, the problem owner already is an expert about the problem. What he or she is seeking from the group is new ideas. If the problem owner overloads the group with too much information, they will become just as stymied as he or she is.

> **Newsflash**   *When the group knows as much about the problem as the problem owner does, they can become less valuable resources.*

Problem Analysis Information

1. Background Events Leading to the Problem
2. Rationale for Why It Is a Problem
3. Prior Thoughts of the Problem Owner
4. Problem Owner's Hopes and Expectations for the Session

Figure 3.3   Problem Analysis Information

If a facilitator is present, it is that person's responsibility to get the problem owner to provide sufficient information without overloading the team with too much. If you let the problem owner talk at will, he or she will ramble on and on, eventually putting the group into a dour mindset where, like the problem owner, they are unable to see the forest for the trees.

This point brings us to one of the reasons why organization-wide selling can be so powerful. People who are not traditionally in the selling role bring fresh perspectives to customer situations. They will offer ideas that the sales-related folks have not thought of before or have discarded out of hand. Many of these ideas could have within them the seeds of something big. By encouraging people throughout the organization to continually offer new ideas about customer-related issues, you will end up with lots of approaches you haven't considered in the past.

Newsflash   *When organization-wide selling is working, people who don't know a lot about the sales process offer ideas about customer situations all the time, and the result can be new ways to attack old problems.*

A similar point applies to bringing a problem-solving approach to sales calls. Salespeople know a lot about their products and their industries, but they can't ever know as much about the customer's business as the customer does. For this reason, they can become the same kind of resource to the customer that a "naive" participant can be in a problem-solving meeting. As I'll emphasize repeatedly, offering properly positioned ideas in addition to products and services can be extremely helpful in differentiating a company from its competitors.

Phase 3: Generate Alternatives
Phase 3 is the fun part of the problem-solving sequence, when the floor is opened up for ideas—lots and lots of them. The objective

here is to encourage the participants to relax, opening up new channels for free-range thinking that will approach the problem from new and different perspectives. As a basic guideline, expect *an idea a minute* if the group is cooking on all four burners.

Ideas come from both the participants and the problem owner, who should not be allowed to simply sit back and let the group do the work. The problem owner shouldn't get any more airtime than anybody else, but he or she should be a key contributor.

I believe that the best of all possibilities happens when an original idea from a participant triggers a new idea in the stymied mind of the problem owner. That's because the group initiates the idea, but the problem owner feels a sense of intellectual ownership for the next step. Idea ownership is a powerful factor in energizing problem resolution.

The key to success in this phase is the group's comfort level when speculating. A sure way to keep everyone comfortable is to apply the basic rule of brainstorming: *Suspend evaluation of ideas completely.* It almost always works.

Here's why this rule is so important. When most of us hear new ideas, our knee-jerk reaction is to blurt out why they won't work. That's not because we are inherently negative or narrow-minded, but because we have been conditioned most of our lives to react negatively to almost anything new, untested, or impractical. Do you remember the first time a parent or teacher shot down some wild idea you'd come up with and took pains to tell you why it wouldn't work?

That kind of negative-based feedback runs throughout our education and continues right into our professional lives. I remember years ago, when my older daughter, Andrea, came home from first grade with her first spelling test. She flew through the door and proudly showed me that she had done well—only two answers wrong. On top of the paper the teacher had written, "Two wrong! Nice work!"

It doesn't take Albert Einstein to deduce the message implied in this kind of error-based feedback. I, on the other hand, told her how well she had done because she had gotten twenty-three of the answers *right*. Which approach do you think will encourage initiative and risk taking in the future?

The same thing happened with my other daughter, Deborah, when she was actively involved in dancing. After each recital, all she wanted to talk about were the two or three mistakes she made, not all the things she did well. Needless to say, that is how she was coached by her instructor.

Whether it's on a school assignment, on an activity, or in a performance review at work, highlighting mistakes, errors, and omissions does enable us to evaluate our progress and make improvements. But through this constant conditioning, we end up predisposed to look for what's wrong with something rather than the value that it might have.

This tendency is well documented in videotapes of problem-solving sessions that Synectics has made over the years. Even though the problems are purposely challenging and participants are encouraged to be creative, the tapes show that people tend to automatically disregard ideas that appear to be off the mark. Their natural reaction is to talk about why an idea *wouldn't* work instead of why it *might*. People react this way not solely because of our cultural fault-finding tendencies, but also because they're task-oriented. When they hear an idea that doesn't immediately seem plausible, they point out its deficiencies, hoping to save time by moving on to a more feasible idea.

The trouble is, this attitude is lethal to our ability to solve challenging problems by generating fresh approaches. Not only does it inhibit people from offering their ideas, but it sends shock waves through the atmosphere in the group. Most people don't react well when their ideas are rejected. Sometimes they simply withdraw. Sometimes they get defensive. Other times they get angry and even vindictive. After a few such incidents, the overall climate of the meeting quickly sours.

In contrast, an environment that allows us to offer any kind of idea without fear of rebuke can be a stimulating experience. I once overheard a participant quip about this phase, "So if the facilitator manages the process, and the problem owner does the evaluating and selecting of ideas, then I guess I'm here to just play in the sand box!" He was right, and play you will—in the sense that you can freely speculate, ponder, take risks, stretch your imagination, and express every idea that occurs to you, from the pragmatic to the seemingly absurd.

To reinforce the non-evaluative spirit of this phase, Synectics encourages participants to express ideas using the phrase "I wish. . . ." Strange as it may seem, simply putting those two words in front of an idea results in an extraordinary increase in people's willingness to participate. They feel they have a license to say almost anything without fear of being shot down. Similarly, phrases like "How about . . . ," "What if . . . ," "I'd like . . . ," and "Maybe we could . . ." are all useful tools that increase willingness to speculate.

A perfect example of the ripple effect of this approach was told to me by someone involved in the genesis of the popular 1970s candy, Pop Rocks. As the story goes, Pop Rocks got their start when someone in a creative session asked simply, "What if we had a candy that talked?" Under normal circumstances that person might have been reticent to speak for fear of ridicule, but this was a non-evaluative session.

As implausible as the idea might sound, the individual in charge selected it as the one to develop because of the innovation of selling candy based on *sound*, rather than the conventional lures of flavor, taste, configuration, packaging, or consistency. Good for her! Notice that in the end the original idea wasn't accepted at face value. Instead, it led to a new connection: from *talk* to *sound*. That is a wonderful way to respond to ideas: by withholding criticism and seeing where they lead. Often it results in genuine innovations.

So how did the idea become reality? As it happened, another group within the company (General Foods at that time) had in the past tried to invent a carbonated form of Kool-Aid by encasing carbon dioxide gas in a sugar shell. The two groups got together, and the result was the invention of one of the hottest-selling fad candy products anybody can remember.

What follows from all this is that the single most important behavior to monitor in groups is the way participants greet and treat ideas. Sales teams, in particular, spend a lot of their time in meetings generating ideas, whether they are building strategies, responding to an RFP (request for proposal), developing new products, or trying to come up with ways to be more competitive. Such sessions will be more fruitful if everyone learns to treat the ideas that are offered with respect. That doesn't mean pretending to like ideas that aren't appealing. It simply means capturing any and all ideas during the idea-generating phase without evaluating them. As we'll see, selecting which ideas to develop into solutions comes later. If you make sure that all ideas get a respectful hearing, you'll be amazed at how much more willing team members are to participate.

Newsflash   *Nothing can diminish the creative potential of a group or team faster than disrespect for ideas. Participants need to be tolerant, supportive, and encouraging of one another's ideas and perspectives.*

So how long should all this merriment last? Well, if the goal is to leave the meeting with a specific number of solutions, then phases 1 through 3 should last no longer than a third to half of the total allotted time. As allotted times get longer, this percentage decreases, as you always want more time to grapple with ideas than to generate them.

Phase 4: Evaluate the Selected Ideas

This is probably the most difficult yet rewarding part of the problem-solving process, because this is the time that selected ideas are transformed into solutions. Why is it difficult? Because there is a huge difference between an idea and a solution. Clichés like "There is no such thing as a bad idea" are baloney. There are lots of bad ideas. The daily paper is full of bad ideas that were tried and went wrong. But while it's plainly false that every idea is a good idea, it's both true and important that *every idea does have value*. The key is to find the value in an idea that, on its face, isn't yet a solution, and then *develop* it into a workable solution.

> **Newsflash**   *If you are willing to look for it, you can find value in almost any idea.*

So how does the group choose which idea to develop out of the dozens it has generated? This is a crucial question, because too often the selection is made arbitrarily. In general, ideas can be selected in one of four ways:

1. The problem owner alone can select the idea to develop.

2. The problem owner can select after hearing from the group.

3. The group can decide with input from the problem owner.

4. The group can decide without input from the problem owner.

Which option is best? Well, Synectics encourages the problem owner to make the call. After all, it's that person's problem, and he or she has to live with the solutions that are developed. The group's input can be valuable (option 2), but the ultimate decision belongs to the problem owner.

Once the problem owner has selected the idea to develop, the group's job is to support that decision and do what it can to help develop it into a solution. In short, the group should be responsible *to* the problem owner, but not *for* the problem owner. If the problem owner seems happy, then, by golly, everyone else should be happy, too.

Once the selection is made, *how* ideas are developed becomes crucial. Through their research on problem solving, Synectics came up with an approach that had an extraordinary impact on the successful development of ideas. It has become the standard for virtually anyone involved in group problem-solving situations.

Synectics suggested that ideas fall on a continuum that ranges from "worthless" to "perfect." Since few, if any, ideas are either worthless or perfect, for all practical purposes, all ideas fall somewhere within these two poles (see figure 3.4).

Somewhere on the continuum between worthless and perfect is a point called the "threshold of acceptability." This threshold is defined ahead of time using specific criteria that vary depending on the situation. *Newness, feasibility,* and *commitment* are the key criteria that Synectics uses. The problem owner usually determines the specifics prior to the session. (See figure 3.5.)

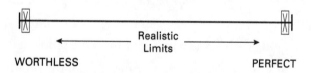

Figure 3.4   An Idea Continuum

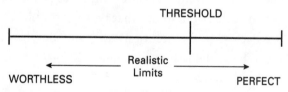

Figure 3.5   The Threshold of Acceptability

Now, most ideas fall short of this threshold, and our conditioned tendency is to reject those ideas automatically. That's something the group has to guard against. But even if an idea is selected precisely because of its intrigue or uniqueness, it can still be difficult to get people to exhibit the diligence required to transform it into a solution. The selection of a *new* idea usually means that there is a lot of work to do in order to improve upon it and make it feasible. Most people would prefer to select obviously feasible ideas rather than invest in trying to develop new ones. That's unfortunate, because it is usually the new and different idea that eventually becomes a breakthrough solution.

For this reason, it's vital for everyone involved to treat ideas as *dynamic* rather than static entities. Ideas are not fixed in their original form, but develop and mutate—one hopes to the point where they cross the threshold of acceptability. The group's task is to keep enhancing the selected idea, moving it along the continuum toward the threshold.

Newsflash   *If groups treat ideas as dynamic, not static, it will be easier for them to transform ideas into solutions.*

When it is time to develop the idea, the group is asked first to identify the value of the idea and then to raise whatever issues or concerns they think of. At this stage they are asked to fight their tendency to focus on why the idea won't work. The rationale is that they first need to identify what parts of the idea to keep before they determine what needs to be fixed.

As the group identifies value in the idea, each positive attribute is noted. Represented by the plus signs in figure 3.6, these "pro" considerations explain why the idea falls where it does on the continuum. Issues or concerns are represented as gaps (denoted by 0s in the figure). These gaps need to be filled with new thoughts and approaches.

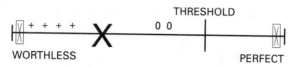

Figure 3.6 Developing Ideas

The challenge in developing ideas this way is that groups tend to think that ideas are static. They tend to identify the positives, then the negatives, and end up treating all the ideas as if they were wallowing in mediocrity.

To get around this tendency, Synectics cleverly developed a process that asked the group to express each concern in the form of an *invitation* for more ideas. Said another way, they suggested treating each concern as a "mini-problem" instead of as a reason to dismiss the idea. In this way, each concern becomes a reason to work harder to overcome it.

Newsflash   *Concerns about ideas can be transformed into "invitations" that keep the process moving forward instead of closing it down.*

For example, if someone voices the concern that a new product idea is *too narrow* in scope, the concern is rephrased as an invitation: "We need to determine how to *broaden* the appeal of the concept." Or if the concern is that a new product is *too expensive,* it is recast as "How do we produce it *for less?*" Proceeding in this way, the group generates positive ways to enhance the original idea, rather than selling the car because it has a flat tire. The result? An upbeat attitude and often an exciting new solution.

Some people call this step "reframing." It's an important concept to grasp, particularly if you want to apply this kind of thinking to customer interactions. The most exciting solutions that I have seen emerge from problem-solving sessions (not to mention sales calls) were often loaded with concerns initially. But the group rolled up its sleeves and went to work to make the metamorphosis happen. They nailed one concern at a time until they were all resolved, transforming a beginning idea into an exciting solution. You can probably see how this process can apply directly to customer interactions.

The idea evaluation process I've described has been called a myriad of names—"balanced assessment," "pro/con," "upside/downside," "balance sheet," and "pluses and wishes." Synectics calls it the "itemized response." Whatever you choose to call it, maintaining a positive attitude leads to positive results.

Once the selected idea has been honed into a solution, it needs to be reviewed for the benefit of the group. The last step is to state the solution and create an action plan, as outlined in phase 5.

Before we look at that final phase, let's briefly relate this idea development and evaluation process to selling. Could it have helped Sal in his interactions with Betty? Like Sal, most salespeople complain that their customers aren't as open-minded as they would like. Certainly, Betty wasn't. But always keep in mind that the tendency to react negatively to something new is cultural, not personal. The challenge is to avoid becoming defensive, tense, aggressive, cynical, or passive, and to use the problem-solving methodology to overcome the objection.

Now that doesn't mean that Sal should have asked Betty to find the value in what he had to say. That would be silly, not to mention a non-starter. But when we investigate objection resolution later in the book, you'll see how process skills could have helped Sal deal with Betty's negative response. In spite of what they say and how they say it, a customer or prospective customer may actually like much about a salesperson and his or her ideas. The trick is to ferret out and focus on the parts that the customer doesn't like in a *non-emotional way*. So, rather than being buffaloed into blabbering about how great his company and its offerings were, Sal could have understood Betty's reaction and *reframed* her concern the way groups do in problem-solving meetings:

> So it sounds to me, Betty, that before we go any further, you need to know what we can offer that you're not getting now. Is that correct? Perhaps if I ask a few questions first, and learn more about your situation, I can better explain how we can help.

Rest assured, we'll discuss this point a lot more later on. For now, just keep in mind that what works in problem-solving groups works with customers, too.

Phase 5: State the Solution and Action Plan

In the final phase, the group reviews the solutions it has developed and formulates an action plan to ensure their implementation. If a solution hasn't been reached, the group puts together a summary statement and corresponding action steps to keep the momentum moving forward.

Don't underestimate the importance of this phase. All of us can remember attending upbeat meetings in which great, exciting ideas were developed, and then hearing the disheartening news, weeks or months later, that nothing had happened. That is probably because the problem-solving group failed to develop a specific action plan.

To avoid this all-too-common result, two important things must happen during phase 5. First, the problem owner needs to demonstrate that the idea has indeed been transformed into a solution, that is, that it meets the criteria established ahead of time. Second, the problem owner should detail the necessary follow-up steps and announce a timetable for performing them.

Meeting the criteria for a solution is the easy part, but be cautious. Often a frustrated problem owner will tell a group that they have a solution in order to avoid working on the task any longer. Really all the group has is an idea that is still in need of development. In cases like this, the facilitator can get the problem owner to acknowledge that he or she is fatigued and that it would be best to continue another time—as long as the group takes the time to summarize where things stand and identify the next steps in the process. But it doesn't do anybody any good to pretend an idea is a solution when it isn't.

The action plan part of phase 5 is more complicated. I believe strongly in assigning point-specific next steps at the conclusion of any meeting. This procedure allows the problem owner to get individual commitments from members of the group to assist in the implementation of the solution. Although people may be willing to participate in a meeting, often they are reluctant to commit their time to actually help, particularly in this day of lean organizations. The conclusion of a meeting, when people are feeling the euphoria of having successfully resolved a difficult problem, is a great time to get them to commit.

An action plan can take any number of forms, but I like to keep it simple. With that in mind I present the "four Ws":

1. *What* must be done?
2. *Who* should do it?
3. *When* must it be completed?
4. *Who* will assist?

OK, so "who" sneaked in there twice, but you get the idea. The rationale behind this "four Ws" list is that if we can get these four answers assigned for each step of the solution, and we assign three or four specific steps, then the chances of the solution actually becoming a reality are high.

Synectics founder George Prince strongly believed in assigning a "champion" to implement a solution. The champion assumes a *passion* about the solution and vows to do everything within his or her power to make it happen. Ideas that have a passionate champion behind them are most likely to survive through implementation.

Tom Peters also stresses the need for champions to make things happen, particularly new things that involve change.

However you do it, the bottom line is, *Never leave a problem-solving meeting without a well-developed action plan.* The specificity and commitment involved in a good action plan ensure that the momentum will continue, and the plan lets the group know that their efforts had tangible results.

So there it is—a structured approach to problem solving. As you can see, there's nothing magical here. You put the group at ease and let them know what's going to happen. You briefly discuss the problem. Then you generate ideas and suspend evaluation. Next you develop the ideas you like most, using a process that works. Finally, you state your solution(s) and formulate a specific action plan.

But even if it isn't magical, this structured sequence does have amazing power. I strongly recommend that sales teams be trained in how to use it. Like any other team or work group, sales teams must learn how to problem-solve effectively and efficiently. And if you adopt the company-wide approach to selling, it will be even more important for the members of your organization to know how to work successfully together to develop creative solutions to customers' problems. It isn't enough to bring the right people together to solve problems. They have to know how to go about it.

Using a specific approach like the one detailed in this chapter and encouraging the team members to play the game by the rules will result in more than just better meetings. It will result in better teamwork, which results in better ideas, better solutions, better strategies, and ultimately, better customer relationships.

In the next section of this book, you'll see in detail how to take the problem-solving approach we've described into interactions with customers. And when you do that, you'll really set your organization apart.

MEMO TO MANAGEMENT

There are other successful problem-solving methodologies besides the one described in this chapter. You may have your own approach that you use throughout your organization, and that's fine—as long as your people can use and apply it regularly. That's the key.

The fact is, most groups in most organizations do not reach their potential when they sit down to solve problems. They don't have the methodology. They don't have the skills. They don't under-stand roles and responsibilities. And they don't have the necessary process sensitivity. The people at Synectics know this, because every time they teach the subject, they start by asking the group to work on a problem and then videotape what happens. Obviously, most groups do some things well. But for the most part, they quickly realize how much there is to learn.

It's up to managers to instill the process, awareness, and skills of effective problem solving. If you want to have an organization that is committed to providing outstanding customer satisfaction, and one in which everybody accepts their role as part of the sales process, then skill in problem solving is critical. Invest in making it happen. Train your people, or as Tom Peters says, "Train *and retrain*" your people. They need to know how to bring a problem-solving mindset to every interaction, whether it is internally or externally focused.

And, once again, don't forget how important it is for you to model this behavior. "Do as I say, not as I do" just won't fly if you are trying to change cultures and create new ways to enhance cus-tomer relationships. If your patience is tried sometimes, or if you have that nearly universal tendency to dismiss ideas that seem out of left field, remember to trust the process. And don't let your pragmatism and decisiveness get in the way of taking the time to turn ideas into well-specified solutions and action plans. The time and energy you invest in solving problems effectively will be more than compensated. Just think of all the time and energy you've already lost on ideas that didn't work or were never implemented!

SECTION II

Putting It Across to the Customer

CHAPTER 4

Needs-Driven Selling

With this chapter, we begin a detailed exploration of how to put across the problem-solving approach when interacting with customers. This knowledge is crucial to organization-wide selling, because it's the people in the front lines—the sales force—who have the first (and quite often the last) opportunity to position the company in the minds of customers. It won't do any good to develop a problem-solving mentality throughout the company if salespeople and their teams don't represent this approach in a credible way. And, once again, getting customers to regard your organization as a problem-solving resource is the best way to differentiate it from the competition.

If you're an executive or sales manager, you can think of this section of the book as a mini training manual for the people in your sales organization. If you're a salesperson, you'll find these chapters directly applicable to what you do every day. And if you're a member of another department who has been recruited onto a sales team, you'll need to understand and be part of this approach to interacting with customers.

Most of section II details the specific skills involved in applying problem-solving skills in sales calls. But before we get to the nitty-gritty of managing interactions with customers, there's one more bit of philosophy we need to put in place.

The Needs-Driven Philosophy

If you want to instill a selling mentality throughout your organization, then everybody needs to be thinking about the customer all the time. And that means that everybody has to be thinking about the *needs* of the customer all the time. That is where the needs-driven philosophy comes into the picture.

I first heard the expression "needs-driven selling" almost twenty years ago in a speech by Dick Kovasavitch, later the chairman and CEO of Wells Fargo Bank. As the phrase implies, the idea is that the customer's needs—*not* what the salesperson has to sell—drive the entire interaction. In fact, the philosophy behind needs-driven selling is that until the salesperson has a solid understanding of a customer's needs, he or she doesn't have the *right* to present any products or services.

That last statement is a deliberate echo of the phrase "the privilege to consult" that I cited from *Webster's Dictionary* in discussing consultative selling in chapter 1. A needs-driven approach is a key element of consultative selling, and it's the only way to succeed in today's marketplace. Manipulative, self-serving approaches to sales are as obsolete as electric hair curlers.

If salespeople are focused on understanding customers' needs, they are more likely to avoid the temptation of premature presentation, which is the antithesis of a needs-driven, consultative stance. Though many sales managers and salespeople will deny giving in to that temptation, purchasing managers and other customers complain day in and day out that most salespeople they meet with are not needs-driven at all and quickly fall back on that tired standby, the canned pitch. With the barest of nods to the customer's needs, salespeople present their product lines and services without knowing whether or not what they have to offer is appropriate for that customer.

Newsflash   *Most salespeople present too early—much too early.*

The canned pitch amounts to a calculated and well-rehearsed *guess* at what *might* work. Not only does it make the customer feel that the salesperson really doesn't care about him or her specifically, but at best the canned pitch is just a shot in the dark. One client describes it as the "spray and pray" approach.

Another way to think about this point is to distinguish between *needs-driven* selling and *product-driven* selling. Don Beveridge, the dynamic sales presenter, compares product-driven selling to "filling the sky with flack in the hope of maybe hitting something." In contrast, needs-driven selling is like "using a guided missile to hit a target." A corollary to this idea is that in needs-driven selling, each and every presentation of the very same products and services will be a little (or a lot) different, based on an individual customer's needs. That's exactly the opposite of a canned pitch.

One caveat is in order: Although needs-driven selling demands that salespeople avoid talking about products and services until they have earned the right to do so, it leaves open the notion of presenting the company as a whole. Often customers challenge sales professionals to provide an overview of their company before *allowing* the salesperson to determine the customer's needs. These are sometimes referred to as "credentials presentations." In such cases, the introduction of the company should be made in general terms, avoiding the "Here's how we can help you" trap. That's what torpedoed our pal, Sal, in chapter 1. Accommodate the customer's request, but don't let it turn into a "Whatchagot?" trap that destroys your needs-driven approach.

Determining Customers' Needs

Right about now, you might be wondering, "What's the news here?" After all, the concept of needs-based selling has been around for a long time. If you ask your salespeople the most important aspect of their job, the majority will probably say "determining, understanding, investigating, or satisfying the needs" of their customers. Most will state unequivocally that they're *good* at this crucial part of their job. What's more, in training programs, salespeople excel in exercises that ask them to do nothing but determine the customer's needs.

Well, if we're all so good at it, why is it that in countless interviews, customers say that salespeople are usually *not* effective at determining their needs? As one purchasing manager said, "They ask a question or two, find out one relatively unimportant piece of information, then start selling their socks off! They think they know precisely what I'm looking for, when in reality, they don't have a clue." If salespeople are so convinced that they do a good job at this, how can their customers disagree so vehemently? Who's right?

The truth is that both groups are correct . . . to a degree. Salespeople *do* uncover many of their customers' needs through the questions they ask and through their ability to listen during their sales calls. However, too often they only gain an understanding of *superficial* needs and never hear the less obvious needs that may actually be of greater importance in relating to that customer.

When buyers say that salespeople don't really understand their needs, I interpret that to mean the *needs the salesperson missed.* In fact, the salesperson may have uncovered several needs related to the customer's situation, but because he or she missed a few big ones, the customer walked away unimpressed and disappointed.

This failure to uncover customers' needs is all the more disturbing because of its impact on the whole organization. The salesperson is the member of the sales team who is primarily responsible for finding out what customers need. If he or she does not do as good a job as possible, the sales team will never be able to reach its potential. The same is true of the rest of the organization. If people in the company don't know what the real needs of their customers are, they can't possibly think of new and better ways to address them.

> **Newsflash**   *Most salespeople think they are needs-driven when in reality, they are not.*

So What Exactly Is the Problem Here?

Still not convinced that all this applies to you and your organization? Let's try an experiment. Read the following story:

> An agitated customer walked into a hardware store on a Saturday morning at 9:00 A.M. When the owner of the store arrived, the customer started rambling on about how he just bought a house the previous week and now, on his second day living in the house, he had awakened to a funny noise in the basement. Upon investigation, he found the basement was under six inches of water. "The floor is starting to buckle, the paint is peeling off the walls, and the furnace looks like it's about to short out," he screamed.
>
> He went on to say that this was his first house, and he knew nothing about home repair. He had tried to reach the realtor who sold him the joint, "but she's probably showing other awful houses to unsuspecting victims." He lamented how he had spent "every nickel he had to get into this disaster" and didn't know how he could pay for any materials needed. The house was over 100 years old, and he had convinced his wife to make the move in spite of her reservations. "So on top of all this water stuff, my wife thinks I'm an idiot!"

Now think about the *needs* expressed by this exasperated customer. Take a minute to write down as many needs expressed in his plea as you can. Feel free to reread the story as many times as you like. Do it now—I promise you'll learn something. Approach this as a "needs analysis" exercise to see how good you really are at determining needs. No cheating. Just do as I ask. You will see why.

I've conducted this exercise in perhaps thousands of training programs, workshops, and speaking engagements. When I ask a group to list this hyperventilating homeowner's needs, the answers are always things like:

- A sump pump
- A WetVac
- New flooring
- Paint and brushes
- A cup of coffee
- Tools
- Do-it-yourself books
- A friend
- A lawyer
- An insurance adjuster
- A plumber
- A marriage counselor
- A pistol

One participant in a session I conducted for a pharmaceutical company earned a big laugh from the group by shouting out, "That guy could use Prozac!"

Unfortunately, in today's competitive environment, responses like this one, and all the others on the preceding list, are just not going to cut the mustard. Why? Because every one of these answers represents a *solution,* not a *need*.

Can you remember talking about a personal or work problem in some social situation, and having some clown blurt out a solution or two before you even finished explaining the problem? If so, you were probably annoyed or frustrated. The impression the other person gave is that he or she could quickly solve a problem that you had been agonizing about. In other words, that person was smarter or more creative than you. Possibly the preferred solution was a good one—but that doesn't mean you were ready to hear it.

That's the same effect salespeople have on clients when they respond too quickly with ideas and solutions before taking an adequate inventory of the customer's needs.

> **Newsflash**   *There is a big—no, make that a huge—difference between a need and a solution.*

Needs Versus Solutions

To illustrate the difference between needs and solutions, let's return to our panicked homeowner. If your list of needs included some kind of pump to fix his problem, you reacted the way most people do, and the way I did the first time I participated in this exercise. The idea-generating machine in your head kicked in and started churning out solutions before pausing to determine the poor fellow's needs.

Let's try again. One of the constraints highlighted by the homeowner was that he didn't have a lot of available cash, since he had sunk all his money into the house, which, as far as he could tell, was sinking itself. Since he had just moved in, he didn't know much about the inner workings of the house, or its history. What he knew at this point was that he had a very wet basement. Since he probably didn't want to spend much money, a pump might not be the best solution. Maybe the house already has a pump that needs to be repaired or perhaps simply turned on, or maybe he could rent one. In light of the circumstances, a mop and a few buckets might be the best solution, or perhaps some kind of economical siphon.

Or maybe there was a clogged drain in the basement. A low-cost solution could be to call the fire department to pump the water out of the basement. Or maybe he could get the help of the neighbors.

Whoops. Once again, all of these ideas are *solutions*, not *needs*. See how easy it is to get off track? The trouble is that solutions aren't what this man needs to hear, nor what a needs-driven salesperson should be offering at this early point in the relationship. A truly "needs-driven" salesperson would be thinking only in terms of understanding the customer's needs, and would then express them verbally.

Just what are the homeowner's needs? Here are some—you can probably come up with more.

- To get the water out of the basement
- To repair the floor
- To restore the walls
- To protect the furnace from shorting out
- To know where the water is coming from
- To know how to prevent this mess from happening again
- To learn about being a homeowner
- To learn where to go for help
- To figure out how to regain esteem in his wife's eyes
- To learn how to feel better about buying such an old house

Remember, the house has been standing for a hundred years. Chances are that a wet basement at this moment won't cause the structure to collapse or go floating down Main Street. Therefore, our unhappy homeowner has a few additional needs:

- To calm down
- To get a grip on the situation
- To understand that the problem is manageable
- To feel good about himself

So there are many expressed needs on the table, as well as needs that aren't expressed directly but are certainly there. The challenge is to understand what those needs are and convey that understanding to the customer *before* worrying about how to address them. Approaching problems in this way requires discipline, but it's likely to lead to solutions that are a better fit for the customer's real needs—and to better relationships as well.

Here's the point: As human beings, customers aren't looking for solutions from salespeople very early in the relationship. Like a new love interest, they need to be courted first. They're looking for sales professionals who understand their needs and as a result can offer understanding now, and thoughtful solutions later—even if it's in a subsequent call.

In addition, presenting solutions prematurely can be misinterpreted as caring more about *your* company, *its* products, and *your* needs than the customer's needs. Fairly or not, it can be interpreted as showboating or some perverse variation of one-upmanship. Not a good relationship-building technique. Even when a customer seems to be impatient for a quick solution, salespeople will be more successful if they first verbalize the relevant needs as they have come to understand them.

Newsflash *What the majority of customers want most is to see that you understand what they are talking about.*

To counter the inherent tendency to think of solutions first, when you realize that you've just thought of a solution, ask yourself, "What is the *need* that triggered this solution?" If Prozac is the *solution* for someone in an agitated state, then the *need* might be to be in a better mood, or at least to calm down. Short of prescription drugs, a better mood might be achievable by assuring the customer that the problem is fixable, or explaining that after a thunderstorm many houses in the area have wet basements and the basements always dry out, or telling him there are ways to prevent this from happening again (remember, at this juncture, he's in the soup over buying the house in the first place). Still another way to improve his mood would be to explain how problems like this are usually simple and not terribly expensive to resolve.

Notice, by the way, how solutions tend to be *nouns*, while needs are usually *verbs*. Look at the two lists I've presented: "sump pump" is a noun; "to get the water out of the basement" starts with a verb. There are exceptions to this rule, of course, but it holds most of the time.

> **Newsflash**   *If you express what you think is a need as a noun, it is probably a solution.*

Understanding the difference between needs and solutions is an important first step in understanding the needs-driven philosophy. In chapter 5, we'll begin to translate that philosophy into a specific sequence of steps that parallels the problem-solving model introduced in section I. Although the precise sequence is less important than the skills that make it work, sequences are useful because they keep us on track. The sequence we'll develop will serve as a good starting point on the journey to becoming a problem-solving resource to customers and prospects.

MEMO TO MANAGEMENT

In a sales-driven, customer-focused organization, everybody must be thinking all the time about the needs of customers and how to address them. The first point of contact, however, is the salesperson. We employ salespeople to create and build relationships with our targeted customer base, and to find out their needs. One of the serious issues management must learn to resolve is the ironic fact that most salespeople think they understand their customers' needs when in reality they don't. The result is lots of missed opportunities—every day.

What makes this even more ironic is that the same thing that makes salespeople good problem solvers works against their ability to understand the customer's needs completely. They hear a need and respond with a solution before they truly grasp the situation. The result is usually a recommendation that is off the mark. And when they behave this way, their good intentions and desire to help don't count. They show the customer that they are really no different than the rest of the pack—which is not the image you want to create for your organization.

Think about your own responses to the unhappy homeowner exercise earlier in this chapter. If you derived a long list of needs, you're the exception, not the rule. By far, the majority of people go right for the solution. Try the exercise with your own people, and watch what happens. You'll be amazed as solutions come shooting at you like phone calls from an aggressive telemarketing company.

This is not an issue that only your salespeople need to worry about. It happens to everybody within the organization. The difference between a need and a solution can be quite subtle. That's why I've used the "verb versus noun" method of distinguishing them. It isn't 100 percent perfect, but it can be a very useful tool.

As a manager, one of your responsibilities in making organization-wide selling become a reality is to do whatever you can to reinforce the needs-driven philosophy. When your people come up with ideas for product refinements or new services or procedures, ask them what customer needs those ideas address. Encourage them to express those needs as verbs. If you do this often enough, they will begin to do it themselves without your having to ask.

When business issues arise that relate directly to the customer, challenge your people to list the key customer needs that their solutions or conclusions address. Explore whether the issue that has come to their attention is the result of their *not* paying close enough attention to those critical needs in the past. I don't mean that you should do this in a punishing way. The idea is simply to reinforce, at every opportunity, the idea that having a customer focus starts with understanding real customer needs.

You can do other things to make the needs-driven philosophy a way of life in the organization. For example, formulate questions that address the issue of understanding and meeting customer needs that you want your people to use in performance reviews, salary increase guidelines, and criteria for promotion. Posters on the walls that ask, "What customer need did you address today?" may sound hokey, but reminders like this can have an extraordinary impact on your people.

Remember, changing organizational cultures is no easy task. And remember once again that it starts with you. Regardless of the level managers occupy within the company, if they don't live and breathe a needs-driven philosophy, it will never permeate the organization. It all comes down to those three simple words, "Lead by example."

CHAPTER 5

Merging Needs-Driven Selling and Problem Solving

This chapter provides a detailed overview of a model for selling that merges the needs-driven philosophy with the problem-solving concepts and methodology introduced in section I. The result is an advanced approach to selling, that will make anyone who uses it more effective in dealing with customers.

For convenience, in the rest of section II, I address the reader as a salesperson. Whether or not sales is your primary sphere of activity, in organization-wide selling, everyone needs to approach customers in a professional manner. And if you participate on (or manage or train) a sales team, you'll need to understand this methodology just as much as the professional salespeople do.

A Needs-Driven Selling Sequence

Let's start by looking at needs-driven selling as a specific sequence of steps. Then I'll show how blending in problem-solving concepts can enrich the traditional model and take it to a higher level.

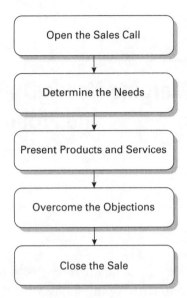

Figure 5.1   Needs-Driven Selling

As shown in figure 5.1, the needs-driven selling process can be thought of as a sequence with five phases. It may well look familiar to you, whether or not you've had formal sales training.

The sequence shown in figure 5.1 is derived from observing successful salespeople in the performance of their jobs. A good sales professional gets the sales call off to a good start, finds out the customer's needs, and presents the products or services that address those needs. Then he or she deals with whatever objections arise and, we hope, closes the sale. All of this can happen in one visit, or it can take years.

Sounds easy, doesn't it? But don't let the simplicity of the model fool you. The truth is that most salespeople don't apply it faithfully. The key to a needs-driven approach to selling is to stay in the "needs-development" phase longer than one's tendencies dictate. Following a specified sequence can help you do that. Take a moment to fix the steps in your mind. We'll improve and elaborate on these commonsense ideas shortly.

One caveat: Like most things in life, the needs-driven selling sequence does not always proceed as smoothly as it looks on paper. I remember calling on a training consultant at a prestigious investment bank not too long ago. It was my second visit there in two weeks. I had met one of her colleagues previously. I was starting the meeting with typical small talk to build some rapport when she abruptly interrupted me with a somewhat challenging statement: "I feel the need to tell you right up front, I was warned about you!"

"Nice start," I thought to myself. When I asked her what she meant, she told me how her colleague had warned her that "if she wasn't careful, she [my prospective client] would do most of the talking."

I quickly explained that in an initial meeting, it is in our mutual interest for me to ask a lot of questions to assess the client's situation, and that I try not to explain how we might help until a subsequent visit. "Well, that is not what will happen today," she said in a way that made me wish someone else had made this call. Again I inquired why, and she said something I hope I'll never forget: "If you think I am going to give you a lot of information and get nothing in return, you're kidding yourself."

Whew! We had barely started, and already I knew that this was going to be one challenging meeting!

So we made a deal. (Investment bankers love deals.) For the first half of the meeting she did most of the talking as I learned what I could about her situation, and for the second half of the meeting I explained how we might be able to help. It is not the way I would have chosen to proceed, but the meeting actually worked out quite well. More significantly, it made me realize that not every customer wants me to be in needs-driven mode all the time. In this case, the person I was calling on wanted to leave the meeting with more than just the assurance that I had learned enough about her situation to present at a later time. She wanted a sense of what I could offer her. And she got what she wanted. Case closed.

> **Newsflash**   *Not all customers will allow you to spend lots of time learning their needs—even if it is the logical thing to do.*

Remember, the sales call is the customer's meeting. We must do what we can to give them what they want. We always want to avoid the canned pitch, but we can't assume that every customer will be willing to answer lots of questions without hearing what we have to offer. The sequence is only a tool; use it as such. Keep in mind that you should be flexible, use common sense, and trust your instincts. If you master the skills associated with this process, it won't matter too much if you have to deviate from the sequence. What matters is being able to call upon the appropriate skills at the precise moment when they're needed.

Combining the Needs-Driven Selling and Problem-Solving Sequences

Before we look at the selling sequence in detail, I want to reformulate the five phases I've presented by blending in problem-solving concepts. We'll move beyond the needs-driven approach you may already be familiar with to another level of selling.

Let's begin by briefly comparing the sequences involved in problem-solving and needs-driven selling.

Comparing the Selling and Problem-Solving Sequences

As you'll recall, the problem-solving process also consists of a sequence of five phases. If we position the two sequences side by side, as in figure 5.2, you can see how much they have in common.

The first phase in the selling sequence *(open the sales call)* is exactly analogous to *positioning the session* in a problem-solving meeting. In each case the objective is to create a healthy climate, make the participants involved feel comfortable, and ensure that they know what is expected to happen and why. And in both situ-

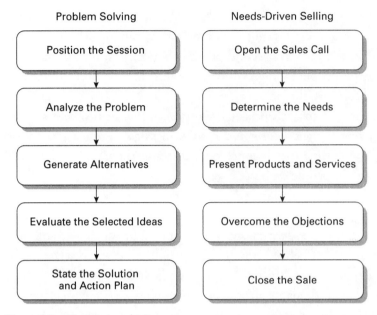

Problem Solving	Needs-Driven Selling
Position the Session	Open the Sales Call
Analyze the Problem	Determine the Needs
Generate Alternatives	Present Products and Services
Evaluate the Selected Ideas	Overcome the Objections
State the Solution and Action Plan	Close the Sale

Figure 5.2   Comparing the Sequences

ations, a key person—the facilitator in the problem-solving meeting, the salesperson in the selling situation—assumes the responsibility for this phase.

The second phase in the selling sequence *(determine the needs)* corresponds to the *problem analysis* phase of a problem-solving meeting. In both settings, the goal is to find out what is needed to move the process forward. In the case of problem solving, the facilitator's task in this phase is to make sure the group gets enough information to begin working on the problem without being burdened by so much information that their creativity is inhibited. This is achieved by asking the problem owner appropriate questions and asking the group to listen for the answers with the sole objective of acquiring the information they need to generate lots of ideas. Similarly, during the needs-determination part of the selling sequence, the salesperson asks the customer as many questions as possible, listening pointedly to determine his or her needs.

Notice how in both cases the problem owner (the customer, in the case of the sales call) does most of the talking at this point. In both cases, too, this second phase is critical. It's during this phase that the people involved obtain the information and insight they need to move the process forward.

Phase 3 in each process—*idea generation* in problem solving, and *presenting products and services* in sales—is clearly the most enjoyable time for all concerned. It is also the part of the process that most people do best.

In sales, being allowed to offer ideas and talk about how one's "products and services" might resolve the customer's problems is the *pièce de résistance* salespeople dream about. With loads of product training behind them, salespeople find themselves safely cocooned in a comfort zone of unassailable facts and figures. And, like the participants in a problem-solving session, they become valuable resources to the problem owner—in this case, the customer. They also get to do most of the talking, which too many people mistake for being in control of the meeting.

In both processes, phase 4 is the hardest phase. In problem solving, we called this phase *idea evaluation*. Some prefer to call it *idea development*. In the selling process, the analogous step is usually called *overcoming objections*. (As you will see later, I really don't like that term, but for now we will use it.) As even a neophyte salesperson knows, our recommendations are almost never accepted without some resistance. We can't close a deal until we've addressed the questions, concerns, and issues that the customer raises before, during, and after our presentation.

Newsflash   *Customers will object even if they feel they are ready to buy, so you must understand how to deal with resistance.*

There's another way to think about this phase, though. When we attempt to manage resistance from a customer, what we're really doing is helping him or her *evaluate* our recommendation, with the goal of *transforming* it into a *solution* that he or she wants to *implement.* This language should remind you of what happens in problem solving, because "overcoming objections" is exactly analogous to what happens during the idea-evaluation phase in a problem-solving session.

With this analogy in mind, I prefer to think of this part of the process in terms of *resolving the issues* rather than *overcoming objections.* A word like *overcoming* suggests something we're doing *to,* instead of *with,* the customer, and that's not at all in the spirit of needs-driven selling—or problem solving, either. So you will see as the process evolves that I'll use "resolving the issues" to refer to this phase.

Another similarity between problem solving and selling in phase 4 is that the airtime is shared by all parties. In a problem-solving session, the problem owner and the group together try to resolve the issues associated with the idea being developed. In the selling scenario, the salesperson works *with* the customer to resolve whatever issues the customer has raised.

The final phase in both sequences is the point at which closure is reached, whether that is the *solution* to the problem or the *closed sale.* In a problem-solving meeting, the facilitator ensures that closure is reached and that an action plan is developed. In the selling situation, the salesperson has this responsibility. In both cases, however, the person for whom we are working makes the final decision.

Problem-Solving Selling

The similarity between the methodologies of problem solving and needs-driven selling leads to a new understanding of the sales process—something I like to call *problem-solving selling.* The goal of problem-solving selling is to *merge* the processes of problem solving and needs-driven selling in order to elevate the activity of selling to a higher, more engaging level than is achieved in traditional needs-driven or even consultative selling. Since the two processes are so compatible and require such similar skills, we can meld the two sequences like the pieces of a jigsaw puzzle, as depicted in figure 5.3.

The result of combining the two processes is the problem-solving selling sequence depicted in figure 5.4. Notice the difference in the titles of the phases. What the figure shows is the traditional needs-driven selling sequence transformed into a higher-level process that requires the salesperson and his or her team to consciously use problem-solving skills in conjunction with traditional selling skills.

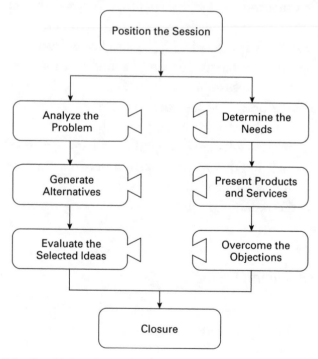

Figure 5.3   Combining the Sequences

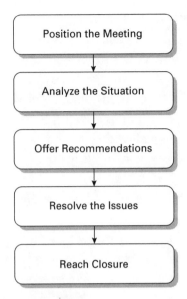

Figure 5.4   Problem-Solving Selling

We'll develop this sequence over the next several chapters. In the remainder of this chapter we take a close-up look at what the melding of problem solving and selling means for each phase in the sequence. Subsequent chapters will probe into the specific skills and tools needed in the implementation of each phase.

A Close-Up Look at the Problem-Solving Selling Sequence

Merging the problem-solving and needs-driven selling sequences gives a new twist to each phase of the sales call. Using our new terminology, let's see exactly how this is so.

Phase 1: Position the Meeting

I've already stressed the idea that the sales call is a *meeting* and that the same dynamics that occur in meetings occur in sales calls. So, instead of thinking in terms of "opening the sales call," think in terms of *positioning the meeting*. That means thinking of yourself as a *facilitator* who manages the *process* of this special type of meeting. And managing the process begins with setting the climate for the session.

There are four steps involved in positioning the sales call, as shown in figure 5.5. First, *put the customer at ease.* A customer who is comfortable with you will talk more freely and answer your questions more directly and openly. He or she is also more likely to hear what you have to say. And of course you know that.

The most common expression for this activity is "establishing rapport." That doesn't necessarily mean customers must consider you a friend. It simply recognizes the reality that buyers buy from people they like and from people who make them feel comfortable. Feeling comfortable means they've privately answered several questions about you that concern such things as dependability, credibility, safety, sensitivity, empathy, and trust. The salesperson who can address these issues to the customer's satisfaction is much more likely to develop a solid relationship—and you should never underestimate the importance of the relationship in selling.

> **Newsflash**   *Buyers commonly make their buying decisions for what most people think is the wrong reason: they buy from people they like.*

1. Put the Customer at Ease
2. Confirm the Agenda
3. Clarify the Logistics
4. Prepare the Customer for Questioning

Figure 5.5   Position the Meeting

The second task in positioning the session is to *confirm the agenda*. An agenda represents a shared understanding of what topics will be discussed and what the objectives of the meeting are. This is a step that even experienced salespeople often skip. But when salespeople fail to explain up front why they are there and what the purpose of the meeting is, customers may well think that they're wasting precious time. In fact, many customers complain about salespeople who inappropriately assume that the customer knows precisely why they have called the meeting.

By the same token, customers must be asked what *they* want to accomplish in the meeting. Otherwise the salesperson is likely to appear completely self-serving. Remember the investment banker I talked about earlier in this chapter? Her agenda was quite different from what I had anticipated. I wasn't crazy about the way she brought it up, but if she hadn't, the sales call would have blown up in my face. In any case, it's amazing how few salespeople take the time to get an agreed-upon agenda on the table. It's just as necessary in a sales call as it is in a meeting.

The third step in phase 1 is to *clarify the logistics*. It always makes sense to confirm how much time the customer has actually allotted to the meeting. It helps to get permission to take notes, to ensure you know how each person present fits into the organization (and why they are there), and, when needed, to explain why you require any specific visual aids or equipment.

Clarifying the time available is important because you never really know how much time a customer has, even if you discussed a specific time allotment when setting up the appointment. Stuff happens. Things change. Nobody has enough time today, and salespeople who are sensitive to customers' time constraints demonstrate in yet another way that they are different from their competitors. And if the customer tells you that he or she has less time than you anticipated, *work with it*. Don't whine about how that messes up *your* agenda. Once more: It's the *customer's* meeting.

The fourth task in this phase is the one salespeople typically leave out most often—namely, *prepare the customer for questioning*. Sometimes you will broaden this step, particularly when you are there to do other things. In most cases, you are setting the stage for questioning. Questioning another person is a delicate matter, one that must be handled with care. Most humans feel uncomfortable when interrogated, so process sensitivity calls for preparing them for this activity.

I learned this lesson the hard way when calling on a small manufacturing company six months after I was assigned my first territory with Union Carbide. I had learned in my first sales training class that it was important to ask lots of questions to learn a buyer's needs. Meeting with the owner, I dutifully started to pound him with one question after another. How much material had he bought? How had he bought it? Who were his suppliers? What he was paying? And on and on, somewhat relentlessly, writing down every response.

In the midst of this onslaught, the customer looked me in the eye said sarcastically, "Are you writing a *book* or something?" At that point, the sales call was over. In hindsight, I realized that I hadn't explained why I needed the information, or what was in it for him to give me answers. He was offended by my approach, and our present and future relationship, not to mention my career, was off to a horrible start. (My clever answer to his question was, "No, sir, I'm not." The call ended in a New York minute.)

To make the process run more smoothly, take the time to explain (1) that you would like to ask some questions in order to learn about the customer's situation, and (2) how the customer will benefit from answering your questions. Most people will comply with a reasonable request *if* they see the benefit and if doing so is consistent with their value system.

Newsflash   *Buyers don't like to be interrogated—or manipulated. They need to know what's in it for them to answer your questions.*

Phase 2: Analyze the Situation

Phase 2 represents the merger of *needs determination* and *problem analysis.* This is the most important part of the problem-solving selling sequence: asking questions and listening effectively to achieve a deep, not superficial, understanding of the customer's situation. And that means learning not only about immediate and obvious needs, but the problems, opportunities, and worries that lie beneath the surface. (Recall the discussion in chapter 4 of how too many salespeople miss the "big" needs that customers have.)

> **Newsflash**   *To differentiate yourself and your organization today, you need to learn more than just customers' superficial needs. You must also learn about their opportunities, problems, worries, and dreams. And the more you know, the more successful you will be.*

There are four steps involved in analyzing the situation, as shown in figure 5.6. The first is the last step in phase 1: *Prepare the customer for questioning,* or better said, *Prepare the customer for needs determination.* Why the repetition of steps? Because if, in your mind, you always begin one phase with the last step of the previous phase, then one phase will naturally flow into the next. Proceeding in this way allows you to be in control of the process without your customer having the uncomfortable feeling of being controlled, or even worse, jerked around. In this case, by preparing the customer

1. Prepare the Customer for Questioning
2. Ask the Appropriate Questions
3. Listen for the Needs and Opportunities
4. Verbally Review Your Understanding of the Customer's Needs and Opportunities

Figure 5.6   Analyze the Situation

for your questions, and getting permission to ask them, you move smoothly into the heart of this phase.

The next step is to *ask the appropriate questions.* Neil Rackham's work clearly showed that the more questions a salesperson asks, the more success he or she enjoys, but the *way* those questions are asked can kill the call as quickly as anything else the salesperson can do. That's why we'll spend considerable time in chapter 7 on the art of questioning.

The third step is to *listen for the needs and opportunities.* Obviously, you can ask intelligent questions and do so in a "process-sensitive" way, but if you're not listening effectively to the answers, all is for naught.

When I say "listen for needs," I mean just that. Fight your tendency to listen for *solutions,* and you can learn to hear *needs* in virtually everything a customer says. Sometimes the needs are obvious. Other times they are not. The bottom line is, your job is to uncover as many of the customer's needs as you can without falling into the trap of premature presentation. It wouldn't bother me a bit if every salesperson who works for me referred to himself or herself as a "needs determiner." And the same goes for all members of sales teams, or anyone else in the organization who interacts with customers.

The final step, and the first step in phase 3, is to *verbally review your understanding of the customer's needs and opportunities.* Reviewing what you learned from the questions you asked is a powerful way to conclude the needs assessment and segue into demonstrating that you now have enough information to make a meaningful recommendation.

This, I believe, is the single most important step in problem-solving selling. That's because everything you do up to this moment, from planning the call to encouraging the customer to talk about his or her problems, was designed to get you to the point where you could demonstrate your understanding of the customer's needs and make unique recommendations for meeting them. In fact, I hear all the time that the customer's inclination to buy begins at this juncture, *before* the salesperson has actually presented anything. Why? Because customers' decisions are dramatically affected by the salesperson's ability to demonstrate a profound and accurate understanding of their situations.

Newsflash	*Demonstrating your understanding of the customer's needs is the single most important step in the sales process.*

One last point about needs determination before we move on to phase 3: If members of the sales team or other resources from the organization take part in the sales call, they can play a significant role by asking questions consistent with their areas of expertise. They can also ask questions that the salesperson might not be able to ask at this stage of the relationship. A guest can do things that the person who manages the relationship can't. The result is a more thorough needs analysis, and an enriched and more effective sales call. But whether you fly solo or with a crew, the more effectively this phase is handled, the more you'll be able to offer ideas as well as products and services when it is time to offer recommendations. And that is a key differentiator in today's challenging environment.

Phase 3: Offer Recommendations

Phase 3 is the time when you make your formal recommendations. Although the heart of this phase is "presenting," *offering recommendations* can mean going beyond describing the company's products and services. With appropriate positioning, you can also provide ideas, perspectives, and suggestions during this phase.

Again, keep in mind the idea of problem solving. Approaching this phase in the spirit of generating alternatives will involve the customer more than conventional selling models, because the customer is encouraged to offer his or her ideas as well.

Phase 3 consists of three steps, as shown in figure 5.7. The first step in this phase is the last in phase 2: *Review your understanding of the needs.* Then, and only then, can you proceed to step 2, *Make the recommendation.*

Step 2 tends to happen naturally, in as many ways as there are clever salespeople. Sometimes a straightforward conversational pitch is appropriate; sometimes a more formal stand-up presentation—complete with slides, overheads, charts, graphics, models, computer-assisted graphics, and even videotapes—is needed. Sometimes salespeople even use copies of a written proposal and walk the customer through it, one item at a time.

However you go about it, the governing concepts for making recommendations are the tried-and-true ideas of "features" and "benefits" (some people prefer "features, advantages, and benefits"). *Features* describe what a product does. *Benefits* explain what the features do for the customer. These terms were invented by A. H. Strong sometime in the 1930s as a way to characterize how the things being suggested are reasonable solutions to the needs the customer has expressed. They have survived the test of time for one simple reason—they work!

The third step in phase 3 is to *ask the customer for feedback.* By the time you're done making recommendations, you will have been doing most of the talking for a while. Now it's time to get the customer involved. Having completed your formal recommendations, you need to hear how the customer feels.

> 1. Review your Understanding of the Needs
> 2. Make the Recommendation
> 3. Ask the Customer for Feedback

Figure 5.7   Offer Recommendations

Most of us don't like rejection, so often we're reluctant to ask for feedback openly. Feedback and the resulting objections, however, can be very useful. Most objections are nothing more than unfulfilled needs, and many of them actually indicate an interest in buying. Viewing objections as "needs in disguise," as Kate Reilly of CRC likes to say, can enhance your willingness to seek customer reactions, because you will have less fear. The result will be a more open discussion with your customer.

Before moving on to phase 4, let me pause to make a couple of points. The first goes back to the ideas of sales teams and organization-wide selling. If ever there is a time to use your resources, phase 3 is it. Many sales team members and other corporate assets have expertise that the salesperson doesn't. That's a primary reason for involving them in the process. The classic mistake made by "rugged individualists" is to neglect such resources when it's time to explain why the company's products and services will be of value. Although presenting may seem like the heart of the salesperson's craft, a true craftsperson uses *all* the resources at his or her disposal.

The second point concerns airtime, or the amount of time any one individual spends talking in a meeting. As the facilitator of the sales call, you need to have a good grasp of what the management of airtime should look like.

In an ideal needs-driven selling situation, airtime distribution would look like figure 5.8. Once the meeting has been positioned, the customer gets the bulk of the airtime. If the salesperson is asking thoughtful, needs-oriented, open-ended questions, the customer will be doing most of the talking. That's what you'd expect during needs determination, since you can't learn about someone's needs if you're doing the talking. Letting the customer talk also demonstrates that you don't have to be talking to be in control.

As you begin to share your understanding of the needs you've just heard, and the customer responds with clarification or confirmation, the two of you are sharing the airtime. Finally, when it is

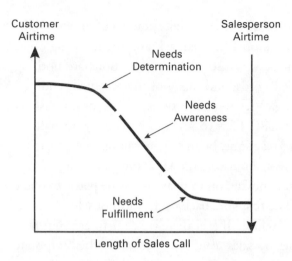

Figure 5.8   Airtime Distribution
Reprinted with permission by CRC© 2000, all rights reserved.

time to make recommendations and present products and services, it is your turn to dominate airtime (along with your team members or other resources). You will have, in essence, *earned the right* to tell your story. You conceded the airtime early in order to own it now.

Phase 4: Resolve the Issues

Phase 4 is what traditionally is called "overcoming objections," which I've recast as "resolving the issues." The key concept here is managing the inevitable resistance that customers will show to our recommendations. Whatever form resistance takes—whether it's objections, misunderstandings, worries, scares, hallucinations, fear of change, or whatever—managing it needs to be treated as a separate and extremely critical part of the selling process.

This phase consists of three specific steps that mirror the idea-development process in problem solving (see figure 5.9). Recall that in problem solving, the task during this phase is to register the group's concerns about a possible solution and to resolve those issues one by one so that the idea crosses the threshold of acceptance. That's the spirit in which I encourage you to approach the

> 1. Ask the Customer for Feedback
> 2. Resolve the Issues
>   - Acknowledge the Objection
>   - Ask the Customer to Elaborate
>   - Transform the Objection into a Need
>   - Respond to the Need
> 3. Invite Other Objections

Figure 5.9   Resolve the Issues

issue-resolution phase in selling. By combining the traditional idea of overcoming objections with the process of idea evaluation and development, you can work *with* the customer in a highly consultative way to resolve whatever issues stand in the way of transforming your recommendation into a workable solution that's adopted by the customer. The customer's involvement in this effort (analogous to the involvement of the problem owner in problem solving) is one of the key things that distinguishes this approach from more traditional types of selling.

You will recall that the last step in phase 3 is *asking the customer for feedback.* This becomes the segue to the issue resolution process and is the first step in this phase. Customers can respond in one of two ways. Either they say they like everything you have said and are ready to move forward (don't hold your breath), or they object to some or all of what you have presented.

Both responses are acceptable because in the first case, you have a done deal, and in the second, you have a chance to work with the customer to reach agreement. Both possibilities are exciting and worthy of eager pursuit.

Assuming the customer takes the far more traveled route and objects to something, it is time to resolve that objection. This is the second step, and it has four specific components, as outlined in figure 5.9. First, you *acknowledge the objection.* That doesn't mean you agree with it. It shows that you understand what he or she has said and that you are ready to problem solve.

Then you *ask the customer to elaborate.* This prevents a sales-person from overreacting to the objection. More important, it increases the likelihood that you will be able to address the objection satisfactorily. Why? Because as the customer elaborates on his or her concerns, you have the opportunity to learn more about what the *need* is that, in the customer's mind, your recommendation failed to address.

Next you *restate the objection.* Giving back what you've heard lets the customer know that you have understood the concerns and are prepared to work on them. That much most people already know. But you can do better. I've already mentioned that objections are really unfulfilled needs. Your task here is to elevate the process of managing resistance by *transforming the objection into a need.*

Remember the notion of reframing concerns in problem solving? Suppose you're participating in a problem-solving session to invent new products, and an idea has been suggested that the group feels has promise. If some tech-head tells the group that the idea isn't safe, chances are the group will abandon the idea. A trained facilitator, however, would treat this statement as an *opportunity* as opposed to a roadblock and say something like, "OK, so what can we do to make it safe?" Similarly, if someone said the idea would cost too much, the facilitator would ask the group, "How can we reduce the cost?" or perhaps, "How can we increase our budget?"

This is what process-sensitive salespeople can do when they encounter resistance. Philosophically, it is much easier to *address a need* than to *challenge an objection,* so the ability to reframe an objection as a need is a key to moving the process toward closure.

We'll spend considerable time later on this skill, because it's a challenging one to acquire. But once you master it, you'll find yourself "resolving issues" instead of "overcoming objections."

After the objection has been restated, you *address the objection,* or as we prefer to say, *respond to the need.* This is the activity that causes salespeople the least amount of difficulty. Once an objection has been reviewed and clarified, there are usually many ways to address it. As you will see later, this can present sales professionals with a wonderful opportunity to use their resources throughout the organization. It is usually the salesperson's responsibility to determine why the customer is resisting a recommendation, but once the objection is well understood, it would be a big miss not to seek the expertise of others in order to address it. At this point, you have resolved the objection.

The third and final step in the issue-resolution phase is to *invite other objections.* Yes, you read that correctly. Look, if there are other objections, don't you want to hear them when you are there as opposed to having the customer think about them later? If the customer has no additional objections, great: You move on. But if your invitation does solicit other objections, you repeat the process you just went through until no more are left. This last step becomes the segue to the final phase, reaching closure.

Phase 5: Reach Closure

For decades salespeople in every field have been saying they wished they were better "closers." Many companies even designate certain people to enter the process in the late stages as closers, much like the relief specialists in baseball who only pitch when the team has a lead in the ninth inning. I never cared for that approach. If the salesperson was able to get to that point, why not let that person close the sale? He or she has earned the right to do it. Fortunately, it's not necessary to anoint special heroes anymore. If the sales professional diligently follows the process and stays deeply needs-driven and problem solving-oriented in his or her approach, closing the sale will be less daunting than it has ever been.

Once you've resolved the customer's issues, it is a natural next move to reach closure: that is, to close the sale or get commitment from the customer to a next step. Again remembering what we

1. Invite Other Objections
2. Ask for the Business
3. Establish Follow-Up Steps

Figure 5.10   Reach Closure

talked about in connection with problem solving, keep in mind that closure doesn't always mean getting *total* acceptance of a proposed solution. It *does* mean that you leave the session with a commitment to advance the process and a specific action plan. Similarly, in sales, reaching closure can mean closing the sale, but it can also mean keeping the process moving forward by establishing specific next steps. Some people think of this as the "big C" (getting the order) and the "small c" (getting commitment to the next step, also known as the interim close).

This phase consists of three steps (see figure 5.10). As usual, the first step—*invite other objections*—is the last step in the preceding phase, resolving issues. The transition to step 2, *ask for the business,* is a natural one, because asking the customer for any additional concerns is tantamount to asking for the business. When the customer finally has no more issues to resolve, it is fair to assume that he or she is ready to commit and that you can ask for the order.

Most of us don't like to ask for the business, in spite of how often our managers, peers, trainers, friends, and instincts tell us to do it. Do it anyway. You've earned the right. Moreover, research suggests that buyers *want* you to do just that! Particularly when you use the problem-solving selling approach, you'll probably find that the answer is affirmative much more often than you imagine.

The final step in this phase is to *establish follow-up steps,* which includes agreeing upon an action plan and a schedule. As in problem solving, this last bit of business is vital to ensuring that the process moves forward (at a minimum) or that the solution—in this case, the sale—becomes a reality.

So there you have it, an approach to selling that combines the needs-driven philosophy with insights gained from the study of group problem solving. It is this combination that brings the selling process to a higher plane and enables the sales professional, the sales team, and all the resources available to them to go beyond conventional selling approaches and differentiate their organization from the competition.

This problem-solving selling process is simultaneously simple (in concept) and complex (in execution). As with the tennis stroke or the golf swing, if you attempt to remember every step in the process while doing it, you could end up in traction. Yet, once you develop a feel for how it all fits together, it becomes straightforward, flowing, and manageable.

Making this sequence work, however, requires bringing process awareness and sensitivity to every selling situation. In a problem-solving setting, the facilitator who manages the process has the advantage of focusing on only that aspect of the session while removing himself or herself from content-related issues. In the context of the sales call, the task is more complicated because the salesperson must engage in the content issues as a participant *and* simultaneously be attentive to climate and process. The fact that, in effect, you've "called someone else's meeting" in arranging for the sales call adds an additional layer of complexity.

What all this means is that each phase of the process has to be approached and managed skillfully, with due attention to the human dynamics. So, now that you have the outlines of the process in hand, it's time to explore the skills involved in each phase in some depth. That's what we'll do in the next five chapters.

MEMO TO MANAGEMENT

For many years, sales managers, vice presidents of sales and marketing, general managers, and company presidents have stood in front of their sales forces and encouraged them to become problem solvers to their customers. With booming voices overflowing with dedication and sincerity, they explained that the salesperson who could truly help customers solve their business problems would attain goals that once appeared to be insurmountable.

These leaders were encouraging their people to perform an admirable task, but too many of them never stopped to think about the enormity of that task. To ask someone to help customers solve their business problems without providing them with the necessary skills is no different than asking a carpenter to build a house without either lumber or tools.

The problem-solving selling model introduced in this chapter combines the best of problem-solving and selling skills. It is designed to enable your people to transform selling situations into problem-solving opportunities. But the model alone won't do it. Conceptually, it's fairly simple. What makes it work are the skills involved in deploying it in real selling situations: interpersonal skills, communication skills, presentation skills, and, not least, problem-solving skills.

Remember, we are talking about elevating the sales process. This means your people have to begin *behaving* like consultants, not just *saying* they are. To change behaviors, you need to provide your people with the skills they need to put philosophy into practice. The model presented here provides the frame for learning the skills introduced in the next five chapters.

The model can help you in another way, too. The key to organization-wide selling is the ability to use as many resources from the organization as possible to provide outstanding customer satisfaction. One of the issues associated with using resources is that people who have chosen not to pursue careers in sales-related jobs often have negative feelings about the sales process. The Willie Loman image is still alive and well in many corridors throughout corporations around the world. The problem-solving approach to selling helps to dispel such negative images. When people from functions like engineering, operations, distribution, credit, financial analysis, and legal start to look at sales as a problem-solving process, they begin to find it more appealing. As a result, thinking of themselves as salespeople, which is the ultimate goal, becomes a more comfortable thing to do.

That's one reason why I've taken pains to reduce the model to an easily understood sequence. Well-articulated sequences help people gain comfort in applying new processes. They are akin to road maps. They let people know where they are in their efforts to get certain things done. For this reason they're extremely useful in teaching and coaching. In conducting a coaching session after joint calls, for example, a sales manager can focus on specific phases of the sequence in analyzing the session and providing feedback. Devoting specific coaching sessions to specific phases can also give such sessions a tight focus that they otherwise often lack.

Beyond that, if salespeople and their colleagues in the organization understand the different phases of the selling sequence and when to apply them, they will work together more effectively. And they can use the sequence to plan how tasks will be distributed among the members of the team: who will be involved in offering recommendations, answering objections, and so on.

So don't let the apparent simplicity of the model deceive you. Because it's relatively easy to grasp, it can put a firm foundation under your efforts to implement organization-wide selling. It can quickly get everyone involved on the same page. At the same time, there's no end to how deep and rich the model can become when it's informed by all the relevant skills, so the concept won't wear out quickly. As we'll see in the next several chapters, there is always more to learn!

CHAPTER 6

"A Table by the Window, Please," or the Importance of Positioning

Transforming interactions with customers into problem-solving opportunities requires state-of-the-art skills. Beginning with this chapter, we'll investigate the specific skills involved in each phase of what I've called *problem-solving selling*.

Although I'll continue to address you as a sales representative, keep in mind that *everyone* who interacts with customers needs to use these skills *all the time* to make organization-wide selling a reality. Whether you're a credit manager calling about an overdue bill, a systems analyst talking to your counterpart, a process engineer dealing with a technical problem—whatever your position may be—you need skills like positioning, facilitating, questioning, listening, offering ideas, managing resistance, and gaining commitment. When everyone who deals with customers deploys these skills, the result is a unified approach that will make the organization stand out head and shoulders above the competition.

Newsflash *Selling skills, which comprise interpersonal skills, communication skills, and presentation skills, must be demonstrated by everyone in the organization every time they interact with the customer. No exceptions.*

This chapter deals with the skills of *positioning*, the first phase in the problem-solving selling sequence. But before we can talk about positioning our meetings with customers, we need to back up and look at the larger context in which these meetings take place—namely, the relationship that you're trying to build with your customers.

It's All About the Relationship

Countless surveys and needs assessments conclude that the *relationship* between the buyer and seller is paramount. If a potential customer or client doesn't feel good about working with you, chances are that person won't do business with you, in spite of what your company has to offer. It's that simple.

So what's the key to a successful relationship? Again, the answer is simple, at least in concept: become a problem-solving resource to your customers. And to do that, you need to go beyond superficial buyer-seller relationships and develop relationships that are based on *trust*.

> **Newsflash**   *To become a problem-solving resource to customers, you must first develop meaningful business relationships that are built on a foundation of trust.*

The Trust Challenge

How do you build trust? Recall that in problem-solving meetings one of the first tasks is to set the climate and get everyone comfortable working with one another. The same concept applies to both the *micro* and *macro* levels of the relationship with a customer. It's important to put our customers at ease every time we interact with them (the micro level). More than that, we want the customer to feel comfortable in the way we work together over time (the *macro* level of the relationship). If we can create a high comfort level of doing business together, we're more likely to be called upon as a source for new ideas when the customer needs help.

The Trust Formula

So what's the secret here? After all, *you* know you're trustworthy. Isn't that enough?

In a word, no. The question is, How do you put that quality across to customers? What does *trust* mean in terms of specific behaviors that the customer observes and responds to?

Here's one answer to these questions. Through the efforts of Bill Cope and John Philipp, Synectics® developed an innovative way to look at trust by putting it into a formula:

$$\text{Trust} = \frac{\text{Credibility} \times \text{Intimacy}}{\text{Risk}}$$

In plain English, trustworthiness is directly proportional to the amount of *credibility* and *intimacy* that people have with each other, and it is inversely proportional to the *risk* associated with the interaction or relationship.

Credibility refers in large part to knowing your stuff, being believable when you make an analysis or a recommendation. The sales team can help tremendously here. Just the fact that you have a team and a customer-driven organization behind you will enhance your credibility. You've got not only your own expertise to fall back on, but also the combined knowledge and experience of all your organizational resources as well.

Intimacy refers to the depth of the relationship, how well people know and like each other. In terms of sales, you can think of it as the comfort level that exists between you and your customer.

Intimacy often takes time to develop, and nurturing it requires sensitivity and empathy, two qualities we'll talk more about in a moment. It is also a function of how much you have in common and the enjoyment you derive from being in each other's company.

Risk is the factor you have the least control over, and yet it is the one that often demands the most from you. Risk is simply the probability (low or high) of making a wrong decision. The bigger the stakes involved, the higher the risk. And as the risks increase for the prospective buyer, so does the need for *credibility × intimacy*. Look back at the formula: If risk is high, then credibility and intimacy need to be high to offset it. Conversely, if risk is very low, trust can be fairly high even without as much credibility and intimacy as you would like.

You already know this. If you're buying a home computer, the risk factor is greater than if you are buying a simple calculator. So you might be willing to buy a calculator from a salesperson without demanding a lot of credibility, let alone intimacy, from that person. But you'd be a lot more cautious about buying an expensive computer from someone who hadn't established his or her expertise in advising you. And between two salespeople who both seem to know their stuff, you're more likely to buy from the one you feel more comfortable talking to. In other words, the one with whom your level of trust is higher.

Beyond increasing credibility and intimacy, you can also work to lower the risk factor directly. Where there is apparent risk in the customer's mind, your challenge is to demonstrate either that doing business with you doesn't entail risk or that whatever unavoidable risk does exist can be minimized.

Newsflash   *Risk is a fact of life in business. Minimizing the risk to your customer makes it easier to trust you.*

How do you reduce the risk for a customer who has never done business with you before? Think about this question for a minute or two, and write down as many answers as you can. Do this before reading further.

Got your list? OK, compare it with what we have observed over the years:

Things to Do to Minimize the Risk of Doing Business with You

- Come with references whom your potential buyer *knows.*

- Highlight your company's years in business.

- Refer to numerous long-term successful relationships you have with your clients.

- Describe situations parallel to the customer's, then describe their outcomes.

- Create incentives that help make up for perceived risks or concerns.

- Start small—one region, one store, one application, one assignment.

- Get other people involved: for example, the customer's manager and your own manager.

- *Share* the risk: for example, clarify your company's warrantees or guarantees and any compensation offered for nonperformance.

- Promise to do everything you can to service the relationship and that there will be no surprises—and back up your promises with a personal guarantee.

- Acknowledge the prospect's fears as legitimate.

- Discuss the *value* of risk: High risk means high reward, as long as the risk is calculated.

Notice how each of these ways to reduce risk increases one or both of the other variables in the equation—credibility and intimacy.

That's part of the beauty of the trust formula. For example, while you might balk at frankly acknowledging risk or candidly discussing its value, doing so appropriately can enhance both of the other variables. The result? Trust goes up.

CREST: Not Just a Toothpaste Anymore

The trust formula gives us a way of thinking about how to cultivate this essential quality, but let's be more specific still. In a review of focus groups and other research in which buyers were asked why they buy, four key attributes emerged that buyers want and expect in salespeople who call on them:

- CRedibility
- Empathy
- Sensitivity
- Trustworthiness

Yep, CREST, just like the toothpaste. In dozens of surveys, buyers said that they would prefer not to do business with salespeople who don't demonstrate these four qualities. End of story. Do I need to add that the same thing applies to *everyone* a customer comes into contact with?

> **Newsflash**   *Everyone in the organization who interacts with customers needs to consistently demonstrate credibility, empathy, sensitivity, and trustworthiness.*

Credibility

We've already touched on credibility in discussing the trust formula. If you're an experienced salesperson, you probably already command a number of ways to demonstrate your credibility. Here are just a few specific suggestions that have emerged from discussions with sales pros:

- Review your relevant work history with the prospect.

- Talk about what is going on in the prospect's industry or business.

- Refer to a mutual contact who knows you and your company's track record.

- Use thoughtful questions to get the prospect thinking about his or her business in a new light; for example: "What's your thinking about the impact of the recent wood pulp price increases?" or "Where do you think this segment of the business will be in five years?" or "What are some of the biggest obstacles you anticipate to reaching your long-term goals?"

- Suggest a professional referral (the most effective referrals tend to be peer to peer).

- Admit when you don't know the answer or don't have a solution. Offer to get back to the prospect, and make good on your offer within a day or two (yes, a day or two; wait a week, and you've blown it).

As I said, you're probably familiar with other ways to establish credibility, but perhaps at least one of the items in the preceding list will get you thinking.

Empathy

The word *empathy* derives from the Greek word for "passion." It refers to a shared understanding that is based on feeling as much as on intellect. You demonstrate empathy when your responses indicate that you "feel with" other people about something important to them.

To display empathy, get prospects to talk about themselves. Look for "hot buttons"—interests and passions, such as hobbies, organizations they belong to, or aspects of what's going on in their business or industry. Since many people have a lively interest in sports, it's a common topic of conversation. But if you use it, go beyond the usual banter about how the home team did last night and discuss strategy or personal involvement in sports.

Many salespeople are trained to look around the prospect's office for hooks into his or her passions. Once again, though, go beyond the obvious "Oh, you play golf?" and ask instead about *how* she got started playing, or how he *felt* winning that trophy. Or show a lively interest in the person's career and work culture: "You've been here twenty years. What has kept you interested?" "Give me an idea of how you and your department develop strategies." Or, "How do you feel in general about salespeople? What would you like from us?"

Not everyone will become engaged with you in this way. But when all else fails, keep in mind that the overlap in your interests can be as simple as the fact that the two of you share the same goal: finding the right product for the right use.

Empathy implies respect. You can show respect in several ways:

- Respect for the prospect's time: Get agreement up front on the time frame for the sales call, and adhere to it.

- Respect for the prospect's information and thought processes: Ask permission to take notes or to ask questions.

- Respect for the prospect's space: Avoid putting things on the person's desk.

- Respect for your competitors: Never put down the competition, because if your prospect is one of their customers, you're actually putting down the prospect.

- Respect for what the prospect says: Let the person know you're listening and have heard what he or she had to say.

Sensitivity

We've discussed sensitivity in the context of managing the process of the meeting, and we'll return to that topic several times. Here are just a few examples of how to demonstrate sensitivity:

- Be cautious about the *kinds* of questions you ask as well as the *way* you ask them (we'll discuss the art of questioning in detail in chapter 7).

- Paraphrase what you understand the person to be saying.

- Verify your understanding of the person's needs.

- Look for signs of discomfort and change course if you see people shifting in their chairs, hesitating in talking, taking lots of phone calls, and so on.

Trustworthiness

We've covered this one. Study the trust formula, and put it to use. Realize that of the four CREST attributes, trustworthiness is the most difficult to demonstrate, yet is considered by most people to be *the* key component of any relationship.

Applying CREST Principles

I was lucky enough to learn the value of several variables within CREST early in my career, when I was selling for Union Carbide. One of my largest customers had warping problems when using our product in an injection molding process. The people at the company had been having problems for several days and were upset about the poor quality and low numbers of usable plastic lids that were being turned out. When they called, I arranged to visit their facility with Charlie Joslin, an experienced technical service manager from our molding and extrusion group.

Charlie checked with quality control to determine that the client's material was on spec. It was. Since no other customers were complaining, we were confident the problem was in their molding shop, somewhere.

When we arrived at the facility, the purchasing manager brought us immediately to the machine where the problem was occurring. The plant manager, quality control manager, molding supervisor, and a machine operator were all there, all stymied. As we watched the complex machine producing the lids, we immediately saw that the warping problem was real. The fact that the machine was old and that the factory was in many ways obsolete didn't matter. Our customers expected us, their primary supplier, to get the process back on track quickly. If not, we would be replaced immediately. They made that extremely clear.

Charlie walked around the machine, using his keen eye and skilled sense of touch. He investigated every pipe, dial, valve, electrical component, and piece of mechanical equipment. After his initial perusal he said, "Well, let's get to work." As he took off his jacket and loosened his tie, I realized we would be there for a while.

Charlie really worked over that machine, methodically experimenting with different settings, twisting every valve, increasing and decreasing the pressure, raising and lowering the temperature—you get the idea.

Three hours later, he had diagnosed the problem. He explained that he had changed a few settings on one of the water feeds. Sure enough, lid after lid came out of the mold like perfect cookies.

After an hour of perfect molding, it was time to leave. The customer was pleased. As we were saying our good-byes, Charlie remarked that those darn temperature readings can be misleading and even went so far as to suggest that we should have warned the customer of this possibility. He provided the customer with reasonable ranges for each setting so they could quickly solve the problem if it happened again. He also promised to submit a report to the customer reviewing what he had done.

When we got in the car, I thanked Charlie for his efforts and for time well spent. That's when he dropped the bomb. Jovially, Charlie confided that he had identified the problem within eight minutes after walking into the plant! Upon first approaching the machine, he had touched one of the key pipes leading to the mold.

"The pipe should have been about 70 degrees Fahrenheit—room temperature," said Charlie, "but it was ice cold. All I had to do was increase the temperature of that feed line and I knew the warping problem would vanish."

Now, I don't know about you, but I probably would have fixed the problem as soon as I noticed it, in the process demonstrating how smart I was and what marvelous technical support I could offer the customer. Not only would I have come across as a hero (or so I would imagine), but with a little bit of luck I could have left on an earlier flight home.

Charlie Joslin's perspective was different. He knew that if he had proceeded in this way, *he* would have looked good, but the molding supervisor would have looked ridiculous. He knew that looking good was less important to the business relationship than saving face for the supervisor. "Look," he told me, "we were already there and the time was allocated, so why not put the time in and avoid embarrassing the plant people?" When I objected that this charade didn't feel right, he put his hand on my shoulder and said, "Son, sometimes saving people's dignity is worth a bit of a charade." He didn't mention that in choosing this route, he had also endeared himself, and us, to the customer.

Charlie, in his instinctive manner, had addressed all three terms in the trust equation. He had demonstrated his *credibility* by taking the machine apart, putting it back together, and eventually solving the problem. Using his nonthreatening approach and acting in a selfless manner, with a bit of self-effacement thrown in, he had proved to be likable and personable, effectively addressing the *intimacy* question. And by taking the time he did, and assuming ownership for the problem, he minimized the *risk* for all involved. I don't even need to comment on how his behavior also demonstrated the key CREST ideas of empathy and sensitivity. In short, he filled the key needs that customers have for the people they do business with.

The Skills of Positioning

We turn now to the skills involved in the first phase of the problem-solving selling sequence: positioning the meeting. Really, positioning begins with everything you do that establishes and nurtures a relationship with a customer, which is one reason why we've spent so much time on that subject. Now, though, we zero in on the specifics of getting a sales call off to a good start.

Positioning is the first step in managing process. Too many salespeople make the mistake of not investing a few minutes early in the meeting to ensure that there are no surprises—at least from a *process* perspective. Positioning the meeting demonstrates respect for the customer and shows that you approach meetings like this in a professional manner. It allows you to manage expectations while ensuring that what you hope will happen does in fact happen. And it provides you with an opportunity to use more effectively the resources who accompany you.

Positioning the meeting includes the four tasks we introduced in chapter 5, shown again in figure 6.1, with a slight twist. As I'm sure you recognize, these are the kinds of tasks handled by a facilitator in a problem-solving session. In a sales call, salespeople need to juggle this role with their role as a participant.

The Salesperson as Facilitator

Try to recall a sales call that involved many people, both from the seller's side and the buyer's side. When these kinds of sales calls begin, they will be much more successful if

- The salesperson makes sure everyone is properly introduced.

- The salesperson takes responsibility for getting the agenda on the table and seeing to it that everyone has a chance to express what they want to get out of the meeting.

> 1. Put the Customer at Ease
> 2. Set the Agenda
> 3. Clarify the Logistics
> 4. Prepare the Customer for What Is
>   About to Happen

Figure 6.1   Position the Meeting

- The salesperson watches the time, makes sure the key points are recorded, and keeps things on track.

- The salesperson concludes the sales call and sets up the next steps.

Obvious, isn't it? In multiperson calls, it's logical for the salesperson to assume the responsibility for facilitation, whether or not anyone calls it that. Yet too often, when the call consists of just a salesperson and a single customer, the salesperson's tendency is to pay little attention to process and to focus primarily on content.

That's not to say that good salespeople neglect process issues. If they did, they would hardly be successful. Chances are, though, that whatever they do to manage process, they do largely by instinct and without conscious intent. I know that I never thought in terms of process early in my career when I was selling at Union Carbide, yet I reached my sales goals every year. I wonder how much better I might have done if I'd known then what I do now.

If you haven't consciously thought in terms of facilitating sales calls, I encourage you to do so from now on. You'll be in control of the process, just as a professional facilitator controls the process in a group meeting. Of course, there are significant differences between the two settings. First, in most sales calls the role of facilitator is not automatically or formally handed off to the salesperson, so it's less clear who is in charge. Second, in a problem-solving session the facilitator ideally behaves in a selfless manner, acting to ensure a good result for the problem owner. In selling situations, you certainly want customers to get what they want, but *you* also have a vested interest in the outcome. Finally, facilitators generally avoid involving themselves in content. As a salesperson, however, you're not only interested in the content, but you provide much of it yourself.

What all this means is that your role in the sales call is more complex than that of either a participant, which is how you've probably seen yourself up to now, or a pure facilitator. Not only do you have two levels of responsibility, but also your facilitation role is one you have to fill without having it formally handed to you. You need to assume it naturally, and that starts with your very first move: putting the customer at ease.

Put the Customer at Ease

I don't need to add very much to what we've already said about this first step in positioning the meeting. Besides, you probably already have a repertoire of ways to put customers at ease. I will say, though, that it makes sense to try to be a little different from everybody else in your approach to establishing rapport. Think in terms of CREST attributes. For instance, what better way to demonstrate *credibility* than to begin the call by talking about an article you've read or a specific event that relates to the customer's business? How about asking about something you know is significant to the customer as a way to demonstrate *sensitivity?* Or talking briefly about a situation parallel to the customer's as a way to build *trust?* Using CREST can help you get the sales call off to a good start and advance the relationship at the same time.

If you're accompanied on the call by members of your sales team or other people in the organization, have your resources participate in the climate-setting process. As your colleagues introduce themselves, they can explain their roles on the team and how they think they can help. As the facilitator, you can always add to what a team member says, particularly relevant information about each person's expertise or experience: "I'm so pleased Kathleen could join us today. She has been involved in this kind of research for almost fifteen years, and I know she will prove to be very helpful." Comments like this show pride in your team members and make a nice impression on the customer.

If you're meeting with several people from the customer side, ask each of them to tell you who they are, what their role in the organization is, and what they want to get out of the meeting. Doing this will allow you to turn a "four-on-one" meeting into four "one-on-one" meetings. For example, when you talk about specifications, you can look at Hal and say something like, "Hal, you were interested in the specs. Let's talk about that for a minute. . . ." If Susan asks about price, you can direct your comments about pricing to her. If your team is with you, you can ask individual team members to address areas that they are particularly expert in.

Set the Agenda

Next, set the agenda—and make sure it's mutually understood and agreed upon. I've already observed that many salespeople make the mistake of not taking the time to explain why they called the meeting and what they hope to accomplish. As one customer put it, "They all come in and go through the small-talk routine and try to establish rapport. Then all of a sudden they start asking questions or talking about their company or product line. And I don't have a *clue* as to *why* they wanted to meet, other than to try to get some money out of *my* pocket and into theirs!"

Tough quote, but one worth remembering.

Even salespeople who do state their objectives often carry on without asking customers what *they* want. What that does is convey the message that *their* agenda is what really matters—namely, making a sale. No wonder salespeople sometimes have image problems! The reality is that most of your customers aren't interested in *your* problem. Remember, it's the customer's meeting—even if you're the one who called it.

Assuming that you *are* the one who called the meeting, which is the usual situation, I encourage you to get your agenda on the table first. Now, this may sound contradictory to the needs-driven approach, but the fact is that often the customer does not have an agenda at all at the outset. Asking customers what they want to accomplish before telling them why you're there is likely to seem foolish. Instead, if it's a needs-determination call, make it clear that you're there to learn about the customer's needs. The same applies to whatever your purpose is, whether it's to make a formal presentation, engage in a little maintenance by stopping in to see how things are going, or correct a problem or respond to a complaint.

I learned this lesson about getting an agreed-upon agenda in place the hard way. In our early days at Consultative Resources Corporation (CRC), the sales training firm I cofounded in 1981, we were heavily involved in working with financial institutions, banks in particular. I remember one case in which the vice chairman referred us to the director of training of a major New York City bank. My partner and I approached the sales call with some anxiety, not only because it was a big opportunity, but because we knew that referrals from senior-level people often create some resentment on the part of middle-level managers. We would be in the training director's office only because someone at a higher level had instructed him to meet with us. So it was likely that he was not all that pleased about seeing us.

Anticipating that resentment, we decided to do our best to demonstrate our process skills. If we could demonstrate how effective we were in using the skills we wanted to teach, perhaps he'd see the potential value of working with us. Oh, how little we knew at this early stage of our consulting careers!

We wanted to get an agenda on the table early, yet we hadn't thought out the concept of whose meeting it was and who had called it. Therefore, after some awkward small talk, I looked at my prospect and in my most facilitative voice asked him what he wanted to get out of the meeting. When he asked me to clarify my meaning, I asked how I could make the best use of his time.

He thought for a moment and then looked at me with an incredulous expression. "Let me get this straight," he said. "You come to *my* office because the vice chairman set up the meeting, and now *you're* asking what *I* want to accomplish, is that right?"

When I responded affirmatively, with what I'm sure was a sheepish expression, he looked me in the eye and said, "What I'd really like to get out of this meeting is to have it end within the next five minutes so I can get back to work instead of answering a bunch of silly questions."

Whoops. Believe it or not, that sales call did not yield positive results. Afterward I realized how ridiculous it was for us to ask the potential client what *he* wanted to get out of the meeting when *we* had called it. He didn't know who we were or how we could help him. He had good relationships with his existing suppliers, and as far as he was concerned his needs were being satisfied. For strangers to come in and ask him how we could make good use of his time meant nothing to him.

Newsflash   *If you call the meeting, get your agenda out first.*

Suppose, however, that it's the exceptional case where the customer calls the meeting. In that case, the customer's agenda goes up first. The customer would not have initiated the meeting if there was nothing to talk about. Your agenda can be stated after the customer's is confirmed.

At this point you have put the customer at ease and established an agenda for the meeting. Before proceeding to clarifying the logistics, though, take into account how much time has passed since the last sales call. To state the obvious, our customers don't think about us as much as we think about them. It's not even close. Our customers are busy thinking about their own problems: *their* company, *their* products, *their* customers. In the average week, it would be safe to say, they spend very little time thinking about their suppliers, except when something goes wrong.

Be sensitive to this reality. In theory, you should make progress on every sales call. The goal of any one call can be anything from getting the opportunity to give a demonstration to closing the sale. But because time has passed since the last meeting, you're bound to lose momentum. Typically you can't pick up exactly where you left off. So, in terms of your goal for *this* meeting, you automatically start behind the starting gate.

For this reason, at the beginning of a follow-up sales call, *review what transpired at the previous meeting.* By doing so, you reduce the inevitable loss of momentum and position the meeting in such a way that you can use the time to move closer to your current goal.

> **Newsflash** *Simply reviewing what happened at the last meeting will significantly decrease the loss of momentum in the sales cycle.*

Clarify the Logistics

The next step is to clarify the logistics for the meeting. That includes the physical setup and any special requirements you might have in order to make your presentation. The most important logistical item, however, is time. Every sales call needs a "time contract." Establishing at the start how much time is available will result in a more effective meeting and will show your consideration and respect for your customer.

Beyond that, the time contract can protect you as well. If you have another meeting coming up and the customer keeps talking, a way to end the meeting is to remind the customer that you've used up the planned time.

This point about confirming the time for the meeting is another hard-earned lesson for me. I remember once driving three hours to Boston to give a formal presentation. I had arranged with my prospective client, a training director for a commercial bank, to give a forty-five minute presentation that would explain how my company could address the needs we had identified in our previous meetings.

The meeting was scheduled for 11:00 A.M., and I arrived about fifteen minutes early. To my surprise, the training director saw me immediately. Remembering that we had contracted for one hour, I figured that with the fifteen-minute bonus I had much more time than my presentation required. So I spent about fifteen minutes talking about the recent conference that we had both spoken at and ten minutes reviewing my understanding of the prospect's needs. I also managed to spend a few minutes empathizing about how the Red Sox were having another disappointing season. Since I had about forty-five minutes left, I stood at the flip chart and said, "Well, I guess it's time to explain how we think we can help you address your needs."

That's when my prospective client said, "You'd better hurry, because you only have fifteen minutes!"

"Whoa," I said. "I thought we had scheduled our meeting to end at noon."

"I'm sorry," she responded, "but my manager called an emergency meeting for 11:30, and I have to be there."

So now I had *fifteen minutes* to explain what we could do to help the bank create a sales culture within the organization. I showed her a few perspectives, rather than formally recommending anything, and rescheduled the meeting for another time several weeks later. For all practical purposes, I had blown the day—three hours to Boston and three hours back—to make a fifteen-minute presentation, and an ineffective one at that!

Great use of time, huh? If upon arriving I had invested just a few seconds to ask whether we still had until noon for the meeting, my wasted efforts would have been avoided. Once I realized that we had only forty-five minutes, I would have moved as quickly as I comfortably could to review the needs and give my presentation.

Newsflash   *Start every meeting with a "time contract." Doing so shows respect for the customer and protects you from surprises.*

Prepare the Customer for What Is About to Happen

The final step in positioning the meeting is to prepare the customer for what is about to happen. The preparation varies depending on the kind of call it is. If it's a needs-development call, it is critical to let the customer know that you need to ask questions and that it will be in his or her interest to let you do so. This step is particularly important when you're asking a series of questions. (Recall our earlier discussion of how interrogation makes people feel uncomfortable.) This is the most common situation, as explained in chapter 5. If it's a presentation call, explain how you intend to proceed and why you are taking that approach. If you're there to attempt to resolve a previous objection, review what you discussed last time and explain how you think you can help. The theme is to demonstrate how what you plan to do will benefit the customer.

Once the meeting has been positioned effectively, you're ready to pursue whatever the agenda calls for. Never underestimate the importance of this step. Many sales professionals have told me that much of their success is the result of how they position their sales interactions and manage their customers' expectations. Good positioning sets the tone for all that follows. It gets you off to a good start and puts you naturally into the facilitator role. Best of all, it starts to differentiate you from the rest of the pack the moment you walk in the door.

MEMO TO MANAGEMENT

In organization-wide selling, everyone in the company thinks of themselves as salespeople, whatever the nature of the contact they have with customers. From customers' points of view, their relationship with your company is a composite of the *many* relationships and interconnections that the people in their organization have with the people in yours. And that means in all departments—not just sales and customer service but collections and engineering and anywhere else where customers have contact with someone in your company, whether by phone, fax, e-mail, or personal meeting.

Of course, not everybody in your organization possesses the interpersonal skills required to develop and maintain successful customer relationships. That's where you come in.

The Charlie Joslin story is about a technical representative who had superb sensitivity and relationship skills. As a result, Charlie developed quite a following among his customers. Sometimes customers would ask for him to visit even when it wasn't necessary because they enjoyed his company and knew he could always help in some way. If you don't have lots of Charlies working for you already, you probably wish you did.

The challenge for you is to instill throughout your company the qualities that Charlie exemplifies—qualities like empathy, sensitivity, likeability, and, of course, extraordinary credibility. Notice how Charlie put these attributes to work in the service of the customer. He thought of the customer's needs before his own. He was less concerned with looking good than he was with the *customer* looking good. He cared more about the *relationship* than he cared about impressing people. Some of that is personality, sure. But a lot of it is skills, and skills can be learned.

Make it a priority to talk to your people about the trust formula and about CREST principles. Do whatever you can to reinforce the behaviors you want them to display, whether it is through coaching, praising them when you catch them doing something right, or, not least, being a good role model. Remember that how you treat your people will often be reflected in the way they treat their customers. Treat your people with respect and dignity, and they're far more likely to treat customers the same way. Like so many of the principles espoused in this book, it starts at the top and cascades down throughout the organization.

Of course, there may be some people in your organization who can't be relied upon to behave in a way that's consistent with the kind of customer relationships you're trying to build. If so, keep them away from the customer. If that's not an option, talk to them at length about how you expect them to behave, and provide timely and specific feedback. There are just too many horror stories about how one individual blew up an entire relationship with a customer. If I can quote my *Star Trek* hero, Mr. Spock, "The needs of the many outweigh the needs of the few." *Nobody* has the right to treat customers in a way that damages their trust. Ever.

As to positioning a sales call, your role here is easy. When you make joint calls with your salespeople—and as a manager I hope you will do that often—bring up the subject of positioning in the planning process. Ask your salespeople how they plan to position each meeting. If they're just learning about positioning, ask them to try different parts of the process on different calls. Respect their role as the facilitator whenever you're along for the ride. At the end of the day, think about the positioning steps as you give them constructive feedback, and find out how they feel about the concept.

Positioning takes little time, yet it has an incredible impact on the probability of success. Do what you can to encourage your people to position meetings consistently, and to do it well. It will pay off.

CHAPTER 7

"Elementary, My Dear Watson," or Analyzing the Situation

Determining customers' needs, or, as I prefer to say, analyzing the situation, is the single most important component of the selling process. Success in this phase rests on two seemingly straightforward sets of skills: questioning and listening. Neither is as simple as it appears.

This chapter describes these two vital skill sets, in addition to the other steps in phase 2 *(Analyze the Situation)* of the problem-solving selling sequence described in chapter 5. As a reminder, the steps of phase 2 are shown in figure 7.1.

To Ask and How to Ask, That Is the Question

Chuck Sulerzyski is passionate about his salespeople understanding the needs of their customers. I have observed Chuck create sales cultures at Chemical Bank (now Chase Manhattan), Banc One, and Provident Bank. He believes that questioning is the most important skill of all: "The ability to ask thought-provoking

1. Prepare the Customer for Questioning
2. Ask the Appropriate Questions
3. Listen for the Needs and Opportunities
4. Verbally Review Your Understanding of the Customer's Needs and Opportunities

Figure 7.1   Phase 2: Situation Analysis

questions and draw the customer out without interrupting is absolutely critical. Our people have to learn the customer's needs. Otherwise they will not be able to make the appropriate recommendations. If they don't ask the right questions in a sensitive way, they won't accomplish their objectives. It is a skill that all our people need to understand thoroughly."

Chuck understands the value of both content and process. Notice how he speaks of asking the *right* questions *in a sensitive way.* That's what makes questioning an art, and it's one at which salespeople need to excel.

Unfortunately, the way salespeople ask questions is one of the behaviors that upsets buyers most. That's partly the fault of the questioners, and partly the nature of questioning.

Careful, You're Walking on Quicksand

I use several exercises to clarify why questioning is such a treacherous activity. One of my favorites involves exploring the way questions cause people to make assumptions. I often ask salespeople to pretend they are sitting at their desks when their manager comes in and says, "What are you doing for lunch?"

I then ask the group to speculate about why they think the manager asked that question. Simple, right? Not at all. Invariably, the group comes up with a wide variety of responses, ranging from the predictable ("She wants to have lunch with me") to the possible but unlikely ("I'm about to be promoted"), to the paranoid ("He's checking up on me," "What he really wants is for me to bring him a sandwich," "I'm about to be fired").

This exercise dramatically illustrates how slippery questions can be. Even a simple six-word question like, "What are you doing for lunch?" can conjure up an amazing array of conflicting possibilities in the mind of the listener.

In sales, as in the rest of life, the questioning process is replete with contradictions, paradoxes, and misinterpretations. It's little wonder that when buyers are asked to zero in on particular behaviors displayed by the salespeople who annoy them most, they always mention too many questions, irrelevant questions, leading questions, inappropriate questions or, worst of all, manipulative questions.

Not that salespeople necessarily do these things with bad intent. Remember Sal the sales guy, from chapter 1? Suppose Sal eventually got around to saying to Betty the buyer, "If I could show you a way that you could get a better deal, would you consider doing business with me?" I'm sure you've heard questions like that. Maybe you've even used them yourself.

On the surface, Sal's question sounds like a decent enough proposal. But Betty can't help but be put off by the tentative, "If I could . . ." followed by the pushy, "Would you . . . ?" On balance, in spite of Sal's good intentions, his query suddenly begins to feel like a manipulation. The way he couched the inquiry makes Betty feel like she's being toyed with—a major no-no in interactions with customers, and one that leads straight to disaster.

This situation illustrates the paradox of questioning in a sales environment. If Sal doesn't ask enough questions to be able to determine Betty's needs, he will be unable to put forth the kind of information she requires in order to say, "Yes!" But if he asks the wrong questions, or asks the right ones inappropriately, he may lose her enthusiasm altogether.

Newsflash   *The type of questioning you practice will make or break the vital connection between you and your buyers.*

So What's the Problem Here?

Why is questioning so complex? One reason is that we've been conditioned from early in life to be suspicious of questions, particularly those that seem to mask statements instead of being genuine questions. Parents often speak to young children in rhetorical questions, the intent of which is to *tell*, not ask. For example, Little Jamie, age four, is in the living room playing with her Malibu Barbie. In walks Mommy, who says, "Are you ready to eat now, sweetie?" Without waiting for an answer, Mommy proceeds to serve Jamie dinner. Her question wasn't really a question at all. It was a statement of intent. The real message is, whether Jamie wants to eat or not, she will soon find herself sitting in front of a bowl of pasta.

This parental behavior can persist long after toddlers stop toddling. A vibrant example came to my attention not too long ago in an article about a man who had just turned forty. It sounded something like this: "My mom and I were strolling through Manhattan's Central Park. As we walked, Mom said, 'Do you always walk so fast?'—her way of asking me to slow down. Then she asked, 'You don't walk through the park at night, do you?'—her way of suggesting that I not do something that she perceived as dangerous. Later, she asked, 'Aren't we near Tavern on the Green?'—her way of letting me know that she was ready for a cocktail at the famous pub. Finally, she asked, 'Haven't we walked enough for one afternoon?'—meaning that she was tired of walking."

This story reminded me of my mom, who is also my great pal. We went to lunch at a diner on a Saturday afternoon not too long ago. I was wearing a baseball hat. She smiled at me and said, "You're not going to wear your hat during lunch, are you, dear?" My hat was off my head in a nanosecond. Mom had made it clear the hat was coming off when we sat down to eat.

Of course, this behavior isn't limited to parents' interactions with their children. All of us hear questions that aren't really questions. But in a sales interaction with a customer, it's important to avoid asking questions that might be perceived as manipulative, controlling, or anything less than a sincere effort to find out needed information.

> **Newsflash** *Straightforward, compassionate questioning that is genuinely an intellectual inquiry, with no covert agenda, works best in all selling situations.*

A special case of the question-as-statement is what I've learned to call "YSI questions," where YSI stands for "You stupid idiot." The idea comes from an excellent sales trainer and colleague, Laura Daley-Caravella. Laura became fascinated by questions that can come across as insulting. She observed that in tone and content many of these questions could be followed by a comma and the words, "you stupid idiot." In other words, there was a judgment, and not a positive one, implied in the very structure of the question. And she pointed out that any question that fits this description probably isn't asked to obtain information. Instead, it makes a statement.

Here's an example of what I mean. I ask groups to identify the questions they would like to ask but are reluctant to. I then investigate the reluctance. Often, it turns out that this hesitancy grows out of fear of the customer's reaction. And for good reason: the questions are YSI questions. For instance, a question such as, "Why did you decide to do business with those people in the first place?" can easily be followed by "you stupid idiot." The question implies disapproval. In fact, most questions that begin with the word *why*, even though intended positively, can be perceived as challenging.

> **Newsflash** *If you can hear "You stupid idiot" after one of your questions, so can your customer. Questions like that get you an "E" ticket to the parking structure.*

In addition to how we phrase individual questions, there's the issue of how we manage the entire process of questioning. Not long ago, my company was about to buy a new videotape system. We were interviewing potential suppliers when I met with a young, bright salesperson, Joe, from one of the major manufacturers. Joe made a pretty good first impression when he reviewed our existing system and pointed out some good things about it, as well as identified some of the deficiencies.

Eventually, Joe began to ask questions (I couldn't help but notice that he could have begun the needs-determination process earlier). He began with fact-finding questions: How often do you use the system? How do you use it? How long is your typical tape? How many different trainers use the system?

Inasmuch as I was a knowledgeable buyer, I was willing to answer these questions, particularly since I understood why Joe had to know those specific things. I would have been more comfortable, however, if he had taken a few seconds to position the questioning by explaining why he needed the information, and what was in it for me to respond.

Then Joe switched to what I call strategic questions, questions about our longer-term needs. Now, this was unusual. None of the other salespeople had asked strategic questions. Here, then, was Joe's sure-fire moment in the sun, a golden opportunity to differentiate himself from all his competitors.

Joe began with a stereotypical, open-ended, "needs-oriented" question that, although contrived, seemed reasonable: "Tell me, Eric, what do you *really* want the system to do for you?"

I thought for a moment and then responded by explaining at some length how reliability was the single most important feature to me. When you videotape salespeople role playing in simulated selling situations, I said, the last thing you want to deal with is a system that goes down.

At that point, Joe, who appeared to be hanging on my every word, had the perfect chance to demonstrate his understanding of my concerns and desires. I had just told him in detail what they were! But instead of following up on my stated needs, Joe said, "Well, everyone wants a dependable system. I'll include that in my proposal. But what do you *really* want the system to do for you?"

Well, at least he had partly heard the seriousness of my request for dependability, so I explained further that I wanted a system that produced better images of people on the tape. I gave him examples and plenty to work with. I really wanted to help Joe help me.

No such luck. Joe's response was, "Even broadcast systems can't get around those kinds of issues . . . but what I really need to know, Eric, is, what do you *really* want the system to do for you?"

At that point, short of telling Joe that I would like the system to do my laundry and cook me breakfast, I had no idea what to say. Quietly I asked, "Would you mind telling me where we are going with this line of questioning? Why don't you just tell me what you need to know?"

Upon realizing that his approach had succeeded in ticking me off, Joe reverted to his usual questioning mode. He tried to take control of the conversation by leading me in the direction he wanted to go—still without giving me any indication why he was asking these particular questions.

The interrogation seemed to go on for days. Finally, I grew weary of his trying to manipulate the conversation instead of gather information. I completely lost interest in him and his company and chose not to work with him.

Moral? Simple. The *process* we use in asking questions is often more important than the *content* of the questions themselves. Had Joe positioned his questions well and made me feel that he was working on *my* behalf, he would have created an environment in which I wanted to hear his ideas rather than question his motives.

Newsflash   *The way you ask questions is usually more important than the questions themselves. Salespeople usually know what questions they want to ask. They don't always know how to ask them.*

The art of questioning, then, has both a process aspect and a content aspect. As we go through the steps of the situation analysis phase, we'll examine both.

Preparing the Customer for Questioning

The first step in analyzing the situation is a pure process move: Prepare the customer for questioning. As you'll soon see, though, in calling this "the first step," I don't necessarily mean that you perform it once and then forget about it. Instead, you weave it in as needed to facilitate the questioning phase.

Good preparation can pave the way for even those delicate questions that are otherwise tricky to handle. For example, one question most salespeople feel discomfort about asking is, "Who makes the decisions here?" Naturally, that makes the person you ask think to himself, "What am I? Chopped liver?"

Yet the question is clearly important. One survey stated that 68 percent of sales calls were made to someone other than the decision maker, the decision implementer, or the decision influencer. In other words, the wrong person.

Why is this percentage so high? One reason is probably that most salespeople are reluctant to ask about the decision-making process because they fear the customer's reaction. The result? They are left in the lurch not knowing how the decisions are made or by whom. But the problem isn't the question, it's the lack of preparation for it.

Pre-Question Statements

To take the guesswork out of the questioning process (and increase your comfort level along with the customer's), I recommend using *pre-question statements* to set up your queries, particularly sensitive ones. Specifically, explain the reason *why* you need the information and how it *benefits* the customer for you to ask it. By explaining the "why," you establish credibility. And by pointing out the benefit, you establish empathy.

Newsflash	*Customers will find it easier to respond to sensitive queries if you use pre-question statements to explain why you need the information and how providing it will help the customer.*

Figure 7.2 shows the process. Here's an example:

Ms. Buyer, I call on many organizations like yours and I notice that every company has its own decision-making process. In order to avoid wasting anyone's time or getting caught up in internal issues I may not understand, could you tell me how the process works here?

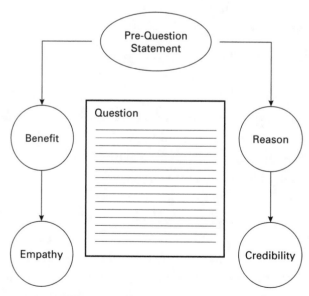

Figure 7.2   Pre-Question Statement

Grouping Questions in Clusters

Another way to prepare your customer for questioning is to group your questions in clusters of related queries. This technique is especially useful when you know you need to ask a lot of questions. Rather than jerk your customer around, focus on one cluster at a time, asking all your questions within that cluster before moving to another. That way, your customers won't feel confused about where you are taking them. You'll also reduce the likelihood of being asked, "What, are you writing a book or something?" (Just for the record, if none of your customers has ever asked you that, some of them have certainly thought it.)

Clusters can include questions about topics like these:

- The customer's product line
- The customer's competitors
- The customer's strategy
- How the customer's company works internally
- What the company wants from its suppliers
- The customer's mission or vision

Questions tend to beget questions. As you stay within a cluster, one question leads to another related one. My friend and colleague, David Michelson, refers to this as "double clicking." You hear something relevant and you double click on it. For example, the customer says something like, "Yeah, but it's risky." You double click on that and say something like, "Could you say a little bit more about why you think it is so risky?" The result is what I call "branching." One question leads naturally to another, like the branches on a tree.

When you move from cluster to cluster, you can use *pre-cluster statements* to prepare the customer for all the questions within that cluster. For example, suppose you've just finished asking several questions about a customer's new product development strategy and you're ready to move on to the next subject. You might say

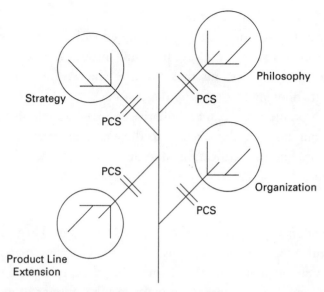

Figure 7.3 Clustering (PCS: pre-cluster statement)

something like, "That was extremely helpful. Now I would like to ask a few questions about the organizational structure, so that I can keep the appropriate people informed. Is that OK?" Additional examples of pre-cluster statements are illustrated in figure 7.3.

Asking Appropriate Questions

Having prepared the customer for questions, the next step is to ask *appropriate* questions. And that brings us to the content side of the ledger.

No rules are carved in stone about what questions to ask. That's why I'm avoiding a plethora of old adages like, "Always ask open-ended questions," and "Don't ask any question that can be answered, 'No'" (because after the first "no," saying "no" gets easier and easier). There are times when closed questions must be asked, and when the answer might be "No." The most challenging question to ask, according to many salespeople, is, "Can I have the order?" Ironically, this is one question that surveys show buyers *want* you to ask. So, let's not get paralyzed with a series of highly specific rules that don't always hold up. Instead, let's concentrate on the *kinds* of questions that advance what you're there to do without annoying or confusing the customer.

In a problem-solving, consultative approach to selling, appropriate questions can be sorted into three categories: transactional questions, needs-clarification questions, and problem-analysis questions.

Transactional Questions

Transactional questions are fact-finding questions. They provide you with "account specifications." If you were selling material or equipment to manufacturing companies, these questions would inquire about such things as annual sales, the amount of material the customers buy, who they buy from, how they buy it, who makes decisions, and what price they pay.

You already ask these kinds of questions, as do your competitors. Transactional questions are important, and you have to ask them, but they don't always reveal a lot about the customer's needs. They don't delve deeply into less obvious needs or tell you much more than you could surmise without the customer's help.

Needs-Clarification Questions

As the name implies, these are the questions you ask to uncover customer needs. I don't mean just the expressed needs at the shallow end of the pool. The smart, brave salesperson will swim to the deep end and pull up several complicated needs floating there hoping to be noticed. And the rest of the team can swim along to ask the questions the salesperson might be reluctant to ask.

There are three subsets of needs-clarification questions: strategic questions, speculative questions, and current events questions.

Strategic Questions   These questions have their roots in the world of strategic planning. Strategic planners like to ask the CEO or executive vice president or general manager to speculate about changes they anticipate in the business or the world in general and their world in particular. The rationale is to force thinking about issues that businesspeople typically aren't focused on in their day-to-day activities.

As salespeople we can apply a similar rationale in order to be more consultative. That is, we can use questions to help customers think in broader terms and get them out of the short-term, tactical mind set.

> **Newsflash** *As sales professionals, we can help our customers by encouraging them to think more broadly about long-term issues.*

Many organizations have used a strategic-planning model known as SPOT, which stands for

- Strengths
- Problems
- Opportunities
- Threats

In the past, many organizations have used SPOT as the basis for a discussion among company leaders. Talking about the strengths and problems of their company forced them to look at internal issues. Discussing opportunities and threats compelled them to look at external factors. The result was the development of much good information to use in developing the strategic plan.

You can use a similar approach in selling to uncover customers' deep needs. Asking customers to talk about their *strengths* will allow you to figure out what they see as the critical points of difference between them and their competitors. (For example, "What were some of the reasons that your market share increased 3 percent last year?")

Questions about *problems* should be asked in a more careful manner. They often benefit from the use of pre-question statements. When the climate is appropriate, and customers feel comfortable with you, getting them to talk about problems can be somewhat cathartic for them—and enlightening for you. (Example: "Most brand extensions fail. I know you had one or two disappointments this year. Could you tell me what you think caused these disappointing rollouts?")

Newsflash   *Problem questions open the door for some serious problem-solving opportunities with the customer.*

Opportunity questions are strategic questions that invite customers to look at some area of their business they might not have investigated yet. These questions require some homework on your part, because in order to ask them you must know what is going on in the industry as well as what the customer is doing.

As an example, if I were selling pharmaceuticals to cattle breeders, and had read about an impending decline in beef consumption, an opportunity question might focus on whether the company had even thought about adding chickens to its product line. Even if the question is off base, asking it would show that I was thinking about the customer's situation (empathy again) and might well open the door for other questions.

With both problem questions and opportunity questions, resources can play a significant role. Think about a marketing research person asking about a particular growing market segment, or an engineer asking about the age of the equipment in the plant. To repeat a point I've made before: One of the great benefits of organization-wide selling is the ability to use your resources to help during the situation-analysis/needs-determination process. Your colleagues from other functional areas will ask questions you never would have thought of. Use them!

> **Newsflash**   *Your resources will think of questions to ask customers that would never occur to you—and that can give you a much deeper understanding of the customer's situation.*

Questions about *threats* are more complicated, proactive questions that ask customers to talk about the risks and challenges they face. You should ask these kinds of questions only when a customer feels safe with you. Not everyone is comfortable talking about whether they feel threatened by the possibility of a hostile takeover or a competitor's aggressive comparative advertising campaign. When asking these kind of questions, then, it makes sense to proceed with caution. Realize, too, that not only are these questions provocative, but they also require the customer to think. So, as a rule, don't ask the customer more than one or two threat questions on a single visit.

Speculative Questions   Speculative questions guide customers to think about what they would *like* to see happen, and then what they *expect* to happen. Usually, people get skittish when they're asked to think beyond "the norm." When we assist them in stretching the usual limits, we can create a new selling paradigm that differentiates us from our competitors. Here are examples:

- "What would you most like to change in the way you do business?"
- "How do you think your customers are changing?"
- "What is your best guess as to what interest rates will do?"
- "If you could change anything about your current supplier, what would it be?"

It's a terrific feeling when the customer is talking freely because he or she feels comfortable working with you. At these times, I suggest encouraging your customer to ask for what they *want,* as opposed to what they think they *should* expect. It's amazing how they'll open up. This technique is analogous to the

Synectics method of asking people to use "I wish" in problem-solving sessions.

Part of speculating is having the customer speculate about you: "Something I'd really like to know is, What do you expect from me? What would be an example of the kinds of things salespeople have done for you in the past that demonstrated they were the kind of people you wanted to work with?" I don't suggest asking questions like these before you gain the customer's trust, but I do recommend asking them early on in the relationship. They can help you get a real understanding of a customer's preexisting expectations.

Again, you can use your resources to help with speculative questions. Senior managers love to ask these kinds of questions, and customers are often flattered when they are asked for their opinions. R&D types, strategic planners, marketing people, and even business analysts can ask speculative questions. What will turn up are deep needs—needs that your competitors may never hear about.

Newsflash   *Ask your customer to speculate and you'll be amazed at what you'll learn. And what you learn may be information your competitor never even hears.*

Current Events Questions   Current events questions invite customers to talk about what is happening in the marketplace, the economy, the country, and the world, and how it is affecting their business. If I ask a shoe manufacturer how he is coping with pricing pressure due to the high number of imports, or ask a software manufacturer how the potential breakup of Microsoft affects his business, I demonstrate credibility and show that I've done my homework, and I open up avenues to finding out about deep needs.

Problem-Analysis Questions

Problem-analysis questions are open-ended questions designed to get buyers talking about a particular problem. These questions ask buyers to give some background and to explain why something is a problem, their prior thinking about the problem, and what they hope can be done about it. Notice these are the same questions Synectics suggests asking the problem owner in a creative problem-solving session. They work well in problem-solving selling, too.

Problem-analysis questions are most likely to be asked with existing customers when the customer has expressed a problem and you want to offer ideas. This is an ideal place to use problem-solving methodology. Get the answers to the four questions just mentioned, and you'll have more than enough information to start generating ideas.

Some Closing Thoughts

Never lose sight of the fact that, asked properly, more questions usually result in more orders. That doesn't mean bombarding the customer with dozens of challenging questions every time, but four or five will certainly make you stand out. And your deeper understanding of your customer's needs will make that person want to do business with you.

Don't get too worried if customers appear a bit uncomfortable when you ask provocative questions that aren't the norm. If you use pre-question or pre-cluster statements, chances are they'll understand why you asked. And after you leave, they might just think about how you made them ponder some things they typically avoid. When you encourage customers to think strategically, you take them places they don't usually go. The results can be extraordinary.

Finally, don't forget about how your sales team and other resources can help you in analyzing the situation. Asking team members to suggest questions for you to ask certainly makes sense. You'll be both surprised and delighted with what they recommend. And when team members visit customers with you, they can comfortably ask questions that you should have asked in the past but never did. As I noted earlier, they can also ask questions that arise out of their areas of expertise—questions you never thought about asking.

> **Newsflash**   *Questioning is such a key element in the selling process that it would be a big miss not to ask anyone in the organization who is available to help to assist in this challenging task.*

"I'm Sorry, Did You Say Something?": Listening for Needs

Step 3 in the situation-analysis phase of the selling sequence is listening for needs and opportunities. We have all heard company leaders talk publicly about how the sales force represents "the eyes and ears of the organization" and how without salespeople the organization is flying blind. These clichés dramatically illustrate how immensely important it is for salespeople to hear what customers say. Ironically, the message often falls on deaf ears.

Like questioning, listening is an art, and it's vital to the selling process. The most brilliant questions in the world are useless if you don't listen to the answers—and that includes listening to both what customers say and what they *don't* say.

> **Newsflash**   *Without excellent listening skills you'll never figure out exactly what your customer's needs are.*

The fact is, most of us need to improve our listening skills. And that might be the biggest understatement in this book.

Barriers to Effective Listening
Before you read further, put down the book and ask yourself why it's so hard to listen to your customers. You know that it is. The question is why. Go ahead, jot down some thoughts. List at least four or five barriers to effective listening.

OK, now that you've thought about it, let's look at what others have concluded. The people at Synectics frequently ask groups to list the reasons why people have difficulty listening during interactive situations. The most common barriers that turn up are these:

- Thinking about what you're going to say next
- Anticipating what the other person will say
- Formulating an idea or a question
- Being preoccupied with something else
- Worrying about another issue
- Being bored with the conversation
- Trying to understand what was just said
- Having preconceived ideas about the task at hand
- Evaluating or judging others
- Thinking about the competition

Notice that the common denominator in all of these is the tendency to listen to *ourselves* instead of to the person who is talking. This tendency is just as deadly even when it is the result of positive intentions, such as trying to be helpful, to understand the situation better, or to make the interaction flow comfortably. Though it may happen without our knowing it, our thinking is directed inward, and as a result we miss the other person's spoken and unspoken messages.

Newsflash   *When you're listening to yourself, it's difficult to hear what the other person is saying.*

My friend Louie—we call him Louie the Listener—knows about this stuff. He says that one of the reasons most of us have lousy listening habits is that our brains process information about six times faster than the average person speaks. According to Louie, we talk at a rate somewhere around 150 words per minute (average radio announcer rate), but we can process information at about 900 to 1,000 words per minute.

When you think about how this relates to customer interactions, the good news is that you can quickly make valuable mental connections to what the customer is saying and be ready to respond momentarily. The bad news is that while you're busy making these connections your mind isn't on what the customer is saying. In other words, you listen for a finite period of time and then drop out.

Synectics has developed a simple yet wonderfully subtle graphic that shows what happens to listening efficiency over time. As shown in figure 7.4, in almost any interaction our listening efficiency is at its maximum early on, when the other person first begins to speak. But this high level of listening efficiency lasts a relatively short period of time, perhaps 30 to 90 seconds. Yep, that's all. After that, listening efficiency takes a major dip.

Needs-Driven Ned   How does this phenomenon play out in a selling situation? Just ask Needs-Driven Ned, the needs-driven equivalent of Quick-Draw McGraw. Ned is intelligent, knowl-

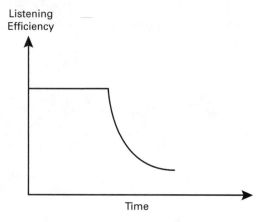

Figure 7.4   Listening Efficiency
Reproduced with permission from Synectics® Inc. ©2000

edgeable, approachable, and organized. He plans every call thoroughly. He keeps up on trends within his industry and is always looking for new and better ways to serve his customers. Ned is just the kind of salesperson most organizations would love to have representing them. Or is he?

Assume for a second that you just became Ned's sales manager. You're surprised to learn that he isn't as successful as you thought. His numbers are disappointing. You read his correspondence and call reports, and he seems to be doing everything right. So why isn't he a sales superstar? To find out, you decide to go on some sales calls with him.

You're impressed by how Ned starts the first call. He positions the call carefully, complete with agenda and time contract. He prepares the customer for questioning and proceeds to ask thoughtful, needs-oriented questions. You nearly fall out of your chair when he asks strategic questions, making a few pre-question statements along the way. What gives? Here's a guy doing everything by the book, yet he can't seem to reach the next level of proficiency.

Suddenly, there it is, like the iceberg that downed the Titanic: the reason Ned isn't the superstar he should be. You watch as Ned tumbles right into the premature presentation trap. After listening to the customer's response to a particularly thoughtful question, Ned jumps all over this first expressed need and starts trying to find a solution for it. Instead of storing the response and continuing to ask questions, he glues himself to the first need that turns up like white on rice, and comes up with a solution that addresses only part of the customer's situation and might even be off base.

Taking this approach, Ned virtually precludes the possibility of ever determining all of his customer's needs or even understanding fully the ones he's heard. Moreover, by presenting too soon, he runs into objections too quickly and starts trying to overcome them instead of treating them as unfulfilled needs. Meanwhile, the needs-determination process has come to a screeching halt.

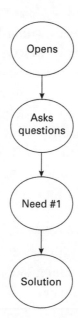

Figure 7.5   "Needs-Driven Ned"

Figure 7.5 shows what Ned's process looks like. Apart from the problems just mentioned, there is another reason why this process is unproductive: *People tend to say what is more important later in the conversation.* Tune out prematurely, and you'll miss the really important stuff.

> **Newsflash**   *People have a natural tendency to say what is most important to them later in the conversation. Don't tune out too soon, or you'll miss out.*

Now you know why Ned isn't the crackerjack salesperson that by rights he ought to be. If Ned's competitor takes the time to fully explore customers' needs before presenting, as depicted in figure 7.6, he or she will achieve a better understanding and offer superior recommendations. And have Ned for lunch every time.

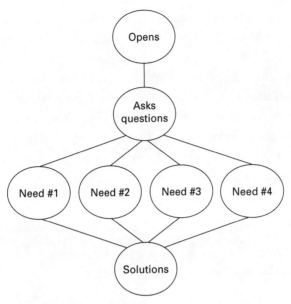

Figure 7.6   A Preferred Approach

Corralling Connections   What happened to Ned happens to all of us, in sales situations and in everyday life. We're constantly making connections. We hear something and it makes us think of something else. That's a valuable talent, and when we're focused, it enhances our productivity. Synectics determined through a series of experiments that if people paid close attention during problem-solving situations, and thereby increased their ability to make connections, they could increase their idea output significantly.

But our ability to make connections is a double-edged sword, because busily making connections is antithetical to effective listening. If you look back at figure 7.4, you can bet that the dip in listening efficiency happens when the listener makes a connection.

In problem-solving situations, Synectics calls this phenomenon "the rehearsal effect," depicted in figure 7.7. When an idea connection occurs, we begin to listen to ourselves as we start to develop our idea. We are, in essence, rehearsing our idea, and we are unable to attend to what the other person is saying at that moment. Once we realize what is happening, we attempt to get back into the conversation. Unfortunately we never get back to our original listening level.

In a selling situation, if some "trigger phrase" from a customer makes you start to rehearse how to present your widgets, listening goes out the window. Now you're thinking about something that you knew about before you walked in. Widgets, after all, are your life. And that means your attention is going to what you already know instead of what you're there to find out.

> **Newsflash** *When you stop listening to rehearse what you are going to say, you put your energy into what you already know at the expense of what you need to learn.*

What you want, then, is the best of both worlds. You want to make connections, most of all to the customer's needs—but without dropping out of listening mode or short-circuiting the needs-determination process.

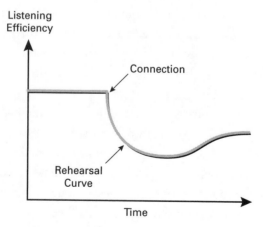

Figure 7.7 The Rehearsal Effect
Reprinted with permission from Synectics® Inc. ©2000

Note Taking   How do you do that? Simple: Take notes. When your neurons fire off a connection, drop out for the second or two it takes to make a note, and then return to the conversation. You'll remember what you were thinking at the time without missing critical information.

Now, right about here, somebody usually brings up the apparent dilemma created by the need to take notes. "Note taking," they'll say, "hinders my ability to make eye contact with the customer. It slows me down, and hampers my spontaneity. It even makes customers suspicious sometimes. At a minimum, it inhibits them and keeps them from really opening up. I hate it."

Yet, when buyers are asked how they feel about salespeople who *don't* take notes, about 80 percent react the way you would if a potential building contractor patiently listened to all your complicated remodeling plans without ever writing anything down. They perceived it as a *lack of interest* on the salesperson's part. I remember one purchasing agent who said that when salespeople didn't take notes he threw away their business cards and refused to see them again!

So the trick is to jot down notes quickly without breaking the connection with your customer. If you look at the revised listening curve depicted in figure 7.8, you'll see a better way to listen that gives you permission to tune out just long enough to take some notes. We call it "listening for needs."

Getting in the habit of writing brief notes can also help you avoid the premature presentation trap. Too many salespeople think that their primary responsibility is to figure out the quickest way possible to satisfy a customer's needs. But that doesn't mean responding instantly to the first need you hear. That's where the gap is between sales professionals' belief that they're needs driven and customers' belief that salespeople really *don't* understand their needs. Remember, both parties are right, up to a point. Most salespeople *do* determine superficial needs—and miss the big ones.

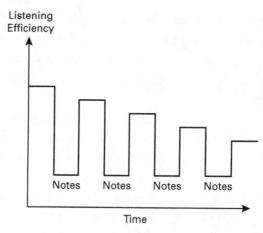

Figure 7.8   Listening for Needs

Want to be different? Then make sure you use your questioning and listening skills to determine *all* of a customer's needs.

Newsflash	*If you want to be successful, don't fall into the "Needs-Driven Ned" trap and present prematurely. Instead, follow the process all the way to the end.*

What You're Listening for: Needs

So far we've been talking about listening as process. Now let's move to the content side of the equation. Just as we categorized questions earlier, here we'll look at the *kinds* of customer needs that we're listening for.

Organizational, Job, and Personal Needs

Buying decisions tend to be based on three different kinds of needs:

- *Organizational needs:* How customers' organization will benefit from the buying decision—simply put, how the decision will affect the bottom line

- *Job needs:* How the buying decision facilitates customers' ability to perform their jobs
- *Personal needs:* How the buying decision affects the way customers feel about themselves

This short list reduces to two broad categories: business needs and personal needs. Business needs are easy to SPOT. Remember the strategic questioning techniques introduced earlier in this chapter? Business needs surface when you get the customer to talk about Strengths, Problems, Opportunities, and Threats.

One way to look at personal needs is to recall Abraham Maslow's famous hierarchy of needs, which you may have learned about in Psychology 101. Maslow concluded that each of us has different levels of needs, and that until one level is satisfied, we can't move on to the next higher level. In case you've not been introduced to Maslow's hierarchy, or could use a refresher, it's pictured in figure 7.9.

If you listen carefully, you may begin to detect at what level a customer seems to be operating in a given interaction. You'll want to approach someone who is driven by security needs differently from someone who is driven by ego or social needs. For example, an insecure buyer needs to know you'll be there for them, a social-driven buyer needs to be liked, and someone who is ego-driven loves to be involved in new product rollouts.

But the main point I want to make here is how important personal needs are in buying decisions. You might think such decisions are all about business. They're not.

Newsflash *Too many people make their buying decisions for the wrong reasons: they decide based on personal needs.*

It goes right back to the CREST concept. People buy from people who make them feel good about themselves. They buy for

Figure 7.9 Maslow's Hierarchy of Needs (SA: self-actualization)

personal reasons. Those aren't always the best reasons to buy. Again, it's all about the relationship.

Obvious and Implied Needs

Another way to categorize needs is one I mentioned earlier: obvious or superficial needs versus implied or hinted needs. Obvious needs are the ones people come right out and tell you ("I need a way to get the water out of my basement"). Implied needs are the ones you put on your Dumbo ears to hear between the lines ("I need a way to feel better about buying this old house").

A subcategory of implied needs is *unconscious* needs. Sometimes a buyer doesn't have a clue about some of his or her important needs. But by listening carefully to nonverbal cues (such as a person's voice sounding hesitant or taking on a wistful quality) and observing body language (a suddenly clenched fist, a worried frown), you may pick up on needs that are below the customer's own level of awareness. Now, addressing such needs has to be done cautiously and sensitively. One way to do it is to work a tentatively phrased statement into your review of needs (the next step in this phase). For example, you might say, "I think you would like an improved software system that will allow you to relax a little more, knowing that people around here will see more clearly what an important job you're doing." Unconscious needs also result from naïveté or even ignorance. The need to understand the risks associated with a big decision can be an unconscious need for a frivolous buyer.

Newsflash *To be as successful as you can be, listen for all of the needs a buyer has, regardless of how they are verbalized.*

The key here is to get past the obvious and understand that there are several categories of needs. A great exercise for any sales team is to take some time to determine as a group what a given customer's needs really are. Identify the organizational needs. Look at the different people within the organization and ask yourselves what their job and personal needs may be. Think in terms of obvious needs and implied needs. Speculate about possible unconscious needs. Your time will be well spent, and you'll capitalize on the expertise and insight of the entire sales team.

After listening for needs, there's one step left in the situation analysis phase. And it's most important of all.

Reviewing Your Understanding of the Customer's Needs

As you may recall from an earlier chapter, many buyers start to make their decisions at the point where the salesperson carefully reviews their needs—*before* the presentation even starts. That's a powerful testimony to how crucial it is to demonstrate your understanding of the customer's needs. You'll be displaying the four CREST attributes—credibility, empathy, sensitivity, and trustworthiness—all rolled into one.

How do you do this? Not by telling customers you know what they want, but by giving back in your own words what you've heard them say. (Be patient. Your turn to show off will come.) Assuming you've listened effectively and taken good notes, your restatement will show customers that you were indeed paying close attention to their responses. Although the main purpose isn't to flatter the customer, as a bonus the proof that you were genuinely listening does tend to have this effect. Psychologist Carl Rogers said that the greatest compliment one individual can pay another in this lifetime is to demonstrate that he or she was listening.

Start your review of the needs by saying something like, "So, if I understand you correctly, it appears that you are looking for . . . ," and paraphrase the needs you've noted. Be tentative with needs that are implied rather than on the surface, so as to avoid saying something the customer takes as a misquotation or misunderstanding. Indicate that you're going beyond the spoken message: "A possible implication I'd like to check out with you, even though you didn't mention this in so many words, is. . . ."

Notice the use of the word *I* in these examples. "I" messages are important, because they signal that what you're saying is what *you* heard, not necessarily what the *customer* said. Even if you're perfectly confident about your restatement, using the "I" formula shows that you're taking responsibility for hearing the customer accurately.

After you get confirmation that you've correctly understood the customer's needs, be certain to review each and every one with the customer. Again, be sensitive when you refer to implied and unconscious needs. If you're unsure whether to explicitly explore personal needs, you may want to omit them from the discussion. But in general, including such needs shows the customer that you genuinely want to understand his or her situation, and it proves that you made connections to what the customer expressed.

To sum up phase 2: The salesperson who asks the best questions, ones that encourage a customer to think about his or her business (without feeling manipulated), and who is capable of identifying as many needs as possible (whether obvious or implied, business or personal) is the salesperson who will earn the buyer's respect and trust. And that means differentiating himself or herself from everyone else.

MEMO TO MANAGEMENT

The skills discussed in this chapter aren't just for salespeople. They're for everyone in the organization who comes into contact with customers. Do you want your whole organization to be a selling machine? Then make sure everyone learns how to ask questions in a sensitive, customer-driven way, how to listen carefully to responses, and how to demonstrate an understanding of customers' needs.

Salespeople, of course, have considerable experience with aspects of these skills, especially questioning. The same cannot always be said for nonsales types. It is easy for them to offend customers without even knowing it. The "you stupid idiot" question has annoyed many a customer of yours, whether you know it or not. (Have you ever had to call a tech support line?)

What this means is that to make organization-wide selling a reality in your company, you will need to invest in appropriate training. You know that. You don't change people's behavior by sending out memos or distributing videotapes—especially when you're dealing with habits that have taken a lifetime to develop.

Beyond that, you've got to reinforce the message—constantly. Take questioning, for instance. The more questions the people in your organization ask customers, the more successful you'll be. Bug your people about this all the time. Become a pain in the neck with respect to how much they know about their customers' situations. Practice your own questioning skills (including sensitivity) by asking *them* questions about their customers. If they don't have the answers, help them figure out ways to get the information they need to know. Encourage them to use you, the sales force, and any other available resources to help analyze their customers' situations. Stay on it. If you demonstrate how important knowing customers' needs is to you, your people will get the message in a hurry.

As for listening, the message to get across is simple. Your people *must* listen to customers. Period. There are lots of Needs-Driven

Neds in your company, well-intentioned people who jump into what they have to say before hearing the customer out. Teach them how to be better listeners. Make them aware of the concept of listening for needs.

I heard someone say once that $10 billion is wasted in American industry every year because of poor listening. He figured it this way: At that time there were about 100 million workers in the United States. Assume every worker made just $100 in listening-related errors per year, and presto!: $10 billion in excess costs and lost opportunities. I figure he was being very conservative.

Enough said. Once again, model the behavior. If it is obvious to you that two of your people are not listening to each other, step in and show them what is happening. Credit the good listeners. Publicize success stories. Do what needs to be done to instill the behavior. You know the drill.

CHAPTER 8

"May I Recommend . . . ?"

OK, now for the fun part. This chapter is devoted to every salesperson's favorite phase in the selling sequence—presenting. I prefer to call phase 3 "offering recommendations" as a reminder that the ultimate purpose of presenting products and services is to develop solutions to the customer's problems and needs uncovered in phase 2 of the problem-solving selling sequence.

As always, keep in mind that real life is often not as neat as an idealized flow chart. The offering recommendations phase of the process includes any communication with a customer or prospect about what your company has to offer. That can be anything from an informal conversation between the salesperson and the customer to a formal presentation in which an entire team talks to a group of twenty or more people. It can be a credentials presentation, a showcase of your products and services, or a final presentation geared toward closing the sale. It can occur on the first call to a customer or the tenth.

Regardless of the circumstances, phase 3 is where you take center stage. It's showtime!

But even though you're both the ringmaster and the main act, you'd be wise to share the limelight. What better way to use your sales team and other expert resources than to have them explain, when appropriate, exactly how you can help customers solve their problems? Of course, the team members need to understand how to offer recommendations and ideas in a problem-solving, customer-driven way. That's why everybody on the team needs the skills covered in this chapter.

The offering-recommendations phase of the selling sequence consists of the three steps shown in figure 8.1. We've covered the first step—reviewing your understanding of the needs—in chapter 7. (The last step in the preceding phase is the segue to the next phase.) Accordingly, we'll devote most of this chapter to the heart of this phase—step 2, making recommendations.

The Joy of Presenting—and the Inevitable Trap

When I conduct sales-training programs, I spend the least amount of time investigating how to present the company's products and services. Why? Simply because most salespeople enjoy and seem the most comfortable with this phase of the selling sequence. I guess inside every salesperson lies an eager-to-perform thespian—in other words, a ham. You like to talk, right? Sure you do. We all do.

The same thing applies to almost every resource the sales professional may call upon for help. When it's time to present, every-

1. Review Your Understanding of the Customer's Needs and Opportunities
2. Make the Recommendation
3. Ask the Customer for Feedback

Figure 8.1   Offer Recommendations

body is available. People love to tell their stories, particularly when they are proud of what they have to offer.

And therein lies the inevitable trap of phase 3. Although a high comfort level is usually a positive thing, it can also be the reason so many of us mess up, causing buyers to doubt whether we're really focused on their needs. Like Needs-Driven Ned, we're too quick to get to the part of the process we feel the best about—presenting solutions—before we understand the customer's problems sufficiently to offer more than obvious answers for superficial needs.

We can fall into this trap even with "needs-driven" and "customer-focused" and similar phrases implanted in our brains. That's what happened to Sal in his encounter with Betty the buyer. Faced with Betty's "Whatchagot?" challenge, Sal tried to differentiate his company by extolling its customer-centered virtues. To establish credibility, he began throwing out impressive statistics about his firm's successes. He described the organization's philosophy, highlighted points of difference it was renowned for, and raved about his sales team and how the company was committed to using all of its resources to help customers solve their business problems.

With a real head of steam up now, Sal went on to share one of his favorite anecdotes, about how one of the kids in the mailroom noticed that a certain customer was spending too much on postage. The kid pointed this out to his supervisor, who in turn informed the salesperson. The salesperson immediately brought this useful information to the customer. Of course, the customer was delighted with this thoughtful demonstration of the value of partnering with Sal's company.

Sal was glowing with pride as he told this story. Although Betty listened politely, she wasn't nearly as impressed as Sal was: The story didn't have anything specific to do with her needs, and she simply didn't relate to it. As Sal went on (and on) about his company, he might as well have been reading aloud from the menu at his favorite Thai restaurant. Betty was already thinking about her next meeting.

Don't get me wrong here. In his own way, Sal was a pro. He wasn't pushy, arrogant, or full of himself. Even Betty would say that he was articulate, knowledgeable, experienced, and likable. He came across as someone who liked what he did and who was genuinely enthusiastic about what his company could do for its customers.

Still, he was dead in the water well before he finally wound up his presentation. Ironically, as he tried to explain how different and customer-driven he and his company were, he only succeeded in demonstrating that he was pretty much like everybody else. Sorry, Sal. No interest. No next steps. No sale.

> **Newsflash**   *Don't let your comfort with presenting get you there too soon. When you present prematurely, your behavior contradicts your needs-driven, customer-focused message.*

The trap Sal fell into is waiting for all of us. But even if we are not maneuvered into presenting prematurely, all the work we've done to determine the customer's needs will be for naught unless we offer recommendations in a way that is consistent with the problem-solving approach. So now let's explore how to do just that.

Let's Customize!

To begin with, in problem-solving selling, no two presentations will look alike. To put it another way, our recommendations should be as different as are our customers and their unique problems.

This point effectively rules out using a canned pitch, the ready-made, one-size-fits-all paean to the company's products and services that so many salespeople fall back on. As far as I'm concerned, the canned pitch is the worst thing that ever happened to the sales profession. (During a recent presentation, the company I was talking to rated it third, behind polyester suits and white shoes with matching belts.)

Sure, there are salespeople who are successful using a canned pitch. You may even know a few. But consider this: There are so many salespeople who use this tired approach that some of them are bound to make a sale, especially if their competitors are no different. But, assuming all other factors are equal, the sales professional who tailors his or her recommendations to a customer's specific needs will bury the canned-pitch virtuoso nine times out of ten.

Newsflash *The canned pitch has probably done more to ruin the image of the salesperson than cigars or three-martini lunches.*

Not only does every buyer have a specific set of needs, but different buyers make decisions for all sorts of different reasons. Some buyers decide on the basis of quality, service, price, or convenience. Many buy because of the relationship. Lots of people make buying decisions for personal reasons, including such things as their tolerance for risk or how they feel about themselves. What makes the buyer tick is what you spent precious time finding out in phase 2. Now the task is to customize your recommendations to the needs and influences you've picked up. Making the transition into the recommendations phase by reviewing your understanding of the buyer's needs, item for item, will help you do that.

Presenting Features and Benefits

The concept of customizing your recommendations brings us back to those old standbys, features and benefits. As you remember, a feature is a descriptive specification of some characteristic of the product or service. A benefit is an explanation of how the feature will help the individual, what its value is to the customer. To put it another way, features answer the question, "What?" Benefits answer the question, "So what?"

Now, we're not about to discard these tried-and-true elements of good presenting. But we do need to know how to handle them.

I've found that most salespeople feel comfortable in discussing the features of a product or service, but are far less comfortable discussing its benefits. That's probably because features are usually "right answers," things you can have down pat, whereas benefits are fluid and relative to the customer. Often they're just educated guesses. Yet benefits are the key to the sale—as long as the customer perceives them as solutions to his or her needs.

This point brings us to an important distinction: generic versus specific benefits. A *generic benefit,* which you would see in a product brochure, explains the item's features and points out how they address the needs of typical buyers. A *specific benefit* is directly related to the *confirmed* needs of an *individual customer.*

Don Beveridge tells a story that illustrates this distinction. Don explains to groups that as a sales manager he did not allow his salespeople to distribute brochures prior to meeting with their customers and determining their needs. *After* the call was completed, the salesperson could send the brochure, but *only* after highlighting the features that addressed that particular customer's specific needs.

Don recognized that customers are looking for specific benefits, not generic ones. Features and generic benefits are about the *product.* Specific benefits are about the *customer.*

Here's another take on this important point. Take a look at figure 8.2, which was developed by Kate Reilly of CRC. We cleverly call it *the four-box model.*

You can think of the upper left-hand box, which represents the specific needs of the customer, as being filled in during the last step of phase 2 and the first step of phase 3. The two boxes at right represent the various things you have available to recommend—in other words, your products and services—and their corresponding features and generic benefits. Essentially, you come to any sales

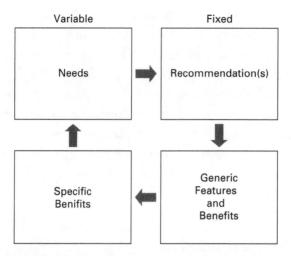

Figure 8.2   The Four-Box Presentation Model. Reprinted with permission of CRC, ©CRC all rights reserved.

call with those boxes already filled in. The lower left-hand box represents specific benefits to the customer. That's the box you'll fill in based on the customer's needs, whether impromptu, like a good jazz artist, or through a carefully prepared symphonic presentation with a fully worked-out score.

Notice that in this model, everything on the right side is *fixed* information. That's the sort of thing that would be in a brochure. In contrast, everything on the left side is *variable*. Every customer has different needs, and there are correspondingly different specific benefits to be derived from the same product or service. That's why every presentation must be different and why the canned pitch falls so far short. With a canned pitch, all you have to work with is the stuff on the right—information that applies only to a mythical Generic Customer.

Newsflash   *The same product or service should be presented differently to every customer, with emphasis on benefits that are specific to that customer's needs.*

The importance of specific benefits, by the way, is the reason that all those predictions of some years back—that salespeople would soon go the way of the dodo bird—were so wrongheaded. We're living in the age of information and service. People to whom service is important want to interact with *other people,* not voices on the phone, direct-mail flyers, catalogs, or even Web sites. They want a real live human being to explain to them how a product will be of value to them based on *their* particular situation. That's why salespeople still have jobs, and why they won't be extinct in my lifetime, or yours.

Speaking to Be Listened To

Since you and your team members will be doing most of the talking during the recommendations phase, you want to speak in a way that maximizes your chances of being heard and understood. To do that, keep in mind what we learned about the listener's half of the interaction in chapter 7.

Recall our human tendency to mentally drop out of a conversation early on, as we start listening to the buzz in our own minds instead of to the speaker. If it happens to you and me, it happens to customers as well—probably more so, since we at least are *trying* to be good listeners as part of our job.

If you relate this observation to the presentation process, one implication quickly surfaces: In offering recommendations, you'll be more successful if you pay close attention to the *order* in which you present them. You want to present your most important ideas at the moment when you have your listener's full attention. And that means resisting the natural tendency to "save the best for last," working your way up to the really important stuff late in the conversation. That's the way a lot of salespeople build their presentations, but it flies in the face of what we know about listening.

Newsflash   *There is a tendency for all of us to save the best for last. Unfortunately, that is when the people we are talking to listen least effectively.*

As salespeople we need to address this notion of a customer's attention span as out of synch with our presentation method. Given the listening curve we looked at in chapter 7, it makes sense to alter our presentation mode when offering recommendations.

Take another look at the four-box model, which I originally introduced as a way to think about *what* you're going to present (the content). Now let's use it as a way to discuss *how* to present (the process). The revised model is shown in figure 8.3

Notice the flow of the arrows. In this revised model, once you've reviewed the need and stated your recommendation, you immediately offer the *specific* benefits. That's right, *before* you describe the *generic* features and benefits. If customers go mentally AWOL because of some connection they've made, at least you'll know they've heard the *most important* information—namely, how

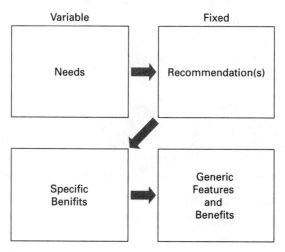

Figure 8.3   Order of Presentation

your recommendation addresses their confirmed needs. Remember, that's the information that is going to motivate the sale.

> **Newsflash** *Whenever you present recommendations to a customer, first review the customer's needs and then immediately discuss your recommendation in light of its specific benefits to that customer.*

Yes, this way of proceeding may seem counterintuitive, and at first it can feel downright uncomfortable. But journalists, public relations people, and advertisers all make use of this principle, putting the most critical information up front, while they still have people's attention. In a sales presentation, following this principle increases the chances of being heard—and what's more important than that?

Using Your Resources

A wonderful way to use your sales team and other resources is to have them participate in offering recommendations and explaining their benefits. After reviewing the needs—that's your job, because you're the one who has determined them—you can defer to your subject-matter experts, who can speak to these points with tremendous credibility and authority. Needless to say, you'll need to fully prep the team so that their remarks are aimed straight at the customer's specific needs.

> **Newsflash** *A powerful way to use sales teams is to have your subject-matter experts participate in offering recommendations and explaining their specific benefits.*

Offering Ideas, Not Just Products and Services

I've maintained that selling reaches its highest level when the sales call is transformed into a problem-solving opportunity. This concept implies that sales professionals must sometimes go beyond reaching into their products-and-services bag to pull out ready-made solutions. Often it's appropriate to offer recommendations in the form of *ideas* as well.

There are two specific situations that merit offering ideas to a customer. One occurs when a customer talks about a problem during the course of the sales interaction, which you can take as an implicit invitation to conduct a one-on-one problem-solving session. The other scenario occurs when the salesperson shows up with an idea to offer that's based on something learned at a previous meeting, or perhaps from another source. Let's look at the process involved in each case.

> **Newsflash**   *A big part of offering recommendations is suggesting ideas, even unexpected ideas, to the customer.*

Want to Solve a Problem? Then Facilitate the Process!

Hmm . . . sound familiar? I told you all those problem-solving skills would come in handy!

To seize the opportunity and help solve a problem brought up by a customer, act as a facilitator does in a problem-solving session. Not by formally claiming that role, of course, but by gently taking responsibility for the *process* aspect of the meeting.

To illustrate, suppose a customer has expressed a concern about some problem he or she is experiencing. At this point a light bulb labeled "Facilitate!" goes off in your mind. You know where to begin: Set the climate. In this case, that means *asking permission* to offer ideas. In general, people aren't too receptive to unsolicited ideas. Think about how you feel when your brother-in-law or next-door neighbor starts spouting off ideas about some problem you have without being asked to do so. Customers feel the same way. But if permission is asked and granted, then the ideas can flow naturally.

So you begin by saying something like this:

> So, what you're saying is [here you paraphrase the concern]. And that sounds like a big concern. You know, I've had some experience in that area. If you're interested, I could make a few suggestions. . . .

Or, if several people are involved in the meeting, you might say:

> . . . and that sounds like a big concern. You know, I'll bet several of the people in the room have some experience in that area. I know my colleague, Janet, does. How about we spend a few minutes just getting some ideas on the table?

As ideas are generated, you take on the role of capturing them on paper. If you want to get fanciful with some of your ideas, that's fine, as long as you let the customer know what you are doing. Explain that at this point the intent is to get as many ideas out as possible, even if they seem far out, and that even a wild idea might have in it the seed of a possible solution.

When you sense that this brainstorming period should wind down, ask the customer to select the idea that he or she finds most interesting, so that together you can work to develop the idea into a workable solution. (Recall the analogous step in group problem solving.)

Next, use the problem-solving methodology to transform the idea into a solution. One approach to identifying the "pluses" of the idea is to ask what about the idea appeals to the customer, or why he or she picked it as the one to develop. Once the positives are noted, then ask what concerns the customer has. Take each concern one by one, and involve the customer in trying to find a way to resolve it. If all the concerns are resolved, the idea will cross the threshold of acceptability, and together you will have derived a *solution* to the task at hand.

Don't forget to review the solution and get agreement on next steps. At that point, you'll have completed the process and pre-

- Customer Expresses Problem
- Salesperson Gets Permission to Offer Ideas
- Salesperson and Customer Generate Ideas
- Customer Selects Idea to Develop
- Customer Evaluates Idea
- Salesperson Reviews Solution and Next Steps

Figure 8.4 Transforming Sales Calls into Problem-Solving Opportunities

sented both yourself and your customer with a terrific reward: problem solved! (For a summary of the process, see figure 8.4.)

Offering Unsolicited Ideas

The problem-solving approach I've just described applies very well when a customer brings up a specific problem. Often, however, you may recognize opportunities to offer customers *unsolicited* ideas, ideas you've thought about outside the meeting and bring in with you. Ideally, there's nothing in these ideas that will benefit you, other than the fact that, to use a Tom Peters expression, you'll "wow and delight" the customer with your empathy and helpfulness.

You'd be surprised how often I hear stories about this from the salespeople I work with in training programs. Recently, a national account manager from a large packaged goods company told about an experience he'd had with a new customer. On his first visit he noticed that behind the buyer's desk was a Mason jar with several dollar bills in it. It was his first call, so he didn't mention it.

Three weeks later, he called upon the same customer. This time he noticed that the Mason jar was about half-filled with dollar bills. He still felt it was inappropriate to ask about it.

On his third call, about two weeks later, the jar was about full. Unable to contain himself any longer, he asked the buyer what it was all about. He figured it had to do with a football pool or something like that.

"I'm glad you asked," she said. "You see, you're still in your grace period. Sixty days after anyone begins calling on me, I insist that they bring one *new* idea to every sales call. If they don't, it costs them a buck. I put the dollars in the Mason jar and when it's full, I give the money to the United Way."

Now, there's one enlightened buyer! Here she was, sitting in the ivory tower of corporate headquarters. The salespeople who called on her worked in the marketplace. She wanted to benefit from what they had to offer. Someone in her position might see thirty to forty salespeople a week. If they all did what she asked, she'd get 1,500 to 2,000 ideas a year. Even if only one out of ten was worth pursuing, she'd end the year with at least 150 new ideas to try out.

Lots of customers want what this buyer came right out and asked for. Yet many sales pros are reluctant to offer unsolicited ideas. The result is yet another missed opportunity to differentiate themselves from the pack.

Newsflash *Your customers want you to bring them ideas—even if they don't say it.*

That doesn't mean customers want to hear ideas without being prepared. As with initiating a problem-solving session, first get the customer's permission. Before ending a sales call, almost as a throwaway, you might turn to your client and say something like, "You know, I've been thinking about that warehousing issue you've been dealing with lately. If you're interested, I have some thoughts I'd like to share with you." Assuming the customer says, "Yes," offer your idea and mention its specific benefits.

Sometimes coming up with a truly valuable idea means doing some homework. Yes, you say, and what for? So I can give away something for nothing?

Yep, that's right: something that may just make your customer's day! Maybe it doesn't put money in your pocket, at least not immediately. On the other hand it hasn't cost you a nickel. As Kent Reilly, an outstanding sales-training consultant, says, "An idea is the only thing I know about that you can give away and still own."

My friend Paul Matik has made a gazillion dollars selling shower curtains. One day he agreed to participate in a focus group that was composed of highly successful salespeople. When asked what the key to his success was, he gave us his answer without skipping a beat. He told us how he never saw a buyer without "shopping" several of their retail outlets. He would always show up with two or three merchandising ideas for his products and his competitor's products. He even brought in snapshots of what the displays looked like in the stores he visited and how they could be improved. He had a knack for merchandising. His customers appreciated it, and he always got the lion's share of the business. And he was successful as a result. He made a lot of money and developed many long-term relationships. And his key to success was his ability to use his innate creativity to help his customers. Need to hear more?

OK. I can't resist. One more story. Consider the case of Jack, a very successful salesperson with a biotech pharmaceutical company who called primarily on oncologists, selling a cancer treatment drug. As you might guess, that's not an easy sales call. Jack would have only a few minutes to speak with the physician between appointments and too often both he and his drug were received with skepticism based on the disappointing results to date.

As part of our needs-assessment process in developing a sales-training program for the pharmaceutical firm's sales force, one of our staff traveled with Jack. He returned from his trip with this wonderful story about Jack:

The oncologist kept us waiting for about thirty minutes. While we were waiting, we heard the support staff complaining about all the patients who had canceled appointments recently. When we finally got in to see the oncologist, he was cold and aloof. Jack attempted to put him at ease, but he was busy writing some notes about the last patient and didn't even make eye contact.

Finally Jack said, "By the way, Doc, I couldn't help but overhear your support staff when I sat in the waiting room. It sounds like you're having a problem with cancellations."

"Yep. It's a real pain in the butt," said Dr. Friendly.

"Well, if you're interested," said Jack, "I may have a way to help you reduce the number of cancellations. Interested?"

At that point, the doctor went through a metamorphosis. He looked up, dropped his pencil, and gave Jack his undivided attention. Jack explained there was a software package available that would automatically call patients, three days, two days, and one day before their appointment. It worked like those automated telemarketing calls or hotel wake-up calls. You programmed it and it did all the work. And experience showed it could help reduce cancellations by up to 60 percent.

The physician was delighted with the idea and asked Jack to get the information. Jack offered to ask the software company's rep to give the physician a call.

From that point on, the doctor was all ears. He gave Jack all the attention he could ever want.

Talk about wowing and delighting the customer! Think it was worth the trouble?

Notice what Jack did. First he got permission to offer the idea. Then he reviewed the need. Then he offered a recommendation and described its features. Then he gave a benefit of the idea that was tailored to his customer. Sounds like the four-box model, doesn't it?

In this case, Jack capitalized on an unexpected opportunity to be a problem-solving resource to his customer. In other circumstances, the beauty of offering unsolicited ideas is that you can prepare beforehand—and get a ton of help from your internal resources besides. In the organization-wide selling approach, everybody is continually thinking about new ideas to present to the customer—provided, of course, that you're continually communicating with the folks in the home office about what you've learned of the customer's needs.

I believe that just about every sales call provides you with an opportunity to offer your customers and prospects new ideas. When there is nothing in it for you, the idea carries even more weight. Salespeople who demonstrate how they genuinely want to partner with their customers—how they truly care about them— are miles head of the competition when it comes to building trusting relationships.

Asking the Customer for Feedback

Once you've made your presentation, the final step in phase 3 is to ask the customer for feedback. You've been playing solo for a while, and now it's time to bring the customer back into the game. Share the microphone.

In a meeting involving several people, it's the salesperson's job to ask for feedback and to decide on the appropriate moment to make this request. It's all part of facilitating the process.

Open-ended questions seem to be most effective for soliciting feedback. To prevent the customer from saying "No" too easily, avoid asking a point-specific question like, "Does that sound like something you'd be interested in?" You want to ask for feedback in a way that keeps the discussion rolling, such as:

- "How does that sound to you?"
- "What are your thoughts about this idea?"
- "Can you give me some feedback?"

Requests for feedback should be genuine and sincere. Remember, in the next phase you're going to use what the customer says here to help resolve his or her concerns. Follow the process, and don't try to move directly to closing. Avoid requesting feedback in a way that suggests that you're attempting to set up your customers, or that you're trying to get them to say something they don't want to say or do something they don't want to do. I don't even like the term "trial close" because it sounds manipulative. Questions like, "Can I ship it on Tuesday or Thursday?" or "Would you like it in bulk or individual packages?" or "I could put in your name or both yours and your spouse's name, which would you prefer?" are both insulting and manipulative. We don't need to manipulate customers. We do need to hear how they feel about our recommendation so we can respond appropriately.

When you ask for feedback, the most likely result is that the customer will generate one or more objections. That's just fine, because it moves you right into the closing phases of the sequence, in which you'll use your problem-solving abilities to resolve the issues and reach closure.

Remember, customers are likely to register objections to your recommendation even if they *like* what you've had to say. Don't let that deter you. You've got them interested. Try to get them to say *something, anything*. Whatever they come up with will give you more information, and information is the key to understanding what the customer *really* wants. It's like needs determination: Don't let an objection propel you into trying to answer it prematurely. Trust the process.

So now we've looked at how to make recommendations and solicit the customer's response. Our next step is to explore in detail the part of the process most salespeople like least—overcoming objections. Whoops there's that expression again. Let's treat it more positively and call it "resolving the issues."

MEMO TO MANAGEMENT

Organization-wide selling asks your salespeople to use all the resources available to them to improve customer satisfaction. This is never more applicable then when they find themselves offering recommendations to their customers and prospective customers.

This point has both an internal and an external application. The internal application refers to the strategy sessions your people conduct to determine how best to address customers' specific needs. Encourage your people to work together to decide what is best for each individual customer.

Externally, your people would be very shortsighted if they didn't bring subject-matter experts with them to the presentation whenever it makes sense and you can justify the cost. The experts wrote the book. They're the ones who can talk most intelligently about the specific benefits of the recommendation. Of course, you need to prepare them and make sure they understand the process and the skills involved in doing a great job.

Make sure, too, that your people understand the power of bringing unsolicited ideas to sales interactions. Think about how one of your customers will react when she learns that the team discussed how they could help her meet her needs and that they've come up with a potentially valuable idea—an idea that benefits only the customer. That is what partnering means. Can you think of a better way to forge a strong bond with your customers?

Think of Jack's interaction with Dr. Friendly and how Jack won the good doctor's gratitude, in the process setting himself apart from his competitors. Remember the Mason jar behind the buyer's desk. Don't dismiss the shower curtain salesman who earned a ton of dough by bringing creativity to the sales process. You probably have some anecdotes like this one in your own organization, and not just in the sales department. Collect them. Give people incentives to submit them. Publicize them. Reward people who come up with creative ideas that solve customers' problems, whether or not the result is an immediate sale. Make cultivating the relationship a way of life for your organization.

Finally, don't let the joy of presenting prevent your salespeople from involving all the resources available to them. Let them enjoy their moment in the sun, but cultivate the mentality that a win is a win for the organization, not just the individual. Remind them, as often as you need to, that presenting, like selling, is a team sport!

CHAPTER 9

Resolving the Issues (Hallelujah!)

I wouldn't be surprised if you turned to this chapter first. Virtually every group I work with wants most to learn about how to manage customer resistance.

Overcoming objections, dealing with customer resistance, resolving issues—whatever we choose to call it, it's the most challenging part of selling. Yet it's also a wonderful opportunity for sales professionals to differentiate themselves from their humdrum competitors.

When we encounter resistance from a customer, the selling process shifts from strictly collaborative to one that has potential for conflict. As one experienced sales professional said, "It is only when I hear the first objection that my *consultant* hat comes off and the *salesperson* hat goes on." This statement captures the kernel of truth in the popular, but somewhat misleading, saying: "Salesmanship starts when the customer says no." Actually, "salesmanship" [*sic*] includes everything we do from the moment when we first plan a sales call. In the early stages, however, selling—especially problem-solving selling—can be thought of as consulting. It's when you ask for the customer's reaction that things can change dramatically.

Any time a potential for conflict arises in a relationship, the danger is that we'll react in a way that doesn't move us toward resolution. In the case of sales, faced with "rejection" in the form of objections to a carefully prepared and reasonable recommendation, our natural tendency is to become defensive, aggressive, or even passive. And as our instinctive "fight or flight" response takes over, our process awareness evaporates.

> **Newsflash**   *If there is ever a time that you may lose your composure (or mind) it is when the customer resists your recommendations and ideas.*

That's one reason why I like to think of phase 4 as *resolving the issues* instead of the warlike phrase "overcoming objections." Doesn't "resolving the issues" sound more positive and less threatening? When we work to resolve issues, we stay in problem-solving mode and use our process skills to work *with* the customer toward a workable solution.

The resolving issues process consists of five steps, recapitulated in figure 9.1. This is presented differently from the way it was in figure 5.5. Any time you encounter resistance, think of these five steps.

In keeping with the idea that we may be offering ideas as well as selling products and services, in this chapter we'll apply the process to both situations. But first let's pause a moment to ask why there are issues to resolve in the first place. Why *do* customers nearly always object, anyway?

Why Customers Object

Suppose you've gone to a hardware store in search of a new electric drill. You've already shopped around, you've decided on the top-of-the-line model, and you've chosen a store you like that has

1. Acknowledge the Objection
2. Ask the Customer to Elaborate
3. Transform the Objection into a Need
4. Respond to the Need
5. Invite Other Objections

Figure 9.1   Resolve the Issues

competitive prices. A no-brainer, right? Yet, if you're like most people who are in a buying frame of mind, as soon as the salesperson starts talking about the model you have in mind, you look at the price tag and start to ask questions: "Do I really need to spend this much for a drill?" "Do I really need two speeds?" "Does it come with a handy carrying case?" "What about that model over there for half the price?"

There you are, with your decision supposedly made and nothing in the way of making the purchase, yet in effect you're raising objections. What's your problem, anyway? Take a second to come up with your own answer to this question before reading on.

OK, here's my answer: The reason you asked all those questions is that you wanted assurance from the salesperson that you were making a good decision. You wanted him or her to explain why the drill was right for *you*. Yes, you "knew" you wanted the drill, but at that moment what you needed was *confirmation*.

As obvious as this point is when we're in a buying situation, when we're selling we don't see it that way. We react instinctively and immediately to the customer's apparent resistance, and our process skills go right out the window.

Switch roles now, and imagine you're the hardware salesperson. Think of the customer as needing confirmation that he or she is making the right choice. How do you respond to the customer's questions? The next heading provides a clue.

Acknowledge the Objection and Ask the Customer to Elaborate

Let's assume you've already completed the segue that moves you to this phase, which is the last step in phase 3, asking the customer for feedback. You've carefully noted each of the customer's concerns and objections. Now what?

My former partner, Jonathan Whitcup, used to say that the most important skill we ever offered was teaching salespeople how to *draw out* their customers' objections. Why? Because if you don't allow customers to talk when they resist, you'll be seen as trying to convince them that you are right and they are wrong. Oops. There goes all that consulting, problem-solving, needs-driven mindset you've worked so hard to create up to this point!

When customers object or resist, avoid the temptation to respond right away. Instead, *get them talking*. You can't resolve whatever their issues are unless you understand *why* they feel the way they do about your recommendation.

Start with Acknowledgment

To get customers to elaborate on their objection, start by *acknowledging* what they've said. I mean just that: acknowledge. Despite what some sales trainers say, that doesn't mean you have to agree with the objection. To my way of thinking, that would show a lack of conviction on your part, and it can cut the ground right out from under you. Nor does it mean subtly implying that you disagree. That only sets up a confrontation, and who needs that?

Acknowledgment means simply giving back what you've heard, without implying a judgment either way. The idea is to show that you *understand* what the customer is saying, that you recognize the customer's right to feel that way, and that you're flexible and willing to discuss the matter further. It's also a nice way to demonstrate empathy.

> **Newsflash** *When you run into resistance, immediately agreeing or disagreeing will inevitably lead to trouble. Stay neutral for a few seconds and you'll have a better chance of getting to the real issue.*

A simple way to acknowledge an objection is to use the customer's language, or paraphrase it closely, without being patronizing. At the same time, you can indicate that the customer's response is reasonable (again, without implying that you agree with it). For example, if the client says, "It costs too much," you might say, "I understand that cost is a big concern. . . ." Other typical acknowledgments can sound like this:

- "OK, I can see why you might feel that way based on what you've heard so far."
- "I know that investing in a new system seems like a daunting task."
- "You know, I've heard other customers raise similar questions, and I think I know where they're coming from."
- "I appreciate your being candid, and I understand why you have that concern."

There are times when it's appropriate to agree with what the customer says without suggesting that this is a reason not to proceed. For example, you may be offering an expensive solution. The customer balks at the price. You can't make believe it's not expensive, but that doesn't mean the customer shouldn't buy it. So you might acknowledge such an objection by saying something like, "Yes, it is expensive. But I think it's worth discussing further whether the cost is worth what it can do for you. So I'd like to ask. . . ."

Keep in mind that acknowledging an objection is the first step in the process and sets the stage for encouraging the customer to elaborate on his or her concern so that you can work to resolve it. In other words, it's another step in the process of problem solving.

Newsflash   *The moment you acknowledge your customer's objection, you demonstrate a problem-solving attitude and approach. What better way to deal with potential conflict?*

Ask for Elaboration

The follow-up to acknowledgment is asking the customer to elaborate. That's right: elaborate. You don't acknowledge the concern just to refute it! Instead, keep the customer talking. Here are several ways to do that.

Use open-ended questions. Don't forget the questioning skills you employ in determining needs. After all, dealing with objections is just a special case of finding out more about the customer's needs.

Open-ended questions are applicable here. It's easier to ask the customer something like, "Why do you feel that way?" than to force a Yes or No response by asking a question like, "Is it because of the problems we had in the past?"

In addition to making your questions open-ended, avoid asking questions that imply a particular thought or judgment. Suppose, for example, that a customer has raised a vague objection, and you respond with, "Is the price structure associated with our recommendation the thing that is troubling you?" Think about how the customer might respond. What you've just done is plant a negative thought in the customer's mind. In effect, you've *created* an objection that might or might not have been there. As a result, you may end up hearing something like this: "I hadn't really thought about the price being too high before, but now that you mention it. . . ."

To avoid such effects, just leave the content out of your questions in the issue-resolution phase. For example, "Can you be more specific?" will encourage the customer to open up without getting you in any trouble.

> **Newsflash** *There is no need to give your customers reasons not to buy when you ask for elaboration. They do this very well without your help, thank you.*

Use pre-question statements. If you need to probe further to find out more about what the customer is thinking, use pre-question statements to set up your requests for elaboration. Taking the time to explain *why* you need the information can put customers at ease and encourage them to talk freely. A good example is one I used a moment ago: "Yes, it is expensive. *But I think it's worth discussing further whether the cost is worth what it can do for you.* So I'd like to ask . . ." Another example is when a recommendation may be complicated. If the customer complains about that, you might say: "Sure it's complicated. But it is also very manageable. Let's discuss this further. . . . "

Use mirroring. Another approach to getting the customer to elaborate in an uncomfortable situation is "mirroring." This means simply repeating the customer's words with a question mark at the end. For instance, suppose a customer says something confrontational like, "This proposal is ridiculous!" Instead of going off like a bomb, you simply look the customer in the eye and say, neutrally, "Ridiculous?" or, "Ridiculous? Why do you say that?" Or, "Why do you think it's ridiculous?" When you use this technique, be sure to mirror the customer's response, not in a judgmental way, but in a tone that suggests you're genuinely curious about the answer.

Use silence. Sometimes you can use silence to get customers to elaborate on their concerns. I find this technique works best in contentious situations. When someone comes on in an inappropriately strong manner, I force myself to keep my mouth shut by counting, "One Mississippi, two Mississippi, three Mississippi. . . ." The silence can have an extraordinary effect as the customer realizes how his or her behavior is not terribly productive. Rarely do I get beyond three or four Mississippis before the customer will say something. And at that point I use what comes out to move us to the next step. (By the way, this approach is much more effective if you do it silently as opposed to out loud!)

Transform the Objection into a Need

Earlier in this book I introduced one of my favorite "big ideas," courtesy of Kate Reilly: *Objections are really needs in disguise.* Think of resistance as expressing an unfulfilled need, and instead of facing a wall, you'll be on the path to continued problem solving.

That is why the third step in the issue-resolution process is to transform the customer's objection into a need. This step is analogous to the "reframing" step in the Synectics problem-solving sequence, where concerns about a proposed solution are treated as *invitations*. The idea is to stay positive and keep the process moving forward. (It may help to remind yourself that "a frown is just a smile turned upside down.")

I'll bet that with a little thought you can take the ugliest objection you've ever heard and see how it is in fact just an unsatisfied need. That doesn't necessarily mean it's a need you can satisfy. Sometimes there are objections that you simply cannot address to the customer's satisfaction. But it does mean that you can transform virtually any objection into a need.

The most common objections I hear from salespeople in training sessions concern such things as price, change, loyalty, procrastination, and lethargy. In other words, the *need* to justify the cost (or to see the value), or a better reason to change relationships, or a more powerful incentive to overcome inertia.

One salesperson told about an objection that was much more personal. A customer told him, "I just don't like you very much."

(Actually, the comment was a bit more abrasive than that. Use your imagination.) Now, nobody wants to hear that the reason a customer is balking is because of, well, you. Nevertheless, the comment can be thought of as an unfulfilled need and dealt with as such. In this case, the customer needed something like greater rapport, credibility, comfort, or trust. Or simply to work with someone he liked.

As always, when you transform an objection into a need, you want to show that you've correctly heard what the customer said. Consequently, your first move should be to restate or paraphrase the objection—but not *as* an objection (that would simply validate it). The trick is to *reframe* the objection in such a way that it states a need. Here's an example:

> *Customer:* Actually, I'm satisfied with my current supplier.
> *Salesperson* [after acknowledging and seeking elaboration]: Oh, so if I understand you correctly, you would need a good *reason* to switch, because you're satisfied with your current supplier, is that right?

Look! Up in the sky! It's an objection! It has been paraphrased! It has been transformed into a need! It's a problem turned into an opportunity! It's the Problem-Solving Salesperson!

Sounds easy, doesn't it? It's not—even when you understand very well what to do. Take it from one who has been there . . . more often than he cares to remember.

Not too long ago an oil company chose our firm for a major sales-training program. We'd been selected from a field of seven training companies that had submitted detailed proposals and given thorough presentations. Naturally, we were delighted.

Once we were selected as the vendor of choice, all that remained was the formality of meeting the senior vice president of sales and marketing. This kind of signoff is fairly routine in our business. We expected to leave the meeting with a signed contract, after which we planned to head off for a well-deserved celebration.

It took only a few minutes for the VP to torpedo our happy anticipation. After the usual bit of "getting-to-know-you's," the VP turned to the manager of management development and said bluntly, "I've decided that these are not the right people for the job. I'm sorry, but we can't go forward."

My partner and I were stunned. So was the management development guy, who had selected us after a long, involved search involving a number of people. In a somewhat confrontational way, he asked the VP why he had rejected the recommendation of the task force. The VP replied, "I don't believe in this videotape garbage, and these guys are making too big a deal about how they use it."

At this point, a voice deep within me urged, "You have to figure out how to get around this guy." Videotaping participants in our training programs as they simulate selling situations in role-play exercises was one of the program's most effective components and a key point of difference from our competitors. Evaluation forms consistently reinforced its value as an effective training methodology. It simply was the right way to go!

With all this going through my head, compounded by the emotions I was feeling, I looked at the VP and said, "I'm surprised to hear you say that about videotape, Bob. Because one of the things we know from having used it for the last twelve years is . . ."

At that moment my partner discreetly put a death grip on my forearm. "Excuse me, Eric," he said politely. Remembering how much I like playing softball and tennis, I had little choice but to let him interrupt. Turning to the VP, he asked, "Just what is your concern about videotape?"

Invited to elaborate on his objection, our client told us how he had always disliked professionally produced videotapes of people selling. He talked about how his people "would see these *actors* making perfect sales calls in faked situations. It would seem unrealistic and hokey, and it would probably de-motivate them as opposed to helping them learn."

The VP's remarks made it clear that he was blissfully unaware of how we used video in our program, which was to tape the salespeople themselves as they practiced the concepts we were teaching. Obviously, he hadn't read our detailed proposal with any great attention.

At this point it would have been easy to ask a "You stupid idiot" question like, "Haven't you read our detailed proposal?" Instead, my partner, having succeeded in getting the customer to elaborate his objection, transformed it into a need: "So, if I understand you correctly, you need to be confident that our use of videotape will be both realistic and motivating, is that correct?"

When the client agreed, my partner apologized that we must not have been clear in our proposal. The way we would use videotape, he explained, would be to put the company's people on tape in practice exercises that would be realistic, motivating, and educational. He went on to say that we didn't like the idea of actors any more than the VP did and that the only people who would appear on the tapes would be the course participants themselves.

Guess what? In a short while we walked out of the office with our signed contract.

Later that day, I thought about how I'd come within one foolish, defensive sentence of blowing the entire deal. Upon hearing an unexpected objection, my immediate response was to come back with an explanation instead of asking the client to elaborate. Even if my explanation was right on the mark, it could well have fallen on deaf ears—particularly if it implied that the VP didn't know what he was talking about. I would have been arguing, not resolving issues—and we may never have reached resolution. And I'm the one who travels the world preaching how to do this stuff!

I try to think about that story before every major presentation. It highlights how, no matter how much you believe in and trust the process, it requires a lot of discipline and commitment to practice it in the face of another human being's objections.

Three Ground Rules for Transforming Objections into Needs
With the basic technique of transforming objections into needs in hand, let's look at three ground rules for making these restatements.

Use "I" Messages. I've already mentioned "I" messages in a previous chapter. As teachers of effective parenting know, "I" messages acknowledge our responsibility for what we're saying and what we've understood the other person to say. It's important to use them when we transform an objection to a need, because we're reframing what the customer said, and we need to take responsibility for that restatement. By using an "I" statement, we indicate that we're expressing our perspective rather than putting words into the customer's mouth. Remember, the last thing we want the customer to feel is that he or she is being manipulated. To avoid that effect, when you restate the objection, use expressions like, "If I understand you correctly . . ." or "Let me see if I have this right" or "Let me try putting it this way. . . . Would you agree with that?"

Use "need" language. The second ground rule is to use the word *need* whenever possible: "So, if I understand you correctly, you need to be sure that the system won't be too hard for your people to learn or operate successfully" or "Let's see if I have this right. When it comes to cost, you need to feel that spending this amount of money is warranted. Is that right?" Remember, it's easier as well as more productive to *address a need* than it is to *challenge an objection.* And take notice of how the needs are once again expressed as verbs.

> **Newsflash**   *Using "need" language turns an objection into something you can work with: an unfulfilled need.*

Seek confirmation. The final ground rule is this: After completing the transformation step, ask for confirmation from the customer. After all, you have changed both the tone and scope of the original objection. You've expressed it as a need, which implies that you think the customer is open to discussing your recommendation further instead of deep-sixing it. It's important to give the customer the opportunity to correct you so he or she will continue to feel involved in the discussion.

Seeking confirmation is straightforward. A simple, "Is that correct?" will suffice. If the customer confirms your restatement, you keep the conversation moving with the customer's buy-in. If the customer corrects your restatement, work with that response (always turning it into a need), and again seek confirmation.

Once the customer accepts the transformation of the objection into a need, you're ready to respond to it. Keep in mind, though, that your answers are less important than predisposing the customer to hear them. If you believe that your recommendation truly addresses the customer's needs, answers to objections will be readily available. The challenge is to prepare the customer to hear them. That's what you'll accomplish when you transform objections into needs that the customer accepts.

Respond to the Need

There are as many ways to respond to objections—or, as we're thinking of them now, to unfulfilled needs—as there are clever salespeople. Often the answer to a reformulated objection will be fairly obvious; it may lie in what you've already proposed, as in the case of the sales-training videotapes I described earlier. At other times, you may need to be more creative to demonstrate how your solution is the right one for the customer's needs. Here are some ideas.

Use benefit statements. Statements of benefits, particularly *specific* benefits, are an excellent tool to use in responding to objections. Sometimes it's enough simply to repeat a benefit that was forgotten or not appreciated during the presentation. Remember, specific benefits explain exactly how your product or service address the customer's *needs*, so it never hurts to review these statements as often as necessary.

Sell yourself. A second technique is to sell yourself. I don't mean getting up on a soap box and bragging about what a marvelous human being you are. But I do mean explaining to the customer how you will do the kinds of things that others won't as a way to justify the higher price, longer lead time, tighter specifications, or whatever reasons you were given not to move forward. You can talk about your commitment, your dedication, or your responsiveness. Remember, we're talking *relationships* here. That can be a major reason for a customer to do business with you.

Sell the organization. If you believe in the organization-wide approach to selling, this is a great time to bring up your sales team and the resources available to you. Demonstrating a positive feeling for your company, especially when you back up your feeling with specifics, almost always makes a positive impression. Explain how your organization's capabilities, strengths, and ways of doing business address the customer's needs.

> **Newsflash**   *Selling yourself and your company is something only you can do, which makes it a unique response to any objection.*

Describe parallel situations. A parallel situation is one in which a similar customer resisted buying for the same reason as your current prospect. Many customers feel better knowing someone else had similar concerns and that you were able to resolve them. So, review how you were able to resolve the issues in the parallel situation. Along the same lines, proof statements, referrals, and testimonials can help you reassure the customer that doing business with you is the right choice.

Involve the customer. It always helps to involve the customer in the process when appropriate. One such occasion is when you're hit with "third party" objections. These are situations where a buyer is happy with your recommendation but has encountered resistance from others. Here is where you can do some serious problem solving. Transform the objection to a need, but this time use a "we" message instead of an "I" message: "So, it looks like *we* have to figure out a way to demonstrate to your associates why it makes more sense to work with *us* as opposed to those other guys, right?" Upon receiving confirmation, you could continue by saying something like, "I have a couple of ideas as to how we might do that and I'd like to hear any ideas that *you* might have as well, OK?" If you take this approach, you will soon find yourself in a problem-solving mode with the customer.

Respond with ideas. If the customer really wants to move forward, but can't for a specific reason, try offering ideas to transform the sales call into a problem-solving session. Set the stage for problem solving like we discussed earlier and get some ideas on the table. For example, if the issue is finding the time to conduct the trial, generate three or four ideas about how to find the time.

Use your resources. Just as your resources can assist in offering recommendations, they can help respond to needs when you are resolving objections. Think how powerful it would be to have someone right there with an expert answer after you have successfully transformed the objection into a need! Obviously, you'll need to prepare your colleagues (a point we'll discuss in the chapter on making joint calls). But if you do succeed in deploying them in this way, you'll experience teamwork beyond and above your wildest dreams.

> **Newsflash** *When you encounter resistance, use your resources! They can help come up with answers in the sales call or can help you strategize about possible answers during the planning process.*

Call a time-out. When you've transformed an objection into a need, it can often be appropriate to call a time-out so that you can prepare an adequate response. After confirming your restatement of the need, let the customer know that you'd like to bring it back to the team, and set up another meeting. Back in the office, meet with your team or any available resources and come up with the best answer.

When you've got a team backing you up, you don't always have to have the answer at your fingertips. That's one of the beauties of team selling.

Invite Other Objections

Once you have resolved an important issue to the customer's satisfaction, the final step in this phase is to invite other objections. Yep, ask for more negative statements—and keep asking until there aren't any more.

Seem risky? Not at all. If the customer has a hidden objection, it's far preferable to hear it face to face and attempt to resolve it than to have the customer think of it when you're long gone and make you come back at a later date to salvage your sale.

So go ahead: invite more objections! But in doing so, be careful about the language you use. Avoid words like *problems, issues, concerns, worries,* or *objections.* You don't want to get customers wondering whether there is something they *should* be concerned about that you haven't told them. Instead use neutral language:

- "Is there anything else we need to discuss?"
- "Do you have any other questions?"
- "Is there anything else on your mind?"

If more objections surface, simply repeat the resolution process for each one. If not, proceed to the next phase and try to reach closure.

Another Look at Airtime

Before we leave issue resolution, let's look again at airtime. You have learned to give up the airtime early in the needs-determination process in order to learn as much about the customer's situation as possible. By giving up airtime early, you earn the right to use it later, when you make recommendations. The same applies to resolving issues (see figure 9.2). *Give up* the airtime when you seek elaboration. *Share* the airtime when you transform the objection

Figure 9.2 Airtime Distribution When Resolving Objections

into a need and seek confirmation. Then you can hog the airwaves when you respond to the need you have agreed upon.

Notice that figure 9.2 is virtually the same diagram as the Airtime Distribution Chart you saw in chapter 5. That's because resolving issues is very similar to determining needs: you ask the customer to talk, you review the needs, and eventually you respond. What a concept!

Think of airtime as an investment. By letting the customer do most of the talking early, you are making a significant investment in the process that will yield profitable dividends later. Or as Joey, one of my favorite old clients in Brooklyn, likes to say, "If you sales guys would shut your big mouths for a second and listen when you walk *in*, you'd have a lot more time to say your piece when the chips are down, before you walk *out*. More coffee?"

Next Up: The Intangibles!
How Do We Resolve Them?

Up to this point we've been concerned with resolving issues that involve what I call "tangibles"—namely, your products and services.

Now let's turn to the intangibles, the *ideas* you offer customers as part of being a problem-solving resource to them.

Suppose you offer an idea to a customer, and you encounter (guess what?) resistance. How do you resolve issues about an intangible like an idea?

Recall from our discussion of idea development in problem solving that ideas can be thought of in terms of a continuum, along which there is a specific threshold of acceptability. Few ideas reach this threshold when they are initially proposed. To put it another way, the group or the problem owner resists them. At that point, the task is to identify an idea's valuable aspects, then the concerns that represent its shortcomings. Each concern becomes a subtask, reframed as an *invitation*. As each concern is resolved, the idea moves forward on the continuum until it crosses the threshold of acceptability and achieves "solutiondom." (For a quick review of the process, see figure 9.3.)

To me, the most meaningful part of this whole notion is that an idea is *dynamic*, not static, and that we can help it progress along the continuum toward acceptance. This task becomes more approachable if we know how to manage what my friend and colleague, Rick Harriman of Synectics, calls "the four levels of idea response."

Four Levels of Idea Response

The four levels of idea response are simply ways in which people can choose to respond to ideas they're not prepared to accept. Rick arranged these levels in the model you see depicted in figure 9.4.

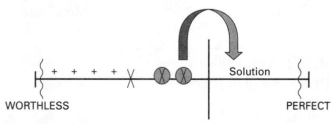

Figure 9.3   An Idea Continuum

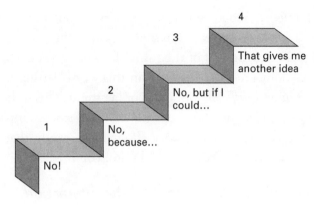

Figure 9.4   Four Levels of Idea Response

A Level 1 response consists of something like, "No! Just plain, No!" This is the simplest form of response to an unacceptable idea. Anyone who has ever raised a two-year-old realizes that it doesn't take much to shoot down an idea. The person says "No" and the discussion ends. No reason given. No explanation offered. End of story. Fortunately, not too many people will respond to your ideas this simplistically.

Level 2 is a response of the form, "No, because. . . ." This is the way most of us respond to ideas we don't like (or new ideas, period: remember our conditioned tendency to react this way to *anything* unfamiliar). Rather than simply saying no, we offer at least some explanation: "It's too much to do at one time," "It takes too long," "It's too complicated," "It's politically unacceptable," you name it. At this level we're looking only at the concerns we have about the idea, without bothering to try to find any value in it.

A Level 3 response has the form, "No, but if I could. . . ." A response of this type indicates that the person finds *some* value in the idea, and is open to seeing how it can be used or modified instead of focusing on why it should be dismissed. Notice that, in this context, the word *but* isn't the negative word that it is in most circumstances. Usually *but* is used as a precursor to dismissal, or as Gerard Nierenberg suggests, to "erase" whatever preceded it: "I like you, but . . ." Following a "no," however, "but" represents an opening to explore. At Level 3, reframing enters into the equation.

A Level 4 response is in the form of, "That gives me another idea. . . ." Someone who responds in this way is letting the idea trigger a *new* and *different idea* in his or her mind. This is the highest level of idea response. We encountered a classic example of it earlier in this book, in the story about how "candy that talks" became "candy that makes sound." Presto! Pop Rocks!

Applying the Four Levels to the Sales Interaction

So how do we use the four-levels-of-response model in resolving issues about ideas? Think of it this way: The truly consultative salesperson is the one who can (figuratively) grab customers by the brains, walk them up the "idea staircase," and reach a *mutually* acceptable solution. If ever you have an opportunity to demonstrate how different you are from the herd, and how much added value you can bring to the relationship, it is when you are using this problem-solving approach to bring ideas to customers and resolve any issues concerning them.

Suppose you're selling sporting goods, and you notice that a particular customer is displaying your product line ineffectively. On one of your calls you offer an idea about a better display for both your line and others. The customer rejects the idea out of hand—in other words, she hits you with a Level 1 response. What do you do?

First, you acknowledge the response ("I see you think that won't work") and then you ask her to elaborate ("Can you explain why?"). When she tells you it's impractical, you're approaching Level 2. Now you know *why* she doesn't like the idea ("No, because . . ."). You probe a little further to find out what *impractical* means. Let's assume that after three questions you learn that it's really a space issue.

You then reframe the idea by saying something like, "So if I understand you correctly, we need to figure out how to take advantage of the impact this new display can have, without taking up too much space, is that correct?" Assume the customer agrees with your reframing. BOOM! You are now at Level 3 ("No, but if I could . . .").

At Level 3, you can offer your own ideas to address the issue *and* seek ideas from the customer. You know the routine: this is just finding ways to express concerns as invitations and then work to resolve each one. Along the way, a workable solution, which may well be significantly different from the idea you walked in with, emerges. Eureka! You're standing proudly on Level 4 ("That gives me another idea . . .").

At this point you've walked your customer up the staircase all the way from "No way!" to a genuine solution that crosses her threshold of acceptability. By using your process skills, you've *transformed* your original idea into a new merchandising approach that benefits both you and your customer. And you've once again demonstrated that you are a genuine value-adding resource, not to mention a swell person besides. (See figure 9.5.)

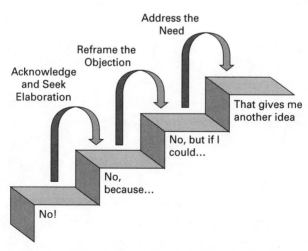

Figure 9.5   Relating Objection Resolution to the Four Levels of Idea Response

Newsflash   *Offering ideas to customers carries the risk that they'll shoot them down. Not to worry. Apply the "four levels of idea response" model and your process skills to help them see the light.*

This completes our discussion of phase 4, resolving the issues. Now let's take a look at the last phase in the selling sequence: reaching closure. You may be surprised at how little I have to say about what too many people think is the key to success in selling. Of course, we need to close. But as you're about to see, closing is nothing more than an extension of the issue-resolution process.

MEMO TO MANAGEMENT

Ask your people what part of the sales process they feel least comfortable with, and the chances are pretty good that they will talk about objections. After all, objections mean the possibility of conflict. And conflict is something most of us don't care for.

So here is where you can do a little reframing of your own. Encourage your people to see objections as *opportunities,* as issues to resolve. And equip them with the means to do it.

The approach presented in this chapter is time tested and extremely applicable to most customer interactions. While some of it may be familiar, the notion of transforming objections into needs is probably a new concept to your people. That is where you can help.

Any time you hear your people talking about why customers are reluctant to buy, ask them what needs they haven't satisfied. Help them look at the reason the customer presents as an opportunity, not a problem. Help them reframe the objection until they get in the habit of seeing objections as *unfulfilled needs.*

Take the same approach with your sales teams. Encourage them to devote time in their meetings to the subject of issue resolution. A terrific exercise is to walk them through the process. First, have them list all the objections they encounter and figure out what unsatisfied needs lie behind each one. Second, have them figure out how they will acknowledge those objections and what questions to ask to get the customer to elaborate. Third, have them brainstorm different ways to transform those objections into needs and how to address them. Get them to use problem-solving skills for this task. I'll bet they come up with some new and exciting solutions.

Don't expect success every time, or all at once. These skills take practice, and even practice won't make perfect in resolving issues. Nobody wins every time. But your people—and your customers—can win a lot more often. And you can help make it happen.

Don't overlook how useful the issue-resolution process can be internally as well. As a manager, you can use it all the time. For instance, when people you're coaching resist one of your suggestions, apply the "four levels of idea response" model. Acknowledge what they say. Encourage them to talk. Paraphrase what you hear as a need ("It sounds to me like you need to hear why I think it's important for you to better use your team members with customers, is that correct?") Then give your best response. Ask if there is anything else to discuss. When you've resolved all the concerns, ask for a commitment to apply what you suggested.

The same principle applies to resolving issues between members of the sales team, or anyone else in the organization. The process described in this chapter doesn't apply only to interactions with customers. It's a tested method for resolving interpersonal conflict. Encourage your people to use the skills all the time, including in their interactions with each other.

Make sure you model the behavior. You'll find yourself in many situations where your people show resistance to something you want from them, especially if you are asking them to behave differently. If you want them to use this approach with their customers and colleagues, you'd better use it as well. 'Nuff said.

CHAPTER 10

Last Call! We're Closing!

I wish I had a penny for every time a salesperson told me how successful he would be if only he knew how to close. I wish I had a nickel for every time a salesperson told me that selling would be easier if she weren't scared to ask for the order. I wish I had a quarter for every time a salesperson told me that he didn't know he had to ask for the business.

The truth is I wish I had a small fortune in pocket change. And I wish that the majority of sales professionals were more willing to ask their customers to commit to the deal when they reach the closing point.

Newsflash *Most sales professionals, no matter how seasoned, are at some level reluctant to ask for the business.*

Closing simply means reaching closure, which is the goal of the entire consultative, problem-solving model of selling that I've been advocating. You may remember the comment in chapter 9 from the sales pro who said that when he meets resistance, his consulting hat comes off and his selling hat goes on. Although it's true that you may take off your consultative hat at this point, it's only to free up your problem-solving machine. You know, the one between your ears. It's the problem solving and issue resolution that do the heavy lifting in this process. Once you've successfully responded to objections, asking for the customer's commitment is a natural next step—so much so that many customers actually *want* you to ask for their business at this point!

So the close doesn't have to be mysterious or daunting. That's why this chapter is short and sweet. Think of the close as I prefer to do: as "reaching closure." Sounds like the natural outcome of a process, doesn't it? As a reminder, it consists of the three steps shown in figure 10.1.

Interim Closes

Sales professionals know that there isn't just one "close." Any time you ask the customer for feedback or for a commitment—even to a next step, not necessarily a purchase—you're "closing." In other words, you're reaching a point of closure.

Most people call requesting feedback during the sales process the "trial close." Yuck! There's another one of those expressions that gives the impression that selling is all about *us* instead of about our customers. "Trial close" says to me that whenever you see a buying signal, stop what you're doing and see whether the customer is ready to buy. After all, the only thing that matters is closing the deal. Right? No, dead wrong.

> 1. Invite Other Objections
> 2. Ask for the Business
> 3. Establish Next Steps

Figure 10.1   Reaching Closure

> **Newsflash** *The "trial close" gives the impression that all that mat-*
> *ters is getting the business. It leaves the customer com-*
> *pletely out of the equation.*

Think about what the phrase "trial close" says. It suggests that you're testing the water to see if the customer is ready to buy. Now, I don't want to get on a high horse and say that there is no validity to this. But there are better ways to think about it.

The Selling Sequence as a Series of Closes

The problem-solving selling approach is geared to the idea that you're *involving* customers in a "win-win" process: when you reach a solution to the customer's problem, both of you win. Requesting feedback is a natural and necessary part of moving this process forward. It's not just a way of dangling bait (with a nasty hook concealed inside) in front of a helpless fish.

Throughout your problem-solving engagement with the customer, you reach a number of milestones, points where you successfully attain specific objectives. One way to look at these milestones is to think of them as "interim closes." Getting an appointment with someone you never met with before is an interim close. Receiving approval from your primary contact to meet with key people in their organization is an interim close. Getting the opportunity to submit a proposal or give a formal presentation is an interim close. In short, an interim close is the fulfillment of any objective that brings you further along in accomplishing the ultimate goal of gaining commitment from the customer.

Contrast this idea with the more limited, and manipulative, idea of seeing whether the customer is ready to buy. I certainly won't object if you want to use "little c" to refer to interim points of closure and "big C" to refer to the final step of getting commitment to buy. The point I want to emphasize is that every one of these "c's," whether big or little, is about the customer and his or her commitment (really big "C") to taking the next step.

> **Newsflash**   *The entire sales process can be viewed as a series of closes. Whenever you make a recommendation and ask for feedback, whether what you're offering is an opportunity to meet, a beginning idea, or a complete solution, you are smack in the middle of the closing process.*

Keep Your Eye on Momentum

The notion of interim closes relates back to the concept of momentum in the sales cycle that we discussed in the context of positioning the sales call (chapter 6). As you recall, the time that elapses between sales calls often results in discontinuity that can cause you to lose momentum away from your ultimate goal of doing business with the customer. For that reason, I recommended that you begin every subsequent meeting with a customer by reviewing what happened the last time you met. I also suggested that you think in terms of a defined goal for each meeting, which might or might not be the ultimate goal of closing the sale. What you want to do is to keep the process moving forward, getting interim commitments along the way that keep your momentum going.

Everything you do to build relationships with customers can be thought of as a series of interim closes. It's analogous to solving a complex problem by breaking it into its component parts rather than trying to solve it all at once. You know you're more likely to be successful if you address each simpler component successfully and build up to a solution. It's the same with the sales cycle. By the time you're ready for the "big C," you'll have successfully reached closure on many smaller steps in the process.

From Objections to Closure

The first step in the closing phase is, as usual, the final step in the preceding phase—in this case, inviting other objections. This segue is actually a natural bridge to the key step in phase 5, asking for the business. To see why, let's return to problem solving just for a moment.

The Synectics folks believe strongly in attacking a complex problem by breaking it down into what they call "springboards." A springboard can be anything from a full-blown, well-developed idea to a freewheeling "wish statement" that is miles away from a workable solution. Some springboards can lead to new and different ideas. By developing those ideas—noting what makes each one appealing and addressing its shortcomings, one by one—you eventually arrive at a full-blown solution to the task at hand.

The same thing applies to the sales cycle. You are continually going to run into resistance. Stay with the process, inviting other objections, acknowledging them, and responding to them until there aren't any more. As you successfully slay each objection dragon, one at a time, eventually you'll find yourself standing on the last of the gasping beasts as it expires.

At this point, the customer's logical move is to accept your solution. Congratulations, you are now ready to close the sale!

How Not to Close

There are scores of expressions describing the style of the close: the "Ben Franklin Close," the "Either/Or" Close, the "Puppy Dog Close," the "Personal Touch Close," and a host of others you've probably heard. The names alone tell you where these styles of closing are coming from. It's the same school of thought that believes that closing is the key to selling instead of the natural outgrowth of a problem-solving process.

Most of these approaches are quite manipulative and wholly inconsistent with the philosophy of problem-solving selling. When you've applied a customer-driven approach to each preceding phase, it would be highly incongruous for you to say in the final phase something like, "Well, that takes care of that issue. Now, I can arrange for delivery next week or the week after. Which would you prefer?"

You don't want to wink and say something like that to your buyer. Not after all the work you've put into putting the customer and his or her needs right at the center of the process. This kind of closing technique reveals Mr. or Ms. Customer-Centered Salesperson as having really been concerned all along about only one thing: Old Number One. Getting the sale. Closing the deal. Hooking the fish.

No matter how glibly you do it, a close like this is insulting. It's demeaning. And it's transparent.

Newsflash   *Manipulative approaches to closing can undo everything you have done in trying to differentiate yourself and your organization.*

The fact is, you don't need tricks. You don't need a kit full of closing techniques. You don't need to play silly cat-and-mouse games. You've worked hard to determine your customer's needs and understand his or her situation. You've offered the appropriate recommendation based on what you've learned, and you've problem-solved diligently to resolve any issues. All that's left is to ask for the customer's commitment in a sincere, straightforward way.

Don't Be a Wimp—Ask for the Business!
I am always surprised to see how few salespeople, particularly those selling services or less tangible products, actually ask the customer to

commit. If they did, they would probably be shocked to see that most customers feel perfectly comfortable about being asked.

I've said it before: Research shows that most customers *want* you to ask for the order. That doesn't mean begging them for their business, or demanding it, either. But let's assume you have resolved the customer's objections. When you ask for others, the customer indicates that there aren't any more. What could be more natural at this point than simply to ask for the business?

It's not only natural to make this request, it's vital to do so. If you don't ask, you might give the impression that you don't want the business. And you force the customer to do *your* job. The customer may simply sit there, or walk away. Simply put, if you don't ask for the business, you're less likely to get it. To say the same thing more positively, one study indicated that the sixth most important reason that buyers buy is that the salesperson *asked* for the order!

Newsflash   *If you don't believe in asking for a commitment, remember one important detail: No one else will do it for you. Asketh and you shall receiveth. Don't asketh and you'reth a wimp!*

OK, so asking for the order doesn't fall trippingly off the tongue. What are the options? You can accomplish the same thing by asking the customer any one of a variety of questions. You can ask the customer's opinion about what the appropriate next step would be, or how you should proceed at this time, or who else needs to approve the decision before you move forward. The key is to get the customer to accept your desire to move the relationship to the next step, which could range from walking out with a purchase order to drafting the contract to bringing in the legal beagles to arrange for you to meet the ultimate decision maker. In any of these cases, you have gained the commitment and, for all practical purposes, closed the sale.

The Assumptive Close

The term "assumptive close" has been used for years to describe a way to proceed when all the issues have been resolved and you can *assume* that the way is clear to close the deal. In essence, the assumptive close says to the customer that it makes sense to you that if he or she doesn't have a reason *not* to buy, then he or she must be *ready* to buy. It works quite effectively if you honestly believe that what you have recommended makes sense for the customer and does in fact address all the relevant needs.

The assumptive close relates well to the notion of thinking in terms of *giving* customers something as opposed to *taking* something from them. I first heard this idea expressed by Len Malkin of Chase Manhattan Bank. Len told his people that if they truly believed in what they had to offer, they did their customers a major *disservice* if they didn't do what they could to get the customers to buy from them. Giving, not taking. I like that.

Newsflash	*When you ask for the business, you give your customer the opportunity to buy the solution you're recommending. If you believe in what you have to offer, you are giving the customer something, not taking something.*

So what do you say? After resolving an objection, you first ask the customer something like, "Is there anything else that we need to discuss?" If the response is "No," your assumptive closing statements can sound like this:

- "That's great! Now perhaps you can discuss with me how we can begin to implement my recommendation?"
- "Well, in that case, perhaps we can begin filling out the paperwork to get the process underway?"
- "Then if everything appears to work, what are the steps required to make it happen?"

- "I'm delighted to hear that. How about giving me an order for the product?"

The exact words matter less than the fact that the customer is being given the opportunity to sign up or agree to buy whatever you have recommended. Again, it's process, not content, that we need to think about. The customer is ready for the next step. Make it easy for him or her to take it.

What If They Say No?

If for some reason a customer *isn't* ready to commit, then you will hear a new objection. You know what to do: Go right back to the objection-resolution process. Begin by acknowledging the objection and probing to get the customer to elaborate. Then work to resolve the objection, and try again to reach closure.

Sometimes, though, the customer has heard enough and "just isn't ready to buy." In such cases, ask how he or she feels about continuing the process. Any time customers simply aren't ready to make a commitment, the logical thing to do is to try to keep the process moving forward in some way. Keep the momentum going, and get an interim close. At minimum, get the next step. Eventually you'll arrive at commitment.

Newsflash *The only time you fail in the selling process is when you don't get a next step.*

And in Closing . . .

It seems funny now, but at one point I thought about not even including a chapter on the closing process in this book. I thought that for the salesperson who uses problem-solving selling, the closing process would just be a natural extension of what they have already learned to do. Consequently, there was really no need to discuss closing.

Later I decided that leaving closing out of the discussion of the selling sequence would have been rather glib. And certainly it *is* a necessary part of the process. But I still believe that the heavy emphasis put on closing by sales managers, sales consultants, sales trainers, and salespeople themselves is exaggerated and unnecessary when you apply the concepts covered in this book.

The key is to give customers what they need and to problem-solve with them to resolve whatever issues they have. If that happens, the reluctance to close fades away and asking for the business becomes something to anticipate with comfort, confidence, and the belief that success is inevitable.

Newsflash *Learn to follow the problem-solving selling sequence, and you'll approach closing with comfort and confidence.*

MEMO TO MANAGEMENT

You may have noticed that this chapter on closing never mentioned anyone but the sales professional. That's because I believe that closing belongs to the salesperson and nobody else.

The salesperson is the custodian of the relationship at the heart of the buying-selling transaction. We don't come up with titles like Relationship Manager, Account Manager, Customer Manager, Account Executive, and the like for nothing. We hire salespeople so they can serve as the liaison between the customer and the organization.

The sales professional spends all of his or her time managing these relationships. The salesperson deals with the day-to-day highs and lows. The salesperson receives recognition when things work out and takes the heat when they don't. That doesn't mean that the sales team and other resources don't enjoy the euphoria associated with big wins or share in the disappointment when things don't work out. But the sales pros are the ones on the front lines. And regardless of the source of the problem, guess who gets the blame when things turn sour?

Let's not forget that it's the salesperson who is caught in a traffic jam with an upset stomach and a budding headache because she's late for an appointment. It's the salesperson who gets blown off by a customer after sitting in the waiting room for an hour. It's the salesperson who shows up expecting a nice, friendly meeting, only to learn about the late shipment or the quality problem or a competitor's low bid.

There are great parts to the job. I personally think it's the best job in the company. When young people ask me about where to start their careers, I'm quick to say, "Sales." But remember what being the point person really means: Day after day, your company is represented, as professionally as possible, by your salespeople. They've earned more than their spurs. They've earned the right to finish the process they've spent so much time and trouble moving toward closure.

The notion of "closer" is old hat. To bring in a product manager or sales manager or senior manager at the end of the deal cuts the ground right out from under the salesperson. Those people can help, but let the salesperson be the one to ask for the business. Closing is part of their role. It should be part of their job description. It's an integral part of the process they've been managing all along. Does it make any sense to have someone come out of the blue to perform only the final step in a continuous, cohesive process?

One of the saddest sales-related stories I've ever heard was about a guy who called on the same customer twice a month for nearly two years. He was about to get his first order, so he brought his sales manager with him. After reviewing the product specs, pricing agreements, inventory guidelines, credit terms, and every-thing else, the logical thing for the sales rep to do was ask for the business. He didn't do that, even though all the buying signals were there. He just kept asking questions.

Finally the manager couldn't stand it any more and blurted out, "Well, then, how about an order?" The customer responded, "What took you guys so long to ask?" They got the order.

So why is this a sad story? Because after almost twenty-five sales calls and a ton of work, the salesperson never felt the gratification of closing the deal. Sure, he was demonstrating closing reluctance, and maybe the manager had no choice. But maybe the manager hadn't set it up right in the first place. Had he trained his people to ask for the order? Had he worked out in advance what their respective roles would be in this climactic meeting? Was the sales-person intimidated by the manager's presence? All I know is, he genuinely resented having the close taken away from him.

So train your people to be consummate professionals, and then let them close the deal. If they need help in strategizing what to do, encourage them to talk to their resources. But make it their job to ask for the business and close. And make it yours to ensure that it happens.

Unleashing the Power of Sales Teams

CHAPTER 11

So What Are These Things We Call Sales Teams?

Throughout this book I've emphasized the use of sales teams in virtually every phase of selling. I've pointed out dozens of ways that teams can participate in the work of the sales pros who are the primary contact with the customer. I've emphasized that everybody on the team needs to understand the problem-solving selling process and the skills involved. But to implement sales teams, you need to know more than just where and when to use the teams and what skills they need to be effective. You need to understand how to set them up and get them working efficiently and productively. That's what this section of the book is about.

If you want to put together sales teams or improve the way your current sales teams perform, you need to look at a number of key variables and ask yourself some serious questions. With that in mind, here are the ten questions I'm asked most often when people want to investigate team selling:

The Ten Things People Most Want to Know About Sales Teams

1. What is a sales team?

2. Why have sales teams?

3. Who is on the team?

4. Which customers, or clusters of customers, deserve their own sales teams?

5. What are the team members' roles and responsibilities?

6. How do the team members work together effectively?

7. How often should sales teams meet?

8. Who runs the show?

9. Who evaluates the team's performance?

10. How are sales teams compensated?

These are big questions, and every company must answer them in ways that fit the organization, the business it's in, its circumstances, and its culture. This chapter will get you started by offering some general observations about sales teams. With these fundamentals in place, the next two chapters will take a close look at how sales teams work together internally and externally.

Question 1: What Is a Sales Team?

Let's first define what a *team* is. My favorite definition comes from *The Wisdom of Teams* (Harvard Business School Press 1993), an extraordinarily insightful and thoughtful book by Jon R. Katzenbach and Douglas K. Smith:

> A team is a small number of people (2–25) with complementary skills who are committed to a common purpose, performance goals and approach for which they hold themselves mutually accountable.

That's a rich definition, packed with big ideas. Notice its key terms:

- *Complementary skills:* Members of a team bring a variety of skills and kinds of expertise to a common task. Katzenbach and Smith talk about the need for three categories of skills: technical/functional expertise, problem-solving/decision-making skills, and interpersonal skills. They do not suggest, however, all these skills are absolute prerequisites when determining who should be on the team.

- *Committed to a common purpose:* Can you say customer satisfaction? Or service excellence? Or organization-wide selling approach, one that marks your company as different from and better than its competitors?

- *Common performance goals and approach:* Very big statement. A sales team exists for a specific reason, and the performance of both the team and its members needs to be measured. Moreover, the team members share a common approach to their collective task (such as problem-solving selling).

- *Holding themselves mutually accountable:* Another big statement. Katzenbach and Smith suggest that "no group ever becomes a team until it can hold itself accountable as a team." In other words, "We're in this together" isn't just a nice slogan. It's a basic ground rule for functional teams.

This definition of teams has two other implications that we should note. First, a team isn't *just* a group. The fact that people work together day in and day out and share some common purpose and even some responsibilities doesn't mean they act or behave like anything that can be called a team. If people can't hold each other accountable, they're not a team. If they're not evaluated for their success as a unit as well as individually, they're not a team. If they don't represent a blend of disparate skills and expertise that are put in the service of a common goal, they're not a team. This point is important, because, as Katzenbach and Smith say, teams usually outperform not only individuals, but other kinds of groups as well.

The second point is that a team is not what is usually called a "task force." Task forces had quite a vogue in past decades. Organizations facing some issue of importance typically would put a group of people together, most of them new to each other, with the objective of resolving the problem. Task forces were charged with meeting a highly specific goal within a specified time frame. The outcome of their work was usually a report that was brimming with great ideas. After that, everybody went back to their previous jobs, while the report gathered dust on some executive's shelf.

I can't emphasize too strongly that a sales team is not a task force. A sales team is a working unit that exists for the long term, with the ongoing mission of providing outstanding customer satisfaction. Moreover, its work is an integral part of the company's day-to-day business. All of which, by the way, answers the question of what a sales team is.

Question 2: Why Have Sales Teams?

Well, here's one answer that I've been alluding to throughout this book: Salespeople today just can't go it alone. There is too much to know. There are too many changes happening every day, too many competitors, too many shifts and advances in technology. Besides, your competitors are probably using teams to enhance their relationships with prospects and customers. So for many organizations, there really isn't a whole lot of choice in the matter.

Here's a more positive answer: Groups usually outperform individuals, and teams usually outperform groups. There's a reason for the cliché, "Two minds are better than one," to which we can add that six minds are better than two, provided they know how to work together effectively. The power of groups is backed up by considerable psychological research. The group problem-solving process, in which a group of people proposes solutions that the problem owner could never have come up with alone, is just one example. With the advantages of being a long-term unit with mutual accountability and the other positive characteristics of teams, sales teams multiply the advantages that groups have over individuals.

> **Newsflash**   *As a rule, groups outperform individuals, and teams out-perform groups.*

Here's maybe the best answer to the question of why you should have sales teams: Sales teams help you provide outstanding customer satisfaction. They enable everyone involved to have a sense of ownership in the customer management process. They allow organizations to leverage their human capital more effectively. And they act as a mechanism to connect the primary point of contact with the customer—the sales professional—and the organization in general, which is made up of people who *should* be thinking about the customer in everything they do. In short, sales teams can play a key role in involving everybody within the organization in the selling effort.

Question 3: Who Is on the Team?

Ideally, a sales team comprises whatever functions touch the customer, either directly or indirectly. Some of these functions are quite obvious and easily play a role on any sales team, for example:

- Sales and Sales Management
- Customer Service
- Marketing/Product Management
- Production/Manufacturing
- Research and Development
- Distribution
- Operations
- Credit

Some functions are less obvious but still can play a significant role on a sales team, depending on the nature of your business. Here again are examples:

- Underwriting (Insurance)
- Broker/Distributor Management (Packaged Goods)
- Advertising
- Design
- Strategic Planning
- Legal
- Compliance (Financial Services)
- Finance
- Quality Control
- Engineering

In short, if the function involves designing, delivering, or following through on providing customer satisfaction or deriving solutions to customers' problems, it has a role to play on the sales team. This doesn't mean, of course, that people from every one of these functions must attend every sales-team meeting or participate in every activity. It does mean that they need to be part of the team and involved in the process whenever their areas can contribute to the task at hand.

> **Newsflash**   *Anybody who touches the customer, either directly or indirectly, has a role to play on the sales team.*

Clearly, the exact makeup of the sales team needs to be tailored to your own circumstances. In the financial services industry, teams can consist of dozens of people. If a commercial bank, for example, has a relationship with a major corporation, it probably needs to have a sales team just for that client. Such teams typically consist of the client executive (bank euphemism for sales professional) and as many as thirty product specialists. The client executive calls meetings and explains the client's needs. The various product specialists then make suggestions about how their products and services might be of value to the customer. These meetings can get rather unwieldy, but they can also produce terrific new ideas that the client executive can bring to the customer.

At the other end of the spectrum is the manufacturing company whose sales team is composed of people from four or five specific functions, such as sales, distribution, customer service, production, and quality control. The idea is to have a smaller, more cohesive team made up of the key people involved in managing the relationships with customers. Others in the company can always serve as resources to the team when they are needed.

Whatever functions you decide to include, one question that people raise all the time focuses on those rather undesirable folk whom nobody enjoys working with. You know the ones I mean—the people who brighten up any room they leave. Well, this may surprise you, but I suggest that you not put a whole lot of energy into looking at personalities when you put together the sales team. If someone has expertise that the team needs, include him or her in the process. Groups have an extraordinary ability to resolve the potential conflict that a negative or recalcitrant or simply annoying person can create, particularly if they're trained in the kinds of skills described in this book. Personally, I'd rather risk potential disruption than lose valuable brainpower. If you trust the team, and the process, the team will probably find a way to self-correct.

Question 4: Which Customers, or Clusters of Customers, Deserve Their Own Sales Teams?

Sometimes this question has a straightforward answer, and sometimes it doesn't. In the packaged goods industry, it's a no-brainer. With mega-customers like Wal-Mart and Safeway, the packaged goods people know they cannot be competitive unless they have separate teams dedicated to servicing those customers. A typical team in that industry is made up of people from functions like category management, marketing, customer service, merchandising, distribution, trade relations, product management, and business analysis, as well as salespeople for the different product lines. In many such companies, there is a team leader who runs the show, in contrast to other sales-team configurations where salespeople take the lead.

In organizations that don't have a Wal-Mart accounting for 40 percent of their business, the answer is not so clear cut. The challenge is to decide how to invest your resources. Sometimes it is worthwhile to devote substantial resources to a specific account. Often it makes sense to have sales teams devoted to a collection of companies in a similar business or to a specific market, including one that is just emerging. Sometimes sales teams tend to be more generic, such as "New Business Teams," whose job is to seek out new customers. Clearly, which customers or clusters of customers should get their own sales teams depends on many factors, not least of which is your company's strategic plan.

Question 5: What Are the Team Members' Roles and Responsibilities?

Let's relate this question to the information introduced in section I about roles and responsibilities in problem-solving meetings.

Think about how these roles apply to the management of the relationship with a customer (see figure 11.1). The customer is always treated as the problem owner. Remember, it's all about the customer. The salesperson is the facilitator, the one who manages the process of whatever happens between the company and the customer. (When we discuss joint sales calls in chapter 13, you'll see how the salesperson continues to facilitate interactions with customers even when senior managers come along on a call.) The resources to the salesperson, the members of the sales team, become the participants. And, of course, the salesperson can always act as a participant as well.

Figure 11.1 Roles and Responsibilities

All this is not to say that the salesperson necessarily takes on the facilitator role every time the sales team meets. Quite often the salesperson will bring an issue to the group and thus assume the role of problem owner for that discussion. In such cases, the salesperson is not in a position to facilitate the meeting effectively. That's why it is so important for all members of the sales team to learn basic facilitation skills: so different team members can facilitate different parts of the meeting when needed.

In my view, the salesperson is the key player on the sales team. Even if his or her manager is on the team, the salesperson is the glue that keeps it all together. Because salespeople are the liaison between the customers and the company, it's up to them to make the team concept work to serve their customers. Or, as I like to say, a salesperson is the customer's advocate internally and the company's advocate externally. I'll have more to say about this point in a few pages, when we talk about who runs the show.

Newsflash *The salesperson is the customer's advocate internally and the company's advocate externally.*

Question 6: How Do the Team Members Work Together Effectively?

To begin with, it's a good idea for a sales team to take the time to define itself by developing a mission statement and corresponding goals and objectives, just the way the organization does. At the organizational level, a mission statement defines the company's reason for being. In spite of the fact that so many look alike and the platitudes can be annoying, well-drafted mission statements let everybody inside and outside the company know precisely what the company stands for. The company's goals and objectives, both tactical and strategic, should be consistent with the mission of the organization.

Sales teams can profit from the same techniques. The members themselves should develop the mission statement. It shouldn't be loaded with clichés and overly optimistic statements ("We will be the best team in the history of the free world"), but it does need to explain what the team is there to do and how it plans to do it. It should certainly make reference to the customer, the company, and the product line, and it should be expressed in terms that lead to measurable goals. Here is one example I came across not too long ago, for a sales team that was dedicated to a single client:

> Our mission is to effectively utilize the collective expertise of the team members to provide outstanding customer satisfaction to ABC, Inc., such that we will maintain our current preferred vendor status. We will maintain or increase our current share of 28 percent of their business. We will constantly work together to develop the best possible products with the highest level of quality. We will consistently perform outstanding customer service and we will do everything possible to reach our profitability and volume targets. And we will work together in a collaborative way that will enable us to enjoy our work and each other.

Once the mission statement is nailed, the logical next step is to develop goals, objectives, and standards. A sales team is a unit just like a division or a department, and it needs the same tools for measuring its performance.

When the team gets to work, a large part of its effectiveness depends on having productive, efficient, and creative meetings. The next chapter is devoted to just this topic.

Although good meetings are important, there is certainly more to the sales team than just getting together on a regular basis. And with team members often situated in remote locations, it isn't always practical to conduct meetings to get things done. Hence, good communication systems and practices are essential.

Communication is always *the* biggest source of problems in any team. Team members need to use whatever means they have available to keep one another informed, for example, by using e-mail to share memos, letters, updates, proposals, and reports. If team members don't know what their colleagues are doing, they can run into big problems.

> **Newsflash** *Keep your colleagues on the sales team informed! Nobody likes surprises when they are part of a team working toward a common goal.*

To ensure that the right information gets to the right people at the right time, the team should establish a central focal point, a clearinghouse for keeping track of who is where on what specific project or task. Although support staff can assist with this essential function, I believe the focal point needs to be the person who is primarily responsible for the team's operation. Yes, you guessed it: I mean the sales professional.

Question 7: How Often Should Sales Teams Meet?
Well, at the risk of sounding glib: As often as they need to.

The truth of the matter is, some sales teams meet several times a week and it isn't often enough, while others meet once a quarter and it seems more than adequate. Meetings aren't always the answer. Whether communication happens by memo, fax, letter, e-mail, voicemail, or just shouting down the hall, what really matters is that everybody involved is on the same page and is getting the information they need to service the customer as effectively as possible.

Again, making sure this happens should ordinarily be the salesperson's responsibility. If the team is kept informed and advised, meetings need to be held only when face-to-face interactions are necessary or advisable. Certainly it's worthwhile to bring the team members together at least occasionally for the sake of charging their batteries and keeping their relationships strong.

Newsflash	*Meet as often as needed in order to do what needs to be done for the customer and to keep the team running smoothly.*

Question 8: Who Runs the Show?

This is a big question, and it can be a big bone of contention. My "default" answer is that it's the sales professional who is responsible for the team's functioning, which includes, among other things, calling meetings, developing agendas, deciding which problems to attack, and implementing the solutions that get developed. Why? Because sales teams are all about relationships with customers, and it's the salespeople who drive that process. Most people in most organizations will tell you that sales "owns" the customer relationship, a point of view I agree with. Obviously, when a team leader to whom the salespeople report manages the team, these responsibilities shift to that individual.

In taking on the responsibility of leadership, salespeople must, of course, be sensitive to the needs of the other players and use their process skills to garner support. Sales teams will find themselves in serious trouble if the sales function takes on a dictatorial or noninclusive approach. But if the sales professionals work with their resources and involve them in the decision-making process, things should work out very well. So if you're looking for an answer, by all means let the sales professionals run the show.

> **Newsflash** *To keep everyone on the sales team informed, establish a central focal point. The sales professional usually takes on this role.*

That having been said, let me share something I heard from John Ward, the charismatic chairman and CEO of American Express Bank. John made it quite clear to me that in his opinion, it's the *company* that owns the relationship, while "the relationship manager *manages* it." He explained that if everybody doesn't feel a sense of ownership, the company will not provide the great service customers demand. Point well taken. But even so, someone needs to have the primary responsibility for making things happen.

Here's another take on this issue, courtesy of Jim Schwarz, president and founder of Compass Management, a consulting firm that focuses, among other things, on sales effectiveness. Jim believes that the reason for using sales teams is "to most effectively deploy the information resources available" to give customers what they need. Jim differentiates *dedicated teams,* which tend to be permanent and use the same resources over and over and have limited flexibility and accountability, from *self-organizing teams,* which are flexible, dynamic, highly accountable, and when necessary, project-oriented. His bias is toward self-organizing teams, because he believes they can be "first to the customer with the best solutions beating the competition." In managing such teams, however, he talks about the role of the resource manager as a replacement for the traditional sales manager. The resource manager "focuses more on customer satisfaction than just hitting the numbers, understands the value of teamwork, and uses a more sophisticated set of skills to get things done."

Jim thinks of the "customer manager" (the salesperson) as the point person, while the team leader or resource manager's role is to "break down the barriers that prevent things from getting done." It's analogous to the manager and captain in sports. The manager may make the decisions. The captain plays a leadership role to get things done. I think that's a useful characterization, worthy of a Newsflash.

Question 9: Who Evaluates the Team's Performance?

Answer: The team members do. So do their managers. So do their customers. In a sense, so does everyone in the organization.

Newsflash	*Think of your sales manager as a "resource manager" who knows how to get things done through the use of the talent within the organization.*

OK, so we need to be more specific. *Of course* the team needs quantifiable measures of performance that are related to its mission, goals, and specific objectives. Performance measurement is a big subject, and for more information I suggest consulting a book dedicated to just this topic. For our purposes, the points to keep in mind are these:

- Include performance measures for both the team as a unit and for the players individually.

- Sales teams need to measure themselves and hold one another accountable. They can do so together in a meeting dedicated to this purpose, or they can do it informally. Peer coaching can be most effective. Either way, they need to step back every so often and do a little healthy self-analysis that includes the process of working together as well as the team's quantifiable performance.

- Don't let any performance measure come into play that does not involve the customer and the team's ability to provide outstanding customer satisfaction.

Question 10: How Are Sales Teams Compensated?

We hope, very generously.

All right, so that's not what you wanted to know. Compensation, especially as applies to teams, is another huge subject. Again, let me refer you to books that are devoted to this issue, while I make just a few key points.

1. The compensation issue has to be dealt with when you first set up sales teams. The team members need to understand precisely how their role on the team affects their compensation.

2. Like performance measures, compensation needs to take into account both individual and team performance. Many organizations are including teamwork as a key criterion when assessing individual performance.

3. Keep in mind what compensation is for, from an organizational perspective. Mathew Kissner, the creative and visionary president and CEO of Pitney Bowes Financial Services, puts it this way: "There are lots of reasons to have incentive programs, but above and beyond everything else, they serve as ways to communicate to people what you want them to do. Of course they also serve as ways to motivate, recognize, reward, and excite your people, but their primary objective should be to communicate precisely what you expect from them."

Key point: Design a compensation and incentive program for your sales teams that clarifies expectations as well as rewarding and recognizing excellent performance.

So there you have it: the who, what, when, why, and how of sales teams. Of course, there's a bit more to be said about the "how" of making sales teams efficient, productive, and successful. That's what the next two chapters are about. Don't even consider touching that dial. There's lots of good stuff coming up.

MEMO TO MANAGEMENT

There is no one way to implement sales teams. The "right" way depends on your business, your industry, your company, your culture, and your people. A manufacturing company will have different kinds of sales teams than a financial services company, whose teams will in no way resemble those within a packaged goods company. In a sense, the way to use this chapter is to take the ten questions we've asked and write your own answers to them. Create a spec for sales teams that fits the nature, size, contours, and talents of your organization.

Give careful thought to the way you put sales teams together. Pay attention to the dicey subject of who plays what role and who is in charge. Encourage the sales team to develop its own mission statement. Figure out ways to measure performance. Be sure to include variables like teamwork, utilization of resources, and team commitment in your performance appraisals and compensation programs.

Once sales teams are up and running, demonstrate both your support and your expectations. Invite yourself to team meetings. Monitor how the team members conduct those meetings, and give them feedback at the conclusion. Publicize success stories. Feature articles about your sales teams in company periodicals. Show through your actions that you believe in the concept of the sales team and are committed to helping your teams succeed. Who knows? You might even make Coach of the Year.

CHAPTER 12

What, Another Meeting?
Count Me In!

If we're going to have sales teams, we're going to have sales-team meetings. As I noted in an earlier chapter, most people say that most of the time they spend in meetings isn't productive. Worse, meetings too often are about as much fun as root canals. I've heard words like *agonizing*, *excruciating*, and *debilitating* used to describe what it is like to sit in some meetings. And those were some of the nicer descriptions.

The irony is that meetings do not have to be disappointing time wasters. Meetings can be terrific experiences. They can be productive. They can accomplish their objectives. They can yield creative and exciting ideas. And they can even be fun.

The secret? Do a good job of managing both *content* and *process*. This chapter will give you some ideas for how to do that.

Planning a Sales-Team Meeting

Productive meetings begin with good planning. And good planning accounts for all the essentials: Why are we meeting? When and where? Who should be there? What is the agenda?

Why Are We Meeting, Anyhow?

Is there anything worse than having to sit in a meeting without know-ing why you're there or what the meeting is supposed to accomplish? Step 1 in planning, then, is to establish a clear goal for the meeting.

Meetings are typically called for one or more of the following reasons:

1. To obtain information
2. To dispense information
3. To make decisions
4. To solve problems

Sales teams meet for all four of these reasons all the time. What you want to be clear about is *which* of these purposes is to be served by *this* particular meeting. If the main purpose is to share information and discuss a couple of issues, then apportion the time accordingly and don't get sidetracked into two hours of problem solving that no one cleared their schedule for. People don't like being sandbagged. If the discussion uncovers a problem to be solved, get the team to agree to another session, or at the very least get everyone's consent to change the agenda. Remember, though, people will come better prepared if they know ahead of time what the meeting is about and what results it is supposed to produce.

Consider, too, whether a meeting is the best way to accomplish whatever needs doing. Meetings consume many valuable person-hours. Are there more efficient ways of achieving your objective, espe-cially if the purpose is simply to gather or dispense information? Of course, there is value in satisfying people's need to spend time with oth-ers and to bond as a team. But chances are they'll get that opportunity simply by meeting when there is real work for the team to do together.

When and Where?

Coordinating the schedules of a number of busy people is always a challenge. Teams should decide for themselves the best time and day of the week to get together. Try to be sensitive to the team members' needs, including travel schedules for the out-of-towners. As you probably know, morning meetings tend to be more productive than afternoon meetings. Avoid, if you can, scheduling meetings for right after lunch. If it's an all-day meeting, do something interactive after lunch to keep everyone involved. If you invite guests, put them on the agenda early so they don't sit there all day worrying about their presentations. The point is, think these things through as part of your attention to creating a productive process.

Answering the "where" question is not always as simple as it looks. Arrange for a comfortable location that accommodates all the purposes of the meeting. Don't forget to make sure *beforehand* that the site has whatever audiovisual support you'll require, whether it's flip charts, a white board, a VCR, or an LCD projector. Account for all the details: pads to write on, marking pens with ink in them, a spare light bulb for the overhead projector, access to an Internet hookup, whatever. If you're in charge, get to the site ahead of time so you can check that everything is there and correct any last-minute problems. Otherwise, you're risking down time, not to mention disgruntled participants.

If your budget allows, consider varying your meeting sites: at headquarters, at the plant, at the R&D facility, at a field office. Meeting at different locations gives team members the opportunity to learn about various parts of the organization and to get to know people from a variety of functions (and for the rest of the organization to learn about the team). Simply by varying the locations you can encourage a feeling of camaraderie and cultivate a mentality of organization-wide selling.

Who Should Be There?

In planning a meeting, be respectful of people's time. Don't insist that every team member attend every single meeting. Work out the agenda in advance, and let those team members whose presence isn't critical decide for themselves whether to attend.

At the same time, be sure to look beyond just the members of the team. Group cohesiveness is a fine thing, but don't let a sales team become a clique. Ideally, the team is continually reaching out to different parts of the organization for ideas and perspectives. One way to accomplish that is to invite non–team members to your meetings. I'll say more about that in a moment.

What Is the Agenda?

Among the most frequently voiced complaints about meetings is that there was no agenda, or that the agenda wasn't thought through carefully, or that it wasn't actually adhered to. Don't let this happen to your sales-team meetings. Plan the agenda carefully, based on what you want the meeting to accomplish. Be sure to give people a chance to prepare by sharing the agenda at least a week in advance.

> **Newsflash**   *Think long and hard about the agenda for every sales-team meeting and distribute it to all concerned at least a week in advance.*

Although the content of the agenda obviously depends on the things the team needs to accomplish, consider making some items a standard part of the agenda for nearly every sales-team meeting. You can even create an agenda template that includes each of these items so that whoever plans the meeting is sure to include them when appropriate. I suggest the following items as standard: The standard items I have in mind are these:

- A warm-up exercise
- Updates: The state of the business and reports from each team member
- A specific customer-related item or issue to problem-solve
- A customer-related issue to discuss
- A guest from outside the team with a topic of interest
- A training or team-building exercise

- Open time for discussion of relevant issues
- Team self-assessment

Warm-up exercise. Any meeting is more effective if you begin by establishing the climate through a warm-up exercise. A warm-up exercise simply involves letting each participant respond to a question you've selected. If you like, you can use a customer-related warm-up to set the tone for the meeting.

Here are several examples of questions you can ask each team member to respond in order to get the meeting off to a good start (usually asking just one is enough):

- What have you done for your customer(s) since the last meeting?
- What have you learned about your customer(s) since the last meeting?
- How has a member of the team or someone else in the organization helped you deal with a customer situation?
- What do you like about your customer(s)?
- What is a frustration you're currently experiencing with your customer(s)?

Updates. Make it standard practice to review the state of business with the customer or customers, or within the market segment. That includes taking a hard look at the numbers and comparing them with last year's results and this year's goals.

Then give each team member the opportunity to briefly update everyone else on his or her function, whether it's distribution, R&D, marketing, merchandising, credit, category management, or any other function represented on the team. Not only will this keep everybody informed, but it will force the team members to plan for the meeting and increase the chances that everyone will show up.

A customer-related item to problem-solve. I recommend arranging in advance for at least one team member to bring a specific customer-related problem to each meeting. That person assumes the role of problem owner for this part of the meeting, while the rest of the group works to help him or her find workable solutions to the problem. The nature of the problem to be solved may help you determine who from outside the sales team needs to attend the meeting.

A customer-related issue to discuss. It would be a real miss if every sales-team meeting did not address at least one customer-related issue. You can solicit proposals for issues that need addressing, and let the "sponsor" of a particular issue assume the role of problem owner for this discussion. Here are some examples of the kinds of issues to consider, along with the functions that might sponsor them:

- Ways to enhance or deepen the relationship (Sales)
- Ways to improve delivery of goods shipped (Distribution)
- New product concepts (R&D)
- Ways of getting customers to give us more lead time (Customer Service)
- Ways to improve our product quality (Manufacturing)
- Ways to keep costs down (Product Management)
- Co-branding opportunities (Marketing)
- Ways to reduce the time required for customers to pay their bills (Guess who?)

Too often problems sit and stagnate in functional silos. Put the team to work at every meeting to address a customer-related issue, and invite resources from elsewhere in the organization to help when needed. Watch what the group can do. You'll be amazed by what they come up with.

A guest from outside the team. If you want to instill an organization-wide sales approach, make it an explicit responsibility of the sales team to identify ways of tapping into organizational resources. One concrete way to do that is to set aside time in sales-team meetings to hear from people from outside the team.

As a basic guideline, I recommend inviting at least one non–team member to each meeting and devoting a specific agenda item to something that concerns that person. To take this idea a step further, get a list of all the functions within the organization and try to invite a representative from each function to at least one team meeting each year. At a minimum, the team is likely to learn something new, while people from other functions will learn more about the team and about their customers. That's a good way to help build a customer-centered consciousness throughout the organization.

A training or team-building exercise. You've probably heard some talk about the need for continual learning in today's world. That certainly holds true for business. Just think of all the skills we've talked about in this book: they take training and practice to master. The training never really stops, partly because new people join the team and partly because everybody needs a refresher course once in a while. Then there are all the new products, services, and procedures your company comes up with, as well as nuts-and-bolts training on things like new technology you want your people to use.

Obviously, time is an issue, and sometimes you'll want to schedule sessions purely for training purposes. But remember, too, that learning can be fun, as well as informative, and building in some new learning as part of your meeting agendas can help keep everybody fresh and involved.

Open time for discussion of relevant issues. When you can, allot some time to open up the floor for broader questions. Encourage team members to note issues the team can profitably explore and bring them to the meeting. They might include items such as these:

- What distribution issues do we need to anticipate?

- How can we capitalize more on our organizational resources?

- How do we deal with a specific market condition?

Team self-assessment. At least once or twice a year, leave ample time on your agenda for some self-assessment work. Like regular tune-ups and oil changes for the family wheels, a little preventive maintenance can go a long way in keeping your team's engine running smoothly.

One approach I find useful in focusing self-assessment discussions is the "Keep/Stop/Start" exercise. This technique permits team members to assess the team's performance in a controlled, low-risk way. Here's how it works.

1. Choose a general task statement that bears on team performance: how the team is working together, customer satisfaction, sales performance, the success the team has had in applying organization-wide selling principles, and so on. For example: Determine ways for us to improve our responsiveness to customer complaints.

2. Break the team into subgroups of two or three people. Ask each subgroup to address the task by generating three lists: the "keep" list, the "stop" list, and the "start" list. The "keeps" are the things that the team is already doing that members feel they should continue to do, the "stops" are the ones they feel they should stop doing because they aren't helping the team reach its potential, and the "starts" are new things to try. All three lists need to relate to the general task statement.

3. Have each subgroup select the items on their lists that they believe are most significant.

4. Have a spokesperson from each group share their results with the entire team. Record all the items on flip charts.

5. Ask the group to vote on which items they think are the most important.

6. Take the top two or three items and turn them into specific task statements. For example, a "stop" like, "Stop submitting the quality control reports so late that they aren't helpful" can be transformed into "Determine ways to ensure that we get the quality control reports on time so we can use them effectively."

7. Have the group problem-solve to resolve the issue that is highlighted by the task statement. Alternatively, the team can either schedule such a discussion for a subsequent meeting or assign the items to groups or individuals to address and report back on at the next meeting.

Apart from their value in improving the team's performance, exercises like this one can be most helpful in the development of a team. They help get issues on the table and prevent gripe sessions. The result is enhanced teamwork, better cooperation, and a happier and more committed team.

> **Newsflash** *When members of a sales team do self-analysis on a regular basis, they prevent little issues from becoming big ones, and they usually figure out ways to work together effectively.*

Conducting Team Meetings

Now we come to a pure process issue: how to conduct team meetings effectively. Remember, it's usually the "how" and not the "what" that gets us in trouble. How will you run the meeting? How much time will you allocate to each agenda item? Who will facilitate? How will you make guests feel welcome? How do you make sure you adhere to the agenda? How do you manage potential conflicts? These and many other questions need to be asked ahead of time by whoever is responsible for planning the meeting.

A key issue is facilitation. Every sales-team meeting should be facilitated. Someone needs to be attending to process, watching the clock, and generally keeping the meeting on track. As you can probably testify from your own experience, lack of effective facilitation accounts for a big part of the discomfort and boredom people associate with meetings.

Up front, make sure everyone on the team learns enough about facilitation to be able to assume that role when necessary. That does not mean that everyone will be equally good at facilitating or that everyone will want to do it, or even should. It does mean that if you instill this skill set among the members of the team, you'll always have someone there who can take on the role. Plus, you'll find that often team members will act as "unofficial" facilitators, making good process interventions even when they're not assigned to the role.

In the context of sales teams, the pure facilitator role, where the person facilitating stays completely out of the content issues, may not be applicable much of the time. The person who runs the meeting—the sales professional or team leader—can do much of the facilitating. You can always designate a facilitator when the discussion seems to require it—for example, for a focused problem-solving session. But for the most part, informal facilitation is more than adequate.

Newsflash   *Pure "content-free" facilitation is not required all the time in sales-team meetings. But some kind of facilitation all the time should become the norm.*

Remember, too, that facilitation exists to serve the process. Sometimes the best facilitation is practically invisible. The facilitator should step in only when it's necessary to intervene in the process. If a group is doing good work, it would be silly for the facilitator to do anything but let them go at it.

You may want to assign other roles, such as scribe or time-keeper, for the entire meeting or a specific part of it. When the meeting becomes a problem-solving session, use the sequence described in section I of this book. Sometimes an unexpected issue that is perfect for the problem-solving process will come up. When that happens, use the skills you've learned. Call a time-out and do all the things the sequence calls for: Position the discussion, have the problem owner give the background, brainstorm ideas, and then let the person who raised the issue select which idea to develop. Ideally, the group will help transform the selected idea into a solution; in this case make sure there's an action plan attached. If not, determine what needs to be done to get the idea to the next level. Don't let a problem-solving discussion end without agreed-upon next steps. There are few things more frustrating than having lots of good issues and ideas tossed around in meetings without any follow-up.

Enlist the energies of your team members in this way, and you'll get some other payoffs as well. There are lots of ways to do team building, for example, but one of the best is to get team members to solve one another's problems. Not only does real work get done, but the team will grow stronger in the process.

> **Newsflash**   *Looking for a way to go about team building? Ask the members of the team to participate in constructive problem-solving sessions. You'll get not only great solutions, but a stronger team in the bargain.*

As a last word on sales-team meetings, let me reiterate that no two organizations or sales teams are exactly alike. Think of this chapter as a menu, and try some things that fit your situation. However you go about it, though, be sensitive to the importance of well-run, enjoyable meetings in keeping your sales team efficient, motivated, and productive. It's worth the effort.

MEMO TO MANAGEMENT

Sales-team meetings should belong to the teams themselves. Your role as a manager is one of providing support and coaching. You can play a helpful role in the planning, but resist the temptation to take over the meetings themselves. Let the sales professional or the team leader fill that role. Keep an eye on process, and if you have suggestions, make them known after the meeting. Use your coaching skills to reinforce what is working well and to offer suggestions about how to improve what isn't.

If you're not a member of the sales team, get yourself invited to meetings every now and again. If you are a power figure within the company, you will flatter the team by asking if you can attend one of their meetings, or better yet, give a presentation about some global issue they need to think about.

Don't let sales teams work in secrecy or become cliques. Encourage the teams to open up their meetings to resources from throughout the organization. Make their accomplishments public knowledge. Constantly remind the team members that organization-wide selling starts with the sales professional, moves next to the sales team, and eventually involves everyone in the organization. Everyone!

CHAPTER 13

The Team Hits the Field: Making Joint Sales Calls

The joint (or team) sales call presents an organization with an outstanding opportunity to differentiate itself from its competitors. Although there are many kinds of sales calls for which additional resources would be superfluous, many sales calls would be greatly enhanced if more people from the selling company participate. In fact, the only reason I accept for *not* making more team calls is that the cost can often be prohibitive. This chapter on making team sales calls effective is for anyone who may be called upon to take part in them.

> **Newsflash**   *The majority of sales calls would be more effective if members of the sales team and other resources from the company participated.*

Why Make Team Sales Calls?

At this point, I hope you don't need much convincing about the value of team sales calls. The obvious benefits include the following:

- By having people from different functional areas present, you make more expertise available to the customer.

- You multiply that most vital of resources, ears. Different people will hear different things.

- You pick up on more needs.

- You show that you care.

- You put on a better show.

- You're able to resolve issues in a more thoughtful and authoritative way.

- You'll do a better job debriefing the meeting.

- You'll prove to senior management that you really were working.

Sorry about the last one. Sometimes I just can't seem to avoid adding something silly to these lists. It's a personality flaw I have learned to live with, much to the dismay of my wife, partner, and various friends.

There are also reasons to do joint calls that are less obvious but just as compelling.

First, for your organization to become a customer-driven selling machine, your people need to know what a sales call looks like, what sales professionals do, and how they behave when they're with customers.

Second, the chance to visit with customers can have a major impact on people who don't ordinarily have this opportunity. Whether they are from support functions, credit, legal, contracts, finance, manufacturing, or even human resources, getting out to see how customers think can change the way they feel and behave when they're dealing with customer-related issues.

Third, remember that involvement enhances commitment. In organization-wide selling, everybody needs to feel a sense of ownership in the customer relationship. Participating in team sales calls will enable non-salespeople to get to know customers face to face and to feel a sense of involvement in the company's relationship with them. As a result, they will be more committed to providing outstanding customer service and satisfaction.

Fourth, joint sales calls allow everyone involved to do some coaching after the meeting. Sales managers know that coaching their people is part of their job description. But coaching doesn't happen enough among people who have no direct reporting relationship. Peer coaching can be very powerful. If all the parties involved look back at the call and talk about what went well and what they could have done differently, everyone can learn from the experience. And if they listen to each other they will probably be that much more effective next time.

> **Newsflash** *There are many reasons to involve people from different functions in team sales calls. Joint calls can produce better customer service both directly and indirectly while enhancing your efforts to cultivate an organization-wide approach to selling.*

One More Time: Can You Say "Facilitation"?

There are four phases of the team sales call: planning, rehearsing, conducting the meeting itself, and debriefing. The sales professional plays the lead role in all four phases, in keeping with his or her responsibility to manage and facilitate the relationship with the customer.

Although in a macro sense the salesperson facilitates the entire interaction, that doesn't mean he or she acts as the facilitator in every phase. As we've seen, during the sales call itself, the customer is treated as the problem owner, the resources are participants, and the salesperson acts as both facilitator and participant. But during

the planning, rehearsing, and debriefing phases, the sales professional becomes the *problem owner*. In advance of the call, the salesperson calls a planning meeting, where he or she briefs the team
on the background, leads the discussion of how the call should go,
and conducts any problem-solving of the customer's issues. The
bottom line is to make sure everyone understands precisely what is
expected of them. Although the salesperson may do double duty
by facilitating the planning session, his or her primary role is to
focus on the content of the discussion. The other team members
are resources who can contribute to the planning effort.

Similar ideas apply to rehearsing the call as well as to debriefing,
in which the discussion centers on how the call went, what the next
steps are, and how to do better in the future. This shift in roles during the different phases makes sense if you remember that *externally*
the salesperson is the company's advocate to the customer (and therefore the facilitator), while *internally* the salesperson is the customer's
advocate to the company (and therefore the problem owner).

> **Newsflash**   *In planning, rehearsing, and debriefing team sales calls,
> the salesperson's primary role is that of problem owner,
> though the salesperson may also facilitate. In conduct-
> ing the call, the salesperson is both facilitator and partic-
> ipant. In all phases, the other team members assume the
> role of participants.*

With these ideas about roles and responsibilities in mind, let's
look at each of the four major phases involved in making team calls.

Planning the Team Sales Call

Good planning for team sales calls attends to the same kinds of
issues as team meetings: why the meeting is being held, who will
be involved, when and where it will take place, what process to
use, and what will be on the agenda.

Why Are We Having This Meeting with These People?

When it comes to team sales calls, the "why" question includes both the specific objective of the call and the reason for involving other team members in it. Remember the customer's perspective: They will expect that anyone who walks into their office has a good reason to be there, and moreover one that serves *them*. So be sure you have a good, customer-centered reason for making the call a *team* call.

That having been said, keep in mind all the ways that team members can be helpful in the various phases of the selling sequence discussed in section II. Perhaps the most common use of the sales team is in the presenting (making recommendations) phase, but the team can also help establish the relationship, determine the customer's needs, resolve issues, and so forth.

So, the salesperson formulates the objectives of the meeting, determines whether it makes sense to involve other members of the team, and, if so, makes sure everyone involved understands the specific objectives of the meeting. Naturally, the salesperson will make all this clear to the customer as part of setting the climate and confirming the agenda during the call itself.

Who Should Be There?

I've just alluded to part of the answer to this question. The salesperson should involve those people who can help make the call a better meeting, whether through their technical expertise or their experience or their perspective or whatever else they bring to the table. What isn't a good idea is to involve people only because it would be fun for them, or for the salesperson, if they came along. Sales managers often go on joint calls, and I encourage them to do so—but they, too, should have a role to play as participants, not just observers. (I'll say more about this point in this chapter's Memo to Management.)

Once the participants have been selected, they need to plan carefully who is going to do what. We'll come back to that point when we discuss the conduct of the meeting itself. Just be sure that everybody involved understands his or her role *before* you arrive at the customer's doorstep.

There's a second part to the "Who" question, however: the customer's side. Unless you're planning a six-on-one meeting, the salesperson should try to establish who will attend on the customer side. Then he or she should let the others participating know who they will be seeing, what those people's jobs are, and what role each person plays in the decision-making process. It helps to know how the people who will attend on the customer side feel about your organization and whether they are supporters or adversaries. Of course, the salesperson won't always know all of this ahead of time, but the more the team members know in advance, the better prepared they'll be to make useful contributions.

Where and When Are We Meeting?

The "where" and "when" of sales calls are usually straightforward logistical questions, but don't overlook the details in your planning. The salesperson should make sure that everyone knows where they need to be and arrange for a conference room or other facility that can comfortably accommodate all the attendees and whatever equipment is required. As simple as this matter is, too often when a bunch of people show up at the customer's office, valuable time is lost trying to locate an appropriate meeting space or something vital like a flip chart or an extension cord. In such cases it's not just the team's time that is being wasted. More important, it's the customer's. Nail the details ahead of time.

As to when the meeting will be held, usually, of course, that's driven by the customer. But salespeople should do what they can to get a favorable time (mornings if you can, but not on Mondays; afternoons if you must, but not on Fridays). The salesperson also needs to make whatever arrangements are required to ensure that *everybody* from your side is there on time, or, preferably, fifteen minutes early. Show your customers the respect they deserve and expect. If somebody on the customer's side has to be late for the meeting, roll with it. But don't let one of your team members be the culprit who disrupts the schedule or forces you to backtrack once the meeting is under way.

What Is the Agenda?

The answer to this question represents the content of the meeting. It has at least five key components (and possibly more, depending on the situation):

1. What are the specific objectives for the meeting?
2. What questions do we need to ask?
3. What are we there to present? (if applicable)
4. What objections do we need to anticipate?
5. What unexpected idea will we bring to this meeting?

I've already emphasized having clear objectives for each and every call and making sure everyone involved knows what they are. With the objectives in hand, it always makes sense to think about the questions the team wants to ask customers. Don't forget how helpful other team members can be in asking questions that the salesperson is reluctant to ask or hasn't thought of asking. Spend some time as a group working out your questions and who will ask them. If the objective of the call is to make recommendations (that is, present), make sure everyone knows who will do what.

> **Newsflash** *When planning a team sales call, be sure to answer the five vital "what" questions to create a solid agenda that everyone understands.*

Similarly, the team will be better prepared to resolve issues if you anticipate objections prior to the meeting. The salesperson should talk with the rest of the team about the objections that may come up. Determine how you will use the process. Give some serious thought as to how you will acknowledge, reframe, and address those issues, and who can help with each step.

Finally, think about unsolicited ideas the team can offer to surprise and delight the customer. Ideally, you've already spent time coming up with ideas in your ongoing team discussions of customer needs. Before the call, spend some time deciding how you will get permission to offer each idea and how you will present it.

Rehearsing the Call

Rehearse the call beforehand? You bet. It always surprises me how reluctant many salespeople are to rehearse their sales calls, even their team calls. That is a big mistake, even if rehearsing seems time consuming and somehow not "cool." Actors and actresses do it. Athletes do it. Presidents do it. The Blue Angels do it. But here is our sales team, about to go after a gazillion-dollar deal, and they don't put the time in to rehearse the intricate interaction they're about to have with customers. I just don't get it.

One of my clients laments that his people have gotten into the habit of what he calls "elevator planning." He explained it this way: "They plan their calls in the elevator on the way to a customer's office. What a missed opportunity!" I hope his comment never applies to your team. That elevator only goes one way, and it isn't up.

Conducting sales calls is like wallpapering a bathroom. The hard part is the prep work. Once the room is cleaned out and prepared, and the paper is cut, putting up the wallpaper is relatively easy. So do the preparation work, including rehearsal—unless of course, your goal is to look like Laurel and Hardy wallpapering a bathroom. In that case, don't bother.

Conducting a Team Sales Call

Here we are, back at process again. How will you make the meeting productive and enjoyable? How do you involve everybody?

How do you ensure that the customers get what they want from the session? How do you handle handing off parts of the meeting to each other? How do you make sure the salesperson stays in control? How do you deal with the unexpected? Just making sure that you ask yourself questions like these, and as many others as occur to you, is a big step toward a more successful meeting.

In a team sales call, everyone needs to know who does what. In my view, there are three things that only the salesperson does; everything else can be shared by all. Those three salesperson-only responsibilities are

1. Confirming the agenda

2. Transitioning from one phase to the next

3. Reaching closure, whether that means closing the sale or getting the customer's commitment to next steps

The person who sets or confirms the agenda also orchestrates the meeting, which includes making the transition from one phase to the next. This, of course, is the facilitation role. If anyone but the salesperson assumes this responsibility, attention will shift to the person who took over, and the salesperson will lose control of the process. That's not what you want to have happen.

You learned earlier how to move from one phase of the problem-solving selling sequence to another in a seamless way. A quick review:

- *Preparing the customer for questions* moves you from Positioning to Situation Analysis.

- *Restating the customer's needs* moves you from Situation Analysis to Offering Recommendations.

- *Asking for feedback* moves you from Offering Recommendations to Resolving Issues.

- *Inviting other objections* moves you from Resolving Issues to Reaching Closure.

Kate Reilly draws an analogy between these steps and using the clutch in a standard-shift automobile. Just as working the clutch ensures that you move from one gear to another smoothly, so do these statements allow you to move from one part of the sales sequence to another while staying in control. Again, this work of facilitation belongs to the salesperson. As the one closest to the relationship, it is up to him or her to decide when it makes sense to move from one phase to the next.

As for closing, I've already emphasized that this job belongs to the salesperson. That's true whether you're reaching an interim close (small "c") or sealing the deal (big "C").

The rest of the team, and any other participating resources, can and should play a role in every other phase of the call. Everybody who comes along can help put customers at ease, ask thoughtful questions, listen intently for needs, assist in making presentations or recommendations, and help with resolving issues. Just make sure that everyone knows what they will be asked to do—and what they *aren't* there to do. What they aren't there to do is watch. They are there to participate.

> **Newsflash**   *A team sales call involves some intricate cooperation and understanding of roles. Make sure everyone involved knows exactly what roles they will play in the meeting.*

OK, so everyone's prepped and understands what to do and what to leave to the salesperson. Now you're there, face to face with your customers. How do you make it a terrific meeting? Or better said, what does the salesperson have to do to make sure that the customer is impressed with the quality of the meeting?

It all begins with positioning. As I mentioned in chapter 6, all the participants on the customer side should introduce themselves, explain their roles in the organization, and say what they want to get out of the meeting. Similarly, the team members introduce them-selves. The salesperson shouldn't do this for them: let customers hear the team members' voices, rather than leaving them sitting there nod-ding and smiling and looking foolish, as if they weren't capable of introducing themselves. But the salesperson has every reason to follow a team member's self-introduction by bragging a bit: "I'm delighted that Jack could join us today. He has twelve years of experience deal-ing with just the kinds of issues we'll be talking about today."

If the purpose of the call is to give a presentation (that is, make recommendations), the salesperson begins by reviewing the cus-tomer's needs. It can be very useful to have these ready on a slide, overhead, or handout. The salesperson then asks whether everyone there agrees with his or her perception of the needs and makes changes if necessary.

As you segue to the presentation, the salesperson should be sure to explain why Jack or Jennifer is going to discuss how a particular recommendation will help. They, in turn, should take great pains to relate the recommendation to the previously highlighted need. If necessary, the salesperson should step in to make the connection. The same point applies to specific benefits. If one or another presen-ter doesn't nail them, the salesperson can help out as needed.

When the presentation is done, the salesperson "works the clutch" by asking for feedback as the first step in inviting and resolv-ing issues. If you've done your homework as a team, you'll be ready to respond to many objections. If one or more come up that the team didn't anticipate, the salesperson will need to be light on his or her feet and call on team members to help out as appropriate.

Whenever an objection has been resolved, the salesperson should ask for others. Keep moving forward until you either close the sale, which rarely happens in formal presentations, or get com-mitment to specific next steps. That again is the salesperson's job.

A word to the salesperson-facilitator: Give your team members a warning before you call on them to speak. They may not be ready, or worse, they may not be paying 100 percent attention. (Remember what we said about how listening deteriorates over time?) Simply use a statement like, "I'm going to ask Marvin to expound on that in just a minute, but before I do, let me say this. . . ." If Marvin is in la-la land, the sound of his name will wake him up, and he'll have a few seconds to get his act together.

> **Newsflash**   *It always helps for the salesperson to give his or her resources a little warning before calling on them just in case they have let their minds drift a bit.*

Remember, as the facilitator, the salesperson is the orchestra leader, the quarterback, the traffic cop, the point guard. You can choose your metaphor. Just be sure to use those facilitation skills if you want a meeting that will delight your customers.

Debriefing

This last phase is one that's easy to overlook. Probably a lot of joint calls are followed with what we might call "elevator debriefing." You can do better than that.

Taking the time to review what happened in each joint call is a necessary part of learning how to be more effective as a team. Whether you use the "Keep/Stop/Start" model introduced in chapter 12 or just conduct a balanced assessment, be sure to discuss all aspects of the meeting, attending to both its content and its process. Keep track of what you learn, and be sure to share the lessons with anyone on the team who isn't at the debriefing session.

Don't let too much time pass before you debrief the meeting. You can do it immediately afterward or within a day or two. If you let too much time pass, you will forget some key points. Plan your debriefing session when you plan for the meeting with the customer.

In addition to a formal debriefing, recognize the value of giving one another feedback after any joint call. Implementing sales teams and organization-wide selling is a journey. It takes effort on everyone's part, and there will be missteps as well as successes along the way. To make it work, you need to give each other feedback in a balanced, straightforward, and nonthreatening way.

> **Newsflash**   *Be sure to debrief and give each other feedback after team sales calls! You'll only learn and improve from the experience.*

Now that we've discussed all the phases of the team sales call, it's time for me to work the clutch again. How's this for a segue? We began this exploration of organization-wide selling by exploring selling as problem solving (section I). Next, we explored the role of the salesperson and the sales team in putting organization-wide selling across to the customer (section II). We've just concluded a closer look at sales teams and how they function both internally and externally (section III). So, following our model of how organization-wide selling begins with the salesperson and radiates out from there, we have only one step left. It's time to talk about making it happen at every level of the organization. Section IV is coming right up.

MEMO TO MANAGEMENT

The team sales call can be a great way to demonstrate just how customer-centered your company is and how professional your people are. It can also be a great way to look bad in front of the customer. Do what you can to ensure that team sales calls work *for* you, not *against* you.

To begin with, don't just encourage your people to make joint calls as a wonderful way to implement organization-wide selling and show customers you care. Practice what you preach. Make joint sales calls with your people. All the time. Once again, become that excellent role model you know you have to be. Many organizations today are boasting about how much time their senior managers, all the way up to the CEO, are spending with customers. If your peer at a competitor is visiting your customers and you aren't, what do you think your customers are thinking? How does it make you look? The question answers itself.

You can also make sure that the team plans and rehearses its calls. When you're involved in the planning process, ask those "W" questions: why, who, when, where, and what. Or, if you're not involved in the planning, check to make sure they've been covered. If you're going to be part of the call, make sure you know what the call is supposed to accomplish and what your role is.

Whenever I travel with one of my people, I always ask what the objectives are for each meeting. If I cannot get a good answer, then I need to know why they have asked me to join them, and why they are taking the risk of wasting the customer's time. A sales call without specific objectives is as unacceptable as any meeting without a purpose or an agenda.

When you're on a team call, or simply a joint call with one of your people, let the salesperson run the meeting. You'll disempower your people if you take over, and you'll give customers the impression that you don't trust your salespeople. The result could be that the customer starts calling you instead of the salesperson when a problem comes up. Bad form.

But *do* participate! I heard a story recently about a salesperson whose boss came along on a joint call and ended up doing more harm than good. The manager shook hands when he came in and said good-bye when he left and did nothing else. The next day, the customer called the salesperson and said: "Next time you bring your manager and he doesn't want to say anything, leave him home. I'll be damned if I'm going to be a guinea pig for your boss to assess your selling skills on my time." Need I say more? If you're at the *customer's* meeting, then be part of it. Just don't take over.

Finally, make sure the team debriefs after every meeting with a customer, and be part of the debriefing. When you go on a call, be sure to provide feedback, particularly to the salesperson. Don't try to do that between customer visits, which can distract the salesperson, unless there's something urgent you simply must get across before the next call. But at the end of the day, or the next day, be sure to work in a coaching session. Attend to both content and process. Reinforce the good things as well as suggesting how to improve areas that need it.

Keep driving the message home: Selling is a team sport. Make sure your teams do what all championship teams do: prepare, practice, and learn to continually improve. Focus on the goal of delivering the best customer satisfaction possible, not on individuals' shortcomings. Make it clear that the point of the game isn't to win individual trophies. It's to gain wins for the team, for the organization, and, most of all, for your customers.

Making Organization-Wide
Selling a Reality

CHAPTER 14

It's All About Culture

By now you should have a detailed picture of how salespeople and sales teams can use problem-solving selling to forge value-adding partnerships with customers. You've learned about the specific skills involved in transforming selling situations into problem-solving opportunities and harnessing the power of sales teams to enhance customer service and satisfaction. Yet there's still one missing piece. A big one.

All the skills and practices we've discussed can't be put into play in isolation. It isn't just the good people in the sales organization who need to adopt a new approach to what they do. Everything we've talked about presumes that the *entire organization* is committed to the problem-solving, customer-centered, organization-wide selling approach. If that commitment is lacking, salespeople and sales teams will run into one roadblock after another. Instead of getting eager cooperation when they reach out to people in other functional areas, they'll get excuses about why something that needs doing in order to address customers' issues creatively and effectively just can't be done.

In short, implementing organization-wide selling isn't just a question of having the right people with the right skills on your sales teams. It's a way of life. It only works if it becomes an integral part of the way people throughout the company do business, every day.

That isn't something that happens overnight. It's the result of lots of effort and lots of learning by lots of people. Training alone won't do it. Inspirational messages alone won't do it. Even modeling the behaviors won't do it. It's a matter of changing the organizational culture.

Cultural change starts at the top and cascades down. That's why this chapter is addressed primarily to managers and executives. The people in the sales organization can play a leadership role by advocating for customer-driven, organization-wide selling, explaining why it's needed and how it will help the company stand out from competitors. In a sense, agitating for cultural change is an extension of being the customer's advocate within the organization. But without direction and support from all levels of management across the breadth of the company, organization-wide selling won't become a reality. So, you can consider this entire chapter a long "Memo to Management."

The topic of how to change an organizational culture is, of course, a huge subject, worthy of a book in itself. I won't insult your intelligence by pretending to supply all the answers here. But I do want to touch on the fundamentals of a cultural change effort as they apply to implementing organization-wide selling.

Culture = Attitudes + Beliefs + Behaviors

Ultimately, making organization-wide selling a way of life means that everybody in the company will *behave* in new ways. But most people in the training business will tell you that to change behaviors, you first have to change attitudes and beliefs. And that isn't easy.

Newsflash   *To change cultures, you need to change attitudes, then beliefs, and finally behaviors. Anyone who has been through such an effort will tell you that it is no easy task.*

One of the prime enemies of efforts to change organizational cultures is the skepticism and even cynicism that people develop once they've been in any organization for any length of time. It's inevitable: There have just been too many new initiatives that started with great fanfare and then petered out, too many grand vision statements that became inoperative before they came close to being realized, too many lofty objectives that never seemed to be translated into new ways of acting, even among the company's leaders. People in organizations acquire skepticism like whales acquire barnacles.

Cutting through layers of skepticism takes persistent effort. Once again, it has to start at the top. The top means the president and CEO, along with the other senior leaders in the company. If the people who run the company don't display a commitment to transforming the organization into a customer-centered, problem-solving selling machine, then the people at ground level certainly aren't going to. And if leaders don't back up their stated commitment with new behaviors, policies, and practices, people's attention will soon fade, and you'll be back to business as usual.

Newsflash   *Cultural change starts at the top and cascades down throughout the organization.*

In the broadest terms, cultural change starts with a strong, clear, consistent message from the top. Then the message needs to be given concrete expression in the way the company does business. Finally, it has to be reinforced day in and day out, not just orally but through appropriate modeling, training, recognition, and rewards. (See figure 14.1)

It Starts with the Message

If the company's senior leaders are committed to implementing an organization-wide selling effort, then the first step is to get the word out. As with any human interaction, getting the message out has two aspects: the content of the message, and the process—the "how" of phrasing the message effectively and making sure it reaches everyone.

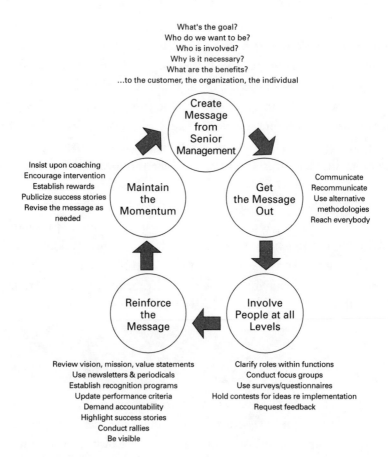

What's the goal?
Who do we want to be?
Who is involved?
Why is it necessary?
What are the benefits?
...to the customer, the organization, the individual

Create
Message
from
Senior
Management

Insist upon coaching
Encourage intervention
Establish rewards
Publicize success stories
Revise the message as
needed

Maintain
the
Momentum

Get
the Message
Out

Communicate
Recommunicate
Use alternative
methodologies
Reach everybody

Reinforce
the
Message

Involve
People at all
Levels

Review vision, mission, value statements
Use newsletters & periodicals
Establish recognition programs
Update performance criteria
Demand accountability
Highlight success stories
Conduct rallies
Be visible

Clarify roles within functions
Conduct focus groups
Use surveys/questionnaires
Hold contests for ideas re implementation
Request feedback

Figure 14.1 Making Change Happen

Content: What Is It You Want to Communicate?

So you want to convey to the people in your organization that you're adopting (or enhancing or revitalizing) the kind of company-wide, customer-centered, problem-solving approach to selling advocated in this book. What, exactly, goes into this message that isn't just a platitude?

Obviously, every organization has to determine for itself precisely what it wants to say. But let me mention several key points to consider making, which may look something like the following:

- Our overarching goal is to cultivate a problem-solving mindset throughout the organization with the specific objective of helping customers solve their business problems. We want to be a value-adding resource that our customers look to for both specific solutions and creative ideas. Such an approach is mandatory to differentiate our company in today's competitive marketplace.

- Solving customers' problems and maintaining a strong relationship with each customer are just other names for good selling. Selling is all about having constructive and fulfilling relationships that help customers meet their needs. In that sense, from now on everyone in the company should think of themselves as salespeople. That includes everybody, from the CEO down to every last worker on the plant floor in Dubuque. Everybody.

- From now on, the company's sales professionals will be asked to use every asset within the organization that can help them accomplish their goal of serving customers' needs. And those assets are expected to cooperate—eagerly.

- Cross-functional sales teams have a critical role to play in fulfilling our promise to customers. Joint sales calls will become part of our routine whenever it makes sense to use them. For this reason, people who are not themselves sales professionals must learn how to become part of the sales process and learn new skills to do this effectively.

- Whether or not individuals are asked to participate in team sales calls, they may be asked to take part in internal problem-solving sessions focused on ways of delivering superior customer service and satisfaction. Responding to such requests to participate in the work of sales teams should be considered a regular part of every employee's job description.

What About Tone?

As with selling, it's not just what you say, it's how you say it. A message from the CEO will almost always capture the attention of the people within the organization. But it needs to be more than just an announcement. A message of this import needs to be passionate and upbeat, demonstrating enthusiasm, excitement, and commitment.

At the same time, company leaders should take pains to explain with great clarity the rationale behind the new approach. If the message sounds like more gobbledygook from the ivory tower, the troops aren't likely to get excited. To get through those barnacles, the message should explain in some detail the specific benefits to the customer, the organization, and the individuals within the organization. It should make clear that organization-wide selling isn't just the latest glitzy initiative, but a transformation in the way the company does business. While not leaving any doubt that everyone is expected to commit to this effort, it should assure people that they will be rewarded for doing so.

How Will You Get the Message Out?

Once the message has been formulated, it needs to be communicated and recommunicated by every effective means: teleconferencing, videotapes sent to every location in the company, road shows hosted by company leaders, white papers, memoranda, e-mail, department and workgroup meetings—whatever mechanisms and media work for you. There is no reason why the message can't get into everybody's hands and eventually into everybody's head.

> **Newsflash**   *If you want to create a company-wide sales process, the word must get out to everyone in the organization. Everyone.*

Many companies have found creative ways to communicate important messages to their people. For those that need help, there are many consulting and public relations firms that work closely with organizations when they are implementing new approaches, policies, or management systems. There are also a number of firms that specialize in helping organizations assess and even change their cultures. Yes, such efforts cost time and money. As I said, changing cultures isn't easy—and we're only getting started.

Involving People at All Levels

Let's not kid ourselves. A message from corporate headquarters, no matter how enthusiastic and articulate, is only the first step toward getting buy-in from people at all levels. Change may start at the top, but to become reality it needs to be implemented from both the top down *and* the bottom up.

Once again, remember that *involvement* is the prerequisite to *commitment.* In the ideal scenario, the CEO's message will explain how the organization-wide selling approach will be developed through the involvement of people at all levels.

There are any number of ways to create that involvement. Different functions within the organization can be assigned the responsibility of determining precisely what their role will be in making organization-wide selling a way of life. Cross-functional focus groups can brainstorm ways of making it work. Some organizations videotape these kinds of focus groups and include summaries and highlights of group meetings in the communications that the CEO sends out. This is one way to show that these ideas come from people at ground level who are informed about the issues. Cross-functional teams can be put together to turn bright ideas into workable solutions and procedures. Questionnaires and surveys can be sent to everyone requesting their views on how to make ideas work. Some companies even have contests for the best implementation ideas.

Obviously these are just a few of the many ways to involve the people within the organization in putting flesh on the concept of organization-wide selling. Whatever mechanisms work for your organization are the ones to use, as long as they involve as many people as is humanly possible.

Reinforcing the Message

Even if all the right things are said in all the right ways, the message will have very little effect if it is not reinforced consistently. Cultural change starts at the top, but it only permeates the organization if every manager plays an active role in making it happen.

Earlier, I said that organization-wide selling needs to be a way of life. That means that the company's statements of vision, value, and mission need to reflect and reinforce this approach to doing business. Company newsletters and other periodicals need to continually refer to organization-wide selling efforts. Success stories need to be publicized. If the kid in the mailroom comes up with an idea that helped a customer, as Sal boasted to Betty the buyer, then everyone in the organization needs to know about it. Recognition programs and awards need to highlight successes in these areas as well.

Have some fun with the change process. Simple rallies at local sites, perhaps with pizza and soft drinks at the end of the workweek, can bring everyone together to hear the same message. Use all your communication resources: posters, messages on coffee cups, an Intranet Web page with information and examples of good practice. The more channels that are used to convey a message, the more likely it is to get across.

Still more has to happen where people really feel it. Performance appraisals and compensation programs need to include measurements that make clear what people are being asked to do to support organization-wide selling. Each year, or however often performance is appraised, people should be encouraged to put in writing their individual goals and objectives in this area, whether they are directly involved in selling or not. And managers need to hold them accountable.

Plan to hold sales teams accountable not only for sales goals but also for reaching out to people throughout the organization. Cross-functional sales teams are key to making organization-wide selling happen, and management needs to keep tabs on what they do. Ask sales managers and sales professionals to explain in their monthly summaries how they are using the resources available to them. Make such outreach one of the accountabilities that goes into the evaluation of team performance. When annual awards are given out to the sales force or any functional group, make sure that there are awards for teamwork, utilization of resources, and, of course, contributions to the organization-wide selling initiative.

The same approach needs to be used with the managers of the functions that the sales teams call upon as resources. Those managers need to be accountable as well. They can be asked to report in detail on a regular basis how they have supported the work of the sales teams. And they should be recognized for successes. I heard of one case in which the CEO created a special President's Award that recognized the person in each functional area who most clearly demonstrated the behaviors required to accomplish a specific objective. Why not create a President's Award for contributing to organization-wide selling?

Finally, if you want a highly visible way of reinforcing the message, appoint a Director of Organization-Wide Selling. These kinds of assignments happen all the time. KeyCorp's Private Banking and Investing Group are so committed to the concept of consultative selling that they created the job of Director of Consultative Selling. Senior Managing Director Kenton Thompson is as sensitive to sales process as anyone you will find in the financial services community. He strongly believes that creating such a position is a powerful way to ensure that he gets a return on his investment in creating a customer-driven sales culture. Think about stealing a page from his book and making a central figure or group of people accountable for coordinating all organization-wide selling activities.

Newsflash   *Consider having some group or some individual play the role of "focal point" to ensure that everyone in the company is doing his or her bit to help create an organization-wide selling effort.*

Implementation Means Training

Everything I've said so far assumes that people *can* do what they are being asked to do and that they can feel competent doing it. No amount of exhortation or assortment of incentives will change people's behavior if the employees don't have the skills required to make the change happen.

That's what most of this book has been about: the specific skills required to execute problem-solving, organization-wide selling. The skills we've discussed fall into four categories: interpersonal skills, communication skills, presentation skills, and, of course, problem-solving skills. All are essential.

Interpersonal skills are critical because, no matter how complicated we try to make the sales process, the bottom line is that customers buy from people they like, respect, feel comfortable with, and trust. Similarly, people work more comfortably with colleagues whom they respect and enjoy. Skills training alone may not make that crabby grouch in the corner cubicle into a likable, delightful fellow, but it will inform him of some ways of behaving that will enable him to work more effectively with both colleagues and customers.

It goes without saying that *communication skills* come into play at every level within an organization and have a major impact on the success of salespeople and their teams. The questioning and listening skills we've discussed are indispensable for learning about customers' needs, comfortably dissecting their problems, and uncovering the information the organization needs to become a viable problem-solving resource. If anyone in the organization touches customers in any way, he or she needs those skills.

Presentation skills are obviously necessary for sales professionals and members of sales teams. At the same time, they're extremely useful to anyone in the organization who is attempting to sell an idea or gain commitment for a recommendation. Even those who have casual interactions with customers can benefit from knowing how to respond to issues or offer ideas in a way that directly relates to the customer's needs.

Problem-solving skills are at the heart of the selling approach I've advocated. Beyond that, they can be applied to managing conflict, resolving issues, or generating creative solutions in any work situation, whether with customers or colleagues. At a minimum, anyone who ever has to deal with a customer complaint needs these skills. Ideally, everyone in the organization gets some training in them. Is there a job in your company that doesn't include one form or another of problem solving? I didn't think so.

One of the challenges involved in imparting the kinds of skills we've talked about is that they are "soft skills." Soft skills are behavioral in nature, and the best way to learn them is through experiential training. They are not the kind of things people learn only by reading a book (not even this one). They need to see the skills modeled and then practice them. Obviously, a commitment to this kind of training involves significant time and money.

But should that stop you? It's funny, but organizations commit huge amounts of resources to training people in all kinds of things that probably have far less impact on the core mission of delivering superior service and satisfaction to customers. It's a little like education. Most of us learn a lot of things in school we may never use. We often don't learn subtle things like how to get along with other people or how to manage conflict or resolve disputes. If we do learn those things, we learn them the hard way—through experience.

If you want people to practice the behaviors called for by your message, don't leave essential skills learning to chance. If your organization is sizable, you probably already have a training function in place. If not, you may need to solicit help from outside. Or you may already be covering many of these skills in the training you offer your salespeople. Now you can think about adapting that training to people in other functional areas.

However you do it, make skills training a keystone part of your initiative, and make sure it includes lots of opportunity for practice. Otherwise, the effort to implement organization-wide selling is likely to go the way of all those other optimistic initiatives that gathered steam for a while, then chugged to a halt, and finally were forgotten.

> **Newsflash**   *If you want your people to behave differently, you will need to invest in training to show them how. It is an investment that can yield huge dividends.*

Keeping It Going

Don't get the ball rolling just to let it roll gradually to a stop. Once you've established the foundation for organization-wide selling and have built it into your training, communication, and accountability systems, create a program of ongoing reinforcement. Here are just a few ideas.

Keep People Involved

You've involved your people in turning organization-wide selling from a concept into a new way of doing business. Now stress continual improvement, and keep everybody involved. On an ongoing basis, employees can be surveyed to solicit suggestions for even more effective ways of implementing the program. Contests can be conducted with prizes for employees who submit the most innovative and workable ideas. Awards can be created for people who do special things for customers, with nominations coming from their peers as well as managers.

You can do things both within and across departments. Have the people within a department identify customer-related problems and challenge individuals or subgroups to come up with the best idea to resolve the issue. Or stage competitions across departments. Imagine, for example, the advertising and market research departments engaged in a friendly contest to determine how best to deal with a customer's image problem. Or the operations folks going head to head with the distribution gang to figure out who can save the customer the most money on deliveries. Publicize the competition and make sure the winners get the recognition they deserve.

I know one organization that encouraged its people to have a "huddle" every morning. At 9:00 A.M., people would stop whatever they were doing and congregate in their work areas to address a "question of the day." Different people took responsibility for determining what each day's question would be, and the questions were e-mailed to each office every morning. For our purposes, the questions could focus on organization-wide selling issues. What would happen if everyone in the organization simultaneously spent ten minutes a day discussing with his or her fellow employees a specific customer-related issue? The possibilities are endless.

Pay Attention to Trust

Trust plays a major role in organizational change. If trust is an issue, an entire project can be put at risk. For example, salespeople need to be willing to introduce people from within the organization to their customers. Sales professionals who are used to going it alone may be reluctant to involve other groups in selling their products because they're afraid the "amateurs" will screw things up. This kind of rugged individualism is inimical to organization-wide selling. If you see signs of this attitude, pounce on it. Talk to the people involved or the managers to whom they report. If people are getting away with behaviors that contradict the vision, it sends a mixed message that can cripple the process.

Similarly, you are missing opportunities every day if people within a specific function aren't talking to their peers on the customer side. Let your engineers talk freely to the customer's engineers. Let your marketing people talk to their marketing people.

Encourage your analysts to talk to their analysts. Keep in mind that the broader the base of a relationship, the more secure that relationship will be. Do what you can to create a climate of trust that allows all this to happen. Of course, that means that you, as a manager, have to be trustful of your people. Yours is the first move.

Newsflash   *Trust your people, and encourage them to trust one another. It's the only way to create the kind of collaboration required in organization-wide selling.*

Use Coaching

Another critical element in modifying behavior and effecting cultural change is coaching. Coaching is one of those things all managers talk about but don't do nearly as often as they need to in order to make behavioral change a reality.

There are any number of books about coaching, so I won't do the subject a disservice by trying to develop it in detail here. I do want to emphasize, though, that coaching needs to be distinguished from other management processes, such as performance appraisals, career reviews, compensation discussions, one-minute managing, and even reprimand sessions. Coaching is the art of using what you know to help someone improve his or her skills. It can and should be done both formally and informally as part of a concerted effort to change the organizational culture.

A formal coaching session is a fifteen- to thirty-minute meeting that is scheduled in advance and that focuses on a specific area. Ideally it consists of reinforcing what the person is doing well and identifying areas for improvement. The manager provides the feedback and discusses it with his or her direct report in a private setting. Then the two people do some problem solving together to deal with the area of needed improvement, with the objective of reaching agreement and appropriate action plans.

Informal coaching happens whenever a manager seizes an opportunity to single out something that the person has done right, or suggest how a particular task could be done better. It can be done orally, in a memo, or in a focused discussion after attending a meeting or participating in a joint sales call. What's for sure is that it can't be left to quarterly one-on-ones and still less to annual performance reviews.

When organizations are instigating change, coaching by managers at all levels is a powerful way to keep the momentum going. Make sure that your managers know how to coach, know what they need to be coaching for, and are held accountable for doing it on a regular basis.

Model the Behavior

I've probably said it one too many times already, but here goes: Managers have to walk the walk. Become a role model. People are often surprised at how, when they make the effort to listen better, the people around them start to become better listeners. When you're more responsive to others' ideas and look for the hidden value in them, people may surprise you by being more open-minded to your suggestions. When you demonstrate customer consciousness, probe into what your people know about customers' needs, invite other resources to participate in solving a customer-related problem, or use your problem-solving skills to develop a vague idea into a workable solution, you're doing some of the most powerful things you can do to keep the process of change going strong.

You probably have your own ideas about how to create meaningful change in your organization. Better yet, you've got all kinds of people around you who have ideas at least as good, or ideas that could become workable solutions with a little development. Hmmm . . . sounds like problem solving, doesn't it? You know what to do.

CHAPTER 15

Putting It in Perspective

As Sal left the sales team training session that had been held in the company conference room, his head was buzzing with new vocabulary and concepts that were familiar in some ways but new and foreign in others. Problem-solving selling . . . using assets from throughout the organization . . . facilitation . . . involving people from other functions in presenting—no, make that "offering recommendations" . . . transforming objections into needs . . . resolving issues. . . . Then there was that "idea development" technique and, what was it? Something about a threshold of acceptance? Sal shook his head ruefully. Oh, for the good old days, he thought, when you just had to know how to charm the prospect, deliver your pitch, and then know how to close 'em. Damn, but I was good at that. . . .

Come to think of it, Sal mused, that old-school stuff hasn't been working too well lately. It sure bombed with old Betty. Maybe it's true that the Salesman-as-Lone Ranger concept has had its day.

Better make that sales*person*, he corrected himself. Funny how so many of our successful sales reps are women these days. That's another big change. One I can live with. They seem to have a better handle on all that process stuff. I am not sure why. How am I ever going to keep it all straight?

As I said at the beginning of this book, there are lots of Sals (and Sallys) in your organization: good people and natural-born problem solvers who probably don't know how much they already know. Although I hope this book has given you, and them, a plethora of new ideas and techniques, and at least a start on acquiring new skills, in the end the essentials aren't all that complicated. A lot of them are common-sense extensions of a single fundamental premise: In a world in which we are all selling commodities, the organization-wide selling approach is a powerful way to make you and your company stand out by delivering the best possible customer service and satisfaction. And that's really what Sal and Sally, in their heart of hearts, have wanted to do all along.

With that in mind, let me just recapitulate briefly the Really Important Stuff, a baker's dozen of the big ideas I hope you'll take away from this book, ponder at your leisure, and return to again and again as your touchstones as you strive to implement the organization-wide selling approach.

> *Big Idea #1:* The rugged-individualist approach to selling isn't just passé, it puts you at a competitive disadvantage. The way to build customer relationships and ensure the best possible service and satisfaction is to involve as many resources as you can.

> *Big Idea #2:* In the organization-wide selling approach, everybody is thinking about ways to improve customer satisfaction. All the time.

> *Big Idea #3:* Customers tend to buy from people (and companies) they like, respect, and trust. If you want to demonstrate that you're different from your competitors, your beliefs, attitudes, and behaviors must all work together to build a relationship with your customer that is founded on trust.

> *Big Idea #4:* Every human interaction has two aspects: content and process. It's the process part that most often

gives us trouble. By the same token, by managing the process in an exemplary way you can stand head and shoulders above your competition. And that goes for anybody who ever deals with a customer, in any capacity.

Big Idea #5: Learning to manage both process and content is a matter of acquiring specific interpersonal, communication, presentation, and problem-solving skills. The key subset of these skills are those that are involved in facilitation. None of these skills is very mysterious, but all take practice to learn.

Big Idea #6: There's no better way to think of selling than as a process of routinely and effectively solving customers' problems—including the ones they don't know they have. The problem-solving selling approach combines the best of selling skills with the best of a proven problem-solving methodology to take selling to a new level, one where selling situations are transformed into problem-solving opportunities.

Big Idea #7: Thinking of selling as problem solving also is the bridge to all the non–salespeople in the organization. Most people like to think of themselves as problem solvers. Put across the concept of problem-solving selling, and you're more than halfway toward the goal of having everybody in the organization thinking of themselves as salespeople, from the CEO on down.

Big Idea #8: The single most important thing you can do in dealing with customers is to show them that you truly understand their needs. Many people's inclination to buy starts at the moment when they feel their needs are understood, *before* the salesperson presents a thing.

Big Idea #9: The single most *challenging* part of the sales process is managing resistance. Repeat after me:

Objections are needs in disguise. Treat them as such, and you'll never use the phrase "overcoming objections" or "handling objections" again. Instead, you'll work *with* the customer to resolve those objections by transforming them into needs and addressing them creatively.

Big Idea #10: The single most *overrated* part of the sales process is the close. In problem-solving selling, reaching closure is a natural outcome of the process you've been engaged in all along.

Big Idea #11: A terrific way to go beyond the usual in selling is to offer customers *ideas* as well as products and services. Walk your customers through the four levels of idea response, and watch a win-win solution happen that turns you and your company into a value-adding (and valued) resource.

Big Idea #12: Making effective use of sales teams is the way to bring more resources to bear on the customer relationship, generate new and better ways of delivering outstanding service, and spread a selling mentality throughout the organization.

Big Idea #13: If you want to implement problem-solving selling in your organization, start at the top—and then build from the bottom, involving as many people as you can. Like selling, changing an organizational culture is a team sport.

That's it, in a nutshell. Let these ideas be your guide, and you won't go far wrong.

Now, if you'll permit me, let me close with a final word to all the Sals and Sallys that I hope read this book, the front-line pros who are the foremost representatives of the organization to its customers, and the primary custodians of that all-important relationship.

We've talked a lot about skills. Keep in mind that acquiring new skills, whether learning to swing a golf club, work a manual transmission, dance the tango, or facilitate the process of a sales call, involves some discomfort at first and a lot of trial and error. Don't try to do it all at once—you may end up tripping over your own feet. Try out one skill at a time. As you get past the initial discomfort, introduce a new one. For example, focus on improving your questioning skills for a while, and then turn your attention to listening for needs. When you make a formal presentation in the near future, try to offer the specific benefits first and see what happens. When you've established rapport with a customer, begin offering an idea or two in addition to your company's products and services. In other words, work your way gradually through the skill set involved in problem-solving selling, and don't expect to get it right the first time every time. Understand your own human tendency to fall into the traps of premature presentation or reacting defensively to objections. It happens to all of us all the time. I know. I've been there. Too often I still am.

So, with all that said, I leave you with four suggestions:

1. Never lose faith.

2. Expect progress, not miracles.

3. Call your mother; she worries about you.

4. If it all seems too good to be true, don't think so much!

Index

A

Accountability in a sales team, 227

Acknowledgment of customer's objection, 190–191

Action plans, 68–70; in problem-solving sequence, 53

Agendas for: joint sales calls, 259, 261; sales calls, 127–130; sales-team meetings, 244–249

Airtime distribution for: determining needs, 103, 104; resolving issues, 202–203

Alvord, John, 11

Analysis phase of problem solving, 56; amount of information needed for, 56–58; fresh perspectives for, 58; in problem-solving sequence, 53

Analyzing the situation (determining customer needs): listening skills for, 152–164; in problem-solving selling sequence, 135, 136; questioning skills for, 133–152

Assumptive close, 218–219

B

Benefits, 171–172; in customized presentations, 171–174; generic, 172–173, 175; specific, 171–174, 175; statements, 30

Beveridge, Don, 77, 172

Brainstorming sessions: basic rule of, 59; "I wish" phrase for, 61; "pinball" factor, 33; in problem-solving sequence, 52; respect for others' ideas in, 62

C

Canned pitch: customized presentations vs., 170–171, 173; needs-driven selling vs., 77

CEOs as salespeople, 11, 19–21

Climate, meeting, 35, 36; creating comfortable, 53–54

Climate of confidence, 12

Closing: assumptive close, 218–219; handling "no", 219; how not to close, 216–217; interim closes, 212–213; manipulative approaches to, 216; momentum in the sales cycle, 214; selling sequence as series of closes, 213–214

Coaching, 284–285

Communication in sales teams, 235

Compensation for sales teams, 239

Consultative Resources Corporation, 128

Consultative selling, 12–15; process skills needed for, 27–28, 36–37

Consultative Selling (Hanan), 12

Cope, Bill, 115

Credentials presentations, 77

Credibility, 115, 118–119

Credit for ideas, 33

CREST attributes: applying, 121–123; credibility, 115, 118–119; empathy, 118, 119–120; sensitivity, 118, 120–121; trustworthiness, 118, 121

Culture, organizational: barriers to changing, 271–273; communicating message of organization-wide selling,

(*continued*) 273–277; involving people at all levels, 277–278, 282–283; reinforcing organization-wide selling message, 278–279, 282–285; training and employee behavior, 280–282
Curiosity, 30
Current events questions, 150
Customer as problem owner, 45, 232, 233
Customer needs: obvious and implied needs, 162–163; organizational, job, and personal needs, 160–162; reviewing, 163–164
Customer needs, determining: listening skills for, 135, 152–164; in problem-solving selling sequence, 135, 136; questioning skills for, 135–152
Customer resistance, managing: acknowledgment of customer's objection, 190–192; airtime distribution for, 202–203; asking for elaboration, 192–194; with benefit statements, 199; to ideas (intangibles), 203–208; inviting other objections, 202; by involving the customer, 200–201; losing composure and, 187–188; resources for, 201; responding to objections, 199–201; by selling yourself and your company, 199–201; transforming objection into a need, 194–198; why customers object, 188–189

D
Daley-Caravella, Laura, 139
Debriefing after joint sales calls, 264–265
Dedicated vs. self-organizing teams, 237
Differentiation, 5–6, 21

E
Edison, Thomas, 33
Einstein, Albert, 32
Emerson, Ralph Waldo, 29
Empathy, 118, 119–120
Error-based feedback, 59

F
Facilitators, professional: role and responsibilities of, 38, 40–41; salespeople as, 44–46

Facilitators: sales-team meeting, 249–250; team sales call, 255–256
Features and benefits, 171–174; how and when to present, 175
Feedback from customers, 183–184
Follow-up, 43
Ford, Henry, 15
Four-box presentation model, 172–173, 175
Four levels of idea response, 204–208

G
Generic benefits, 172–174; when to present, 175
Ground rules for meetings, 55–56
Ground rules for transforming objections into needs, 197–199
Group problem-solving method: general overview of, 52, 53; importance of learning, 51–52; phase 1: positioning the session, 53–56; phase 2: analyzing the problem, 56–58; phase 3: generating alternatives, 58–62; phase 4: evaluating selected ideas, 63–68; phase 5: stating solution and action plan, 68–70
Groups, generation of ideas in: basic rule of brainstorming sessions, 59; "I wish" phrase for, 61; "pinball" factor, 33; problem analysis and, 56–58; in problem-solving sequence, 52, 53; respect for others' ideas, 62

H
Hanan, Mack, 12, 28
Harriman, Rick, 204
How to Make Meetings Work (Doyle and Strauss), 41

I
"I" messages, 164, 197–198
Ideas, evaluation of: choosing idea to develop, 63; idea continuum, 64; ideas as dynamic entities, 65, 204; invitations for more ideas and, 66; in problem-solving sequence, 52, 53; reframing concerns, 67–68
Ideas, generation of: basic rule of brainstorming sessions, 59; "I wish" phrase for, 61; "pinball" factor in groups, 33;

problem analysis and, 56–58; in problem-solving sequence, 52, 53; respect for others' ideas, 62

Ideas, offering: asking permission before, 177–178, 180; situations that merit, 177; unsolicited ideas, 13–14, 179–182

Ideas, overcoming objections to: four levels of idea response, 204–208; idea continuum and, 204

Ideas presented in this book, 288–290

Inquisitiveness, 30

Interim closes, 212–213

Intimacy, 115–116, 117

J

Job needs, 161

Joint sales calls: conducting, 260–264; debriefing phase of, 264–265; planning, 256–260; reasons to make, 253–255; rehearsing, 260; roles and responsibilities in, 255–256

Joslin, Charlie, 121–123, 133

K

Katzenbach, Jon R., 226, 227

"Keep/Stop/Start" exercise, 248–249, 264

Kissner, Matthew, 239

Kovasavitch, Dick, 76

L

Listening skills: barriers to effective listening, 152–158; kinds of customer needs to listen for, 160–163; listening for needs, 152; note taking and listening efficiency, 159; questioning and, 165–166; reviewing customer needs, 163–164; of successful salespeople, 30–31

M

Malkin, Len, 218

Management, author's memos to: closing, 220–222; joint sales calls, 265–267; needs-driven selling, 84–86; needs-driven selling and problem solving, 109–111; objections, 208–209; organization-wide selling, 25–26; positioning skills and trust building,

133–134; presentations, 184–185; problem-solving, 48–49; process for problem-solving, 71; questioning and listening skills, 165–166; sales team, 240; sales-team meetings, 251–252

Managers: as coaches, 284–285; resource, 238; as role models, 285

Maslow's hierarchy of needs, 161–162

Matik, Paul, 181

Meeting climate, 35, 36; creating comfortable, 53–54

Meetings, joint sales call. *See* Joint sales calls

Meetings, problem-solving: climate of, 35, 36, 53–54; content vs. process in, 34–37; ground rules for, 55–56; objectives of, 55; quality of thinking in, 35; roles and responsibilities in, 37–41; roles in selling situations, 41–43; sales calls as, 34

Meetings, process for problem-solving in: general overview of, 52, 53; phase 1: positioning the session, 53–56; phase 2: analyzing the problem, 56–58; phase 3: generating alternatives, 58–62; phase 4: evaluating selected ideas, 63–68; phase 5: stating solution and action plan, 68–70; training for sales teams in, 51–52

Meetings, sales-team: conducting, 249–251; planning, 241–249

Meetings, team sales call. *See* Team sales calls

Michelson, David, 144

Mirroring, 193

Mission statements for sales teams, 234–235

N

"Need" language, 198

Needs-clarification questions: current events questions, 150; speculative questions, 149–150; strategic questions, 146–149

Needs-driven selling: needs analysis exercise, 79–81; needs vs. solutions, 81–84; premature presentations and, 76–77; uncovering customer needs, 78–79

Needs-driven selling and problem solving sequences: combining, 90–93; needs-driven selling sequence, 87–90; problem-solving selling, 93–95; problem-solving selling sequence, 95–109

Nierenberg, Gerard, 205–206

Note taking, 159, 160

O

Objections, resolving: acknowledgment of customer's objection, 190–192; air-time distribution for, 202; asking for elaboration, 192–194; with benefit statements, 199; to ideas (intangibles), 203–207; inviting other objections, 202–203; by involving the customer, 200–201; losing composure and, 187–188; resources for, 201; responding to objections, 199–201; by selling yourself and your company, 199–200; transforming objection into a need, 194–199; why customers object, 188–189

Objectives, clarify, 55

Offering recommendations phase: asking for feedback, 183–184; customizing presentations, 170–171; features and benefits, 171–174; four-box presentation model, 172–173, 175; order of information in presentations, 174–176; premature presentations, 169–170; presentation as, 167; sales team's participation in, 176; suggesting ideas in, 176–183

Open-ended questions: problem-analysis questions, 150–151; resolving issues with, 192; rules about, 145

Opportunity questions, 148

Organizational culture: barriers to changing, 271–273; coaching by managers, 284–285; communicating message of organization-wide selling, 273–277; involving people at all levels, 277–278, 282–283; modeling behavior, 285; reinforcing organization-wide selling message, 278–279, 282–285; training and employee behavior, 280–282; trust between employees, 283–284

Organizational needs, 160

Organization-wide selling, ix, 6–7; CEOs as salespeople, 11, 19–21; consultative selling, 12–15; differentiation, 5–6, 21; problem-solving mindset for, 22–23; sales teams, 15–19; selling as problem solving, 7–12; selling as team sport, 24; summary of advice on, 287–291; "Whatchagot?" sales-call disasters, 3–5, 21. *See also* Organizational culture

P

Participants, meeting, 38, 45

People skills, 29

Performance measurement: in sales teams, 238–239; self-assessment discussions, 247–249

Personal needs, 161–162

Peters, Tom, 70, 71, 179

Philipp, John, 115

Pop Rocks candy invention, 61, 206

Positioning: CREST attributes in sellers and, 118–123; as first phase in problem-solving sequence, 53–56, 114; preparing the customer, 132; putting customer at ease, 126–127; salesperson as facilitator, 124–126; setting the agenda, 127–130; as skill needed by every employee, 113; time contract for, 130–131; trust building and, 114–118

Premature presentation traps: joy of presenting and, 169; in needs-driven selling, 76–77; note taking to avoid, 159; tuning out too soon, 155–156

Pre-question statements, 142–143, 193

Presentations: asking for feedback, 183–184; customizing, 170–171; features and benefits, 171–174, 175–176; four-box presentation model, 172–173, 175–176; as offering recommendations phase, 165; premature, 76–77, 159–160, 169–170; putting critical information upfront in, 174; sales team's participation in, 176; suggesting ideas in, 176–182

Prince, George, 30, 69
Privilege of consulting, 13, 76
Probability of Success (POS) equation, 35
Problem owner: customer as, 45; in joint sales calls, 255–256; as role in problem-solving meetings, 37–40
Problem questions, 148
Problem solving: meetings, 34–37; mindset for organization-wide selling, 22–23; process sensitivity needed for, 27–28, 36–37, 43–47; roles in meetings, 37–41; roles in sales calls, 41–43; salespeople as natural problem solvers, 28–33; selling as, 7–12. *See also* Problem-solving method for groups; Problem-solving selling model.
Problem-solving method for groups: general overview of, 52, 53; phase 1: positioning the session, 53–56; phase 2: analyzing the problem, 56–58; phase 3: generating alternatives, 58–62; phase 4: evaluating selected ideas, 63–68; phase 5: stating solution and action plan, 68–70; training for sales teams in, 51–52
Problem-solving selling model, 93–95; phase 1: position the meeting, 96–98; phase 2: analyze situation, 99–101; phase 3: offer recommendations, 101–104; phase 4: resolve issues, 104–107; phase 5: reach closure, 107–109
Process sensitivity, 37–38; key to consultative selling, 27–28; meeting facilitator's responsibility, 38, 40–41; throughout an organization, 47–48; tool for problem solving, 43–47
Product-driven selling, 77

Q
Questioning: appropriate, 145–151; complexity of, 138; grouping questions in clusters, 144–145; importance of, 135–136, 152; link between success and, 30; preparing customer for, 142–145; process aspect of, 140–141; as treacherous activity, 136–137; "you stupid idiot" questions, 139, 197

R
Rackham, Neil, 30, 100
Rehearsal effect, 157–158
Rehearsing sales calls, 260
Reilly, Kate, xi, 103, 172, 194, 262
Reilly, Kent, 180–181
Rejection, 31–32
Resolving the issues: acknowledgment of customer's objection, 190–192; airtime distribution for, 202–203; asking for elaboration, 192–194; with benefit statements, 199; to ideas (intangibles), 203–208; inviting other objections, 202; by involving the customer, 200–201; losing composure and, 187–188; resources for, 201; responding to objections, 199–202; by selling yourself and your company, 199–200; transforming objection into a need, 194–199; why customers object, 188–190
Respect for the prospect, 120
Results-oriented salespeople, 31
Risk for a customer, 116; reducing, 116–118; in trust formula, 115
Risk takers, salespeople as, 30
Rogers, Carl, 164
Roles and responsibilities: joint sales calls, 255–256; problem-solving meetings, 37–41; sales calls, 41–43; sales teams, 232–233

S
Sales calls: agendas for, 127–130; as meetings, 34; as problem-solving sessions, 7–12; roles and responsibilities in, 41–43
Sales calls, joint: agendas for, 259; conducting, 260–264; debriefing phase of, 264–265; planning, 256–260; reasons to make, 253–255; rehearsing, 260; salesperson's role in, 255–256
Sales calls, "Whatchagot?", 3–5; process skills for handling, 36–37, 45–46; reframing customer concerns in, 66–68, 195
Salespeople: attributes buyers want in, 118–121; CEOs as, 11, 19–21; as facilitators, 124–126, 255–256; as key

(continued) players on sales teams, 232–233; as problem-solvers, 7–12; stereotypical images of, 11; traits of successful, 28–33

Sales team, 15–19, 225–228; communication in, 235–236; compensation for, 239–240; dedicated vs. self-organizing, 237; ideas generated by, 33; leader of, 236–238; meetings of, 235–236, 241–252; mission statements for, 234–235; performance measurement in, 238–239; reasons for, 228–229; roles and responsibilities in, 232–233; selling as team sport, 24; which customers deserve their own, 231–232; who belongs on, 229–231. *See also* Joint sales calls; Organization-wide selling

Sales-team meetings: agenda for, 244–249; conducting, 249–251; frequency of, 235–236; reasons to call, 242; scheduling, 242–243; who should attend, 243–244

Schwarz, Jim, 237

Scribes for meetings, 41

Self-organizing teams, 237

Selling: consultative, 12–15; the organization, 200; as problem solving, 7–12; as team sport, 24; yourself, 199–200. *See also* Organization-wide selling

Selling, needs-driven: needs analysis exercise, 79–81; needs vs. solutions, 81–84; premature presentations and, 76–77; uncovering customer needs, 78–79. *See also* Needs-driven selling and problem-solving sequences

Selling model, problem-solving, 93–95; phase 1: position the meeting, 96–98; phase 2: analyze situation, 99–101; phase 3: offer recommendations, 101–104; phase 4: resolve issues, 104–107; phase 5: reach closure, 107–109

Sensitivity, 118, 120–121. *See also* Process sensitivity

Silence, using, 193–194

Smith, Douglas K., 226

Soft skills, 281

Solutions: action plans and, 68–70; needs vs., 81–84; stating, 68–69

Specific benefits, 172–174; when to present, 175, 176

Speculative questions, 149–150

Spin Selling (Rackham), 30

SPOT strategic planning model, 149

Status quo issue, 5–6

Strategic questions, 146–149

Sulerzyski, Chuck, 135–136

Synectics method of problem solving, 28–29, 34, 57, 61, 64, 115, 150, 151, 153, 154, 157, 194, 215

T

Task forces vs. sales teams, 227–228

Team sales calls: conducting, 260–264; debriefing after, 264–265; planning, 256–260; reasons to make, 253–255; rehearsing, 260; roles and responsibilities in, 255–256

Tenacity, 32

Thompson, Kenton, 279

Time contracts, 130–132

Training: coaching sessions, 284–285; in group problem-solving skills, 51–52; organizational culture and, 280–282

Traits of successful salespeople, 28–33

Transactional questions, 146

Trial close, 212–213

Trust between buyer and seller: CREST attributes in sellers and, 118–121; CREST principles in action, 121–123; formula for, 115–118; importance of, 114

Trust between employees, 283–284

Trustworthiness of salespeople, 118, 121

U

Unsolicited ideas: negative reactions to, 13–14; offering, 179–183

Updates in sales-team meetings, 244, 245

W

Ward, John, 237

Warm-up exercise for sales-team meetings, 244, 245

"Whatchagot?" sales-call disasters, 3–5; process skills for handling, 36–37, 45–46; reframing customer concerns during, 66–68, 195

Whitcup, Jonathan, xi, 190

The Wisdom of Teams (Katzenback and Smith), 226

Y

"You stupid idiot" questions, 139–140, 197

About the Author

Eric Baron was educated as a chemical engineer, having received his B.E. from Stevens Institute of Technology in 1968. Upon graduation, he joined Union Carbide Corporation, where he held jobs in sales, sales management, marketing, and training. In 1976, he left Union Carbide to join Synectics® Inc., an international consulting firm that focuses on creative problem solving, innovation, and teamwork. While at Synectics, he became interested in applying problem-solving skills to the sales process.

In 1981, he left Synectics as vice president of sales and marketing to cofound Consultative Resources Corporation (CRC), a sales and sales management training and consulting firm. He served as president of CRC until 1992, when he left to establish The Baron Group in Westport, Connecticut. The Baron Group clients include American Express, Ogilvy & Mather, Chase Manhattan Bank, Bristol Myers Squibb, Prudential, J.P. Morgan, Citicorp, and Pfizer.

Eric is an internationally known public speaker and provides keynote presentations at sales meetings and conferences around the world. He also continues to serve as managing director of The Baron Group.

Eric lives in Weston, Connecticut with Lois, his wife of over thirty years. They have two grown children, Andrea, who works as a social worker in the Bronx, New York, and Deborah, who is an Outward Bound Leader in Boulder, Colorado.

He also contributes his time regularly to community organizations, including the Westport School System. He is currently chairman of the Fairfield County Division of the March of Dimes Board and serves on several other boards of nonprofit organizations.

About The Baron Group

The Baron Group is a sales process training and consulting firm that provides numerous services for its corporate clients. The majority of the work is in providing training programs for salespeople and sales managers at all levels within organizations.

The curriculum consists of a variety of selling skills programs, including Consultative Selling Skills, Team Selling, and Negotiation Skills. Management programs include Coaching for Sales Performance and Sales Action Planning.

Eric Baron and other members of the firm regularly serve as keynote speakers at National Sales Meetings, Conferences, Client Events, and Recognition Programs. They offer customized presentations consistent with the objectives or theme of the event.

The Baron Group has long-term relationships with its clients, which include such companies as AT&T, American Express, Citibank, Ogilvy and Mather, Bristol-Myers-Squibb, Prudential, Milliken, Pfizer, Banc One, Fleet Bank, Burlington Industries, J.P. Morgan, Chase Manhattan Bank, PriceWaterHouse Coopers, and Research International.

The headquarters is in Westport, Connecticut, at 57 Wilton Road.

Phone   203-227-7907
Fax   203-221-8411
E-mail TBG@Barongroup.com